SUPERVISOR'S
STANDARD REFERENCE
HANDBOOK

Also by the Author:

The Art and Skill of Managing People, 1975, Prentice-Hall.

SUPERVISOR'S
STANDARD REFERENCE
HANDBOOK

W.H. Weiss

PRENTICE-HALL, INC.

Englewood Cliffs, N.J.

Prentice-Hall International, Inc., *London*
Prentice-Hall of Australia, Pty., Ltd. *Sydney*
Prentice-Hall of Canada, Ltd., *Toronto*
Prentice-Hall of India Private Ltd., *New Delhi*
Prentice-Hall of Japan, Inc., *Tokyo*
Prentice-Hall of Southeast Asia, Pte., Ltd., *Singapore*
Whitehall Books, Ltd., *Wellington, New Zealand*

Library of Congress Cataloging in Publication Data

Weiss, W   H
   Supervisor's standard reference handbook.

   Includes index.
   1. Supervision of employees. I. Title.
HF5549.W4313   658.3'02   80-11336
ISBN 0-13-877142-1

Printed in the United States of America

How This Book Can Help You with Your Supervisory Problems

Every supervisor needs a reliable guide to the latest and best answers to supervisory problems. *Supervisor's Standard Reference Handbook* provides the most important reference material for first-level management—practical, down-to-earth techniques and methods for solving everyday problems. Combining the experiences of many knowledgeable supervisors in business and industry has resulted in a desk reference book that the supervisor can consult with confidence, knowing that it will supply the most widely accepted practices and procedures for solving supervisory problems. The information has been organized and presented with two principal objectives:

1. To give you a look at and help you understand the people you must work with in handling a supervisor's job in today's office and plant.
2. To provide answers to problems that will save you time and effort in handling your supervisory duties.

Change is constantly taking place in how people think and act, and what it takes to motivate them. You need to know how to manage people, what to do, and how to do it if you are to get jobs done. Moreover, if you need to have an "instant" answer, a quick solution, at your fingertips—this book provides it.

The *Supervisor's Standard Reference Handbook* is a compilation of tested solutions to your problems, solutions that work. The techniques that this book reveals can be relied upon absolutely because they have been used by many supervisors and proven on the job. Much of what I've put into this book comes from the experiences of supervisors I've known and worked with in the last 30 years. The chapters are organized around the types of problems these supervisors met in their day-to-day work. I show how supervisors have effectively dealt with them in managing people and getting the work out. The material in the book is presented in as concise a manner as possible. There's minimal "background" discussion of a topic, just the key points and the how-to-do-it. You will find a number of "Cases-in-point" which illustrate the solutions to supervisor's problems. The book covers practically all supervisory problems, both office and factory shop types.

This book is intended to be kept on your desk, ready for use. The contents are therefore arranged so that you can locate information quickly. Thus, the material is given not only in the usual manner by chapter and subject, but also by section number. For instance, if you want to know how to combat excuses from your people, and the table of contents or a cross-reference in the text refers you to Section 1.6, you simply turn to the sixth section of Chapter 1. The numbered paragraphs will make it much easier for you to spot items in an instant.

To present know-how and information in the clearest, most concise way, *Supervisor's Standard Reference Handbook* offers you 164 fact-filled sections arranged among 19 chapters:

1. How to Get Action: Proven Methods That Get Results
2. Tested Supervisory Techniques That Keep You in Control of People and Events
3. Training and Development Know-Hows That Assure Results
4. Making Your Point and Making It Stick
5. How Successful Supervisors Use Persuasion
6. How Effective Supervisors Handle People
7. Supervisory Decision Making: How the "Pros" Do It
8. How to Handle Problems of Communication
9. Proven Techniques That Make Giving Orders Easy
10. Guaranteed Methods for Getting Cooperation
11. Positive Techniques for Maintaining Control of Quality and Quantity
12. Sure-Fire Ways to Control Costs
13. Tested Ways for Evaluating Performance: Handling Appraisals Simply and Effectively
14. Proven Methods for Getting Along with the Union
15. Productivity and What to Do About It
16. Successful Ways for Getting the Most from Skilled and "Special" People
17. Working Out Answers to Your Problem People
18. Tried-and-Proven Ways to Handle OSHA Problems
19. Tested Techniques for Adapting to Change

Every effort has been made to fill this book with the latest successful supervisory procedures, covering nearly every conceivable situation or problem you might encounter. Here are just a few of the wide range of subjects included:

Supervisor's Standard Reference Handbook is written to fill all your needs for a standard reference work in this field. Since it covers the full range of supervisor's responsibilities and duties, in almost any type of business—in the office, the shop, or the plant—all supervisors can benefit from using it regularly.

W. H. Weiss

CONTENTS

6. How Effective Supervisors Handle People 73

7. Supervisory Decisionmaking: How the "Pros" Do It 85

8. How to Handle Problems of Communication 99

1

How to Get Action: Proven Methods That Get Results

Supervisors have many responsibilities. One of the major ones is to accomplish their department's objective of getting jobs done. A company looks to its supervisors to get action from its employees in order that the company can be profitable and grow.

You can be an effective supervisor by motivating and organizing your people to do their work efficiently and productively. But you need to do more than this to be successful at getting results. You need to practice good leadership principles on the job and be able to to contend with pressure and stress. You must recognize the value of time and take advantage of it; you must know how to combat excuses. Most of all, you must follow up to see that the action you start with your people gets the job done.

1.1 Sure-Fire Methods for Organizing People to Action

Psychologists and personnel experts say that the key to motivating and organizing people to action is to understand their human needs on the job and to provide a work environment which goes along with those needs.

One of the most basic of all job needs is the satisfaction of knowing one's job well. People need to master their jobs before they can perform them well. You should see that they do this if you want to organize them to action.

People who are going to put a lot of effort into their work also want and need appreciative behavior on the part of their supervisors. They like to feel that their leaders will react the same today to their good work as they did yesterday. Workers, in particular, dislike vacillation. They want a predictability about their leaders and their job environment. They want to be sure that if they do a specific thing, the act will likely lead to a certain consequence.

You must be consistent in the day-to-day performance of your job. A wishy-washy attitude one day, followed by being stubborn on doing things your way the next, destroys people's confidence in you and turns off enthusiasm for the work.

If the people on the job know they are going to get credit and recognition for doing a good job, the work is more attractive and less tedious. The feeling of being valued personally is a strong motivator to action. When a man knows his work is appreciated, it is natural for him to reciprocate by doing his best.

1.2 Successful Ways of Maintaining Leadership

Leadership is a mysterious quality of human endeavor which many people aspire to but only a few attain. With leadership your supervisory skills come to life; without it, your abilities and talents lay dormant and you have little influence on others.

Your company expects you to use your leadership skills, and your people look to you for guidance and direction. Thus, you play a key role in the growth and profitability of the company. You must act the part of a leader day after day in order to be successful as a supervisor.

Here are some guidelines for maintaining leadership and enabling you to run an efficient and productive department:

1. Give priority to requests from above, and inform those concerned of your progress on fulfilling those requests.

2. Get your paperwork done on time. It's a good measure of your efficiency and an effective way to inform people of your accomplishments.

3. Keep up to date on the status of your work and the needs of your people. Continually work towards satisfying those needs.

4. Be predictable and reliable—don't change your position from day to

day. Management likes to have confidence in you, and your people look for consistent behavior on your part.

5. Don't guess at an answer when asked a question. If you don't know, say so. Establish a reputation for knowing what you're talking about.

6. Be a planner. Visualize things that do not exist and figure how to attain them.

7. Coach and train your people. Know how to evaluate the work being done and the people doing it.

8. Be both goal- and group-oriented. Keep your people working toward the goals you've set.

9. Accept new responsibilities willingly and be a person who can be counted on to complete an assignment.

10. Set a good example for your people in the way you handle your job.

1.3 Handling Pressure on the Job

Every supervisor at one time or another feels pressure on the job. If you are a conscientious person it is perfectly normal for you to feel some anxiety and tension. And this is not bad since such feelings keep you on your toes and motivate you to get things done.

However, pressure can be dangerous to your health if it gets to a high level and you are unable to control it. Experienced supervisors have found several ways to handle it. The most simple, although not always possible, way is to withdraw from the situation which is causing it. A respite usually will enable you to tackle a problem with a better frame of mind because the pressure will be less or gone at a different time.

In dealing with pressure, consider the possibility that you may be looking at the situation as worse than it really is. How important is it, for example, that a job be done immediately? Can something be done temporarily or partially to handle the problem? Do other people think it is as urgent or as necessary as you do?

Reconsider where you stand on a problem or an issue. If you yield a bit, other people may also, and the problem may become less severe.

You can lessen pressure on yourself by deciding ahead of time how you're going to handle a problem if it arises. You'll avoid having to decide later when you might be pushed for time.

1.4 Seven Ways to Contend with Pressure

A substantial amount of pressure that a supervisor feels is job tension according to psychologists. You can take a big step toward contending with it if you define and pin it down. Attack the problem by making a list of the things that are causing the pressure. Put down what you must do, when you must get it done, and how much time you think it's going to take. You'll find that by listing what's causing the pressure, you'll reduce its impact—you'll see the problem as simply another job which you have analyzed and now have under control.

Here are seven other ways you can hold down pressure on the job:

1. Get help in handling your problems. Share them with other supervisors and your superior. The advice and help you'll get will make a big difference. Even simply talking about problems without solving them helps.

Case-in-Point: Tom Jackson, supervisor in the maintenance department at one of Goodyear's synthetic rubber plants, found himself continually under pressure at the end of his shift because of the paperwork he had to complete. He mentioned this one day to another supervisor in his department. The other supervisor told Tom that he simply did most of the paperwork and recordkeeping during the shift. Attendance records, time sheets, and reports of jobs completed are examples of the type of paperwork which can be handled at free times during the day. Tom immediately adopted this idea and found that he no longer was under pressure at the end of the day.

2. Handle a problem that arises as quickly as possible. Postponing or delaying taking care of a problem simply results in stacking it up with others which increases pressure. Learn to handle problems automatically instead of setting them aside and you'll wipe them out without as much stress.

3. Develop a system for handling problems and putting them in proper perspective. Know beforehand which tasks you can delegate so that you can immediately pass them off when they come up, and set up a standard procedure for handling others. Filing written procedures where you can easily refer to them will enable you to make such work almost routine.

4. Establish a work pace which suits your temperament and is below the level which causes you to be under pressure. The working level which is comfortable varies from person to person so don't try to set it in comparison with another person's. Watch that you do not start your day too fast. You'll do better at a steady, level pace.

Case-in-Point: Perhaps you've noticed that some company employees who perform a service for people do not change their work pace to match the number of people waiting in line. Most store clerks, airport reservation attendants, ticket sellers, and others on similar jobs have learned to work at a steady pace because a speedup invariably results in stress and mistakes.

5. Maintain yourself physically and mentally. The better condition you are in, the more capable you are of handling problems with a minimum of pressure. Try to avoid fear and worry. Both build pressure, sometimes without you being aware of it. Believe in yourself; believe that you'll be able to contend with future problems when they arise. Keeping your emotions under control will also help you to prevent buildup of pressure.

6. Include relaxation in your day. Get some exercise frequently, even if it's only a short walk. Periodic breaks in your routine are good for relieving pressure. Take a few minutes now and then to think about your family, your friends, and your outside interests. Getting your mind off the job can refresh you and enable you to resume your work feeling less pressure.

7. As a last resort, concede a point or let something happen that you were trying to prevent. You might feel that this is "giving up," and in a way it is, but what you give up isn't as important as your health and well-being.

1.5 What to Do When Your Idea Isn't Accepted

It happens to every supervisor at one time or another, so you may as well be prepared to handle the problem. Your request to one of your people to do something on the job meets with objection. What should you do?

The first and most important thing to do is to be calm and not lose your temper while you try to learn why you or your idea is opposed. Ask yourself several questions in your search for an explanation.

Was your request fair? Were you understood? Did you ask the right person? If you've not been out of line with any of these, you'll have to ask why the person is objecting. Ask for a specific reason.

You may hear that a change has taken place that you didn't know about, one that would make carrying out your request unwise or impossible. Or, the person objecting may have a logical excuse which hasn't been expressed. Then again, the person may simply be irritated. After you allow some time for complaining and blowing off steam, you'll get compliance. You may need only to be patient and not be insistent for a few minutes.

However, if the person is stubborn and simply refuses to do what you've asked without explaining, you have a disciplinary problem on your hands. If you are unable to get your way through persuasion, see if you can get a partial agreement and then work on getting a complete one. If this fails, you have no choice but to start disciplinary action appropriate to the circumstances.

An easy way to get ready acceptance of your idea is to let one of your people "originate" it. Pick the person you want to handle the project, explain the problem, and subtly indicate the line of reasoning you want followed. Once the person presents an idea as his or hers, make him or her defend it—and allow yourself to be won over. This approach will invariably result in the action being carried out enthusiastically.

1.6 Getting People to Follow Your Orders and Instructions

You occasionally are going to run into a situation where your instructions have not been followed as you requested. Although you'll find that the reason is a misunderstanding rather than disobedience, you'll want to take steps to prevent this from happening again. Most often, you must make certain your people really understand what you want. This is not as obvious and simple as it seems.

If you spell out the details of assignments, you must leave nothing to the imagination since any step you omit could cause trouble. It's up to you to anticipate every contingency. But you can ease the unexpected problems which accompany step-by-step instructions if you give assignments in terms of results desired.

Speak the other person's language to get understanding, and don't assume that people always understand what you say. If there is any doubt in your mind, ask them to repeat back to you in their own words what they are being asked to do. This gives you a chance to discover any misunderstanding and correct it.

1.7 Combatting Excuses Painlessly

Supervisors hear all kinds of excuses from people on the job when work is not done on time or at all. One man may say that he didn't have the right tools, another may complain that the job was too tough or he didn't have enough time, and a third may blame it on the material he had to work with. Some workers won't do their best because they think they'll be taken advantage of and end up doing more than their share. Others are afraid someone else might get credit for their efforts. A few don't cooperate because of lack of interest. Whatever, all are excuses and there's few you should accept.

How do you combat excuses on the job? Losing your temper, threatening, and raising a big fuss will usually not change matters without causing hard feelings. What you must do is work on the attitude of the people who make excuses. You can do this most painlessly through communication.

How to Do It: The person who makes the excuse that the work is too hard should be asked to take a little time to study the job. What part is difficult? How much of the whole job is the tough part? Is it lack of proper tools or knowledge that makes the job hard? Is it inexperience?

Get across to the man who makes excuses that life would be very humdrum if he were never challenged, if he didn't run into an occasional problem, if he didn't have to do a little more now and then. He would never get the satisfaction of cracking a tough nut, helping somebody out of a mess, and getting things in better shape.

Along with discussing an excuse, you should, of course, take steps to provide what is needed to make the job easier. You will thus eliminate that as an excuse next time as well as show that you are interested in your worker's welfare, safety, and ease of getting the job done.

To relieve their supervisors from having to continually contend with repetitive excuses, many companies have disciplinary programs which impose increasingly severe discipline, ending with discharge for various types of offenses. Business and industry need such programs to deal with misfits (see Chapter 17), but combatting periodic nonserious excuses is better handled through persuasion and reasoning.

1.8 Proven Ways of Making Good Use of Time

Wasting time is one of our most costly activities despite the fact that each of us can do something about it if we try. There is no such thing as "not enough time." The same amount of time is available to all of us—some people just use their time better.

Since time is valuable, you should figure out how to get the most from it. A few minutes each morning spent planning your day can make you more efficient as well as increase the amount of work you can get done. The executive who accomplishes much usually has his or her time planned days ahead. You don't need to go to that extent, but you can decide daily how you will use your time and also you can adopt timesaving habits.

When you have several jobs to do, start with the one that is most on your mind. The reasoning behind this is logical—your effectiveness and efficiency are not the best when you are concerned or worried, so you should try to relieve such feelings as soon as you can; you will be able to do a better job on your other tasks. If you have a disciplinary step to take with one of your people, do it as soon as possible. If some dirty or unpleasant work faces you, handle it early to get it out of the way.

Always give a high priority to a job which someone has requested of you. Doing work that your boss has requested usually should be put ahead of all jobs that you need to do. After satisfying the boss, give attention to jobs that your people have asked for. Work which needs to be done to satisfy only yourself should be your last choice.

Being punctual is an excellent way to get in the habit of using time effectively. Another is to avoid dawdling at tasks which can be done quickly and without much effort. Take advantage of the time during the day when you are waiting for someone to read. Carry a notebook or pad with you so that you can write down a thought or idea that you want to remember.

Case-in-Point: Helen Taylor, a part-time free-lance writer, in explaining how she was able to write so many stories while holding a full-time job, pointed out, "I always carry a notebook with me. Any time I get a thought or idea that I want to remember, I write it down. Later, when I'm ready to write the story or an article, I have my notes to refer to. This technique saves me a lot of time in trying to recall the words I was going to use and the points I wanted to make."

Slow starters often waste a lot of time. You can overcome this problem by planning or laying out your work the night before so that you don't have to look for things or make decisions the first thing in the morning.

Another way to solve the slow start problem is to begin work on a partially completed job instead of tackling a new one. You can use this idea with your slow starters in the office or shop. Start some project in the afternoon which will arouse their interest but which cannot be finished that day. They'll pick it up the next morning and get going easier.

1.9 How to Reduce Job Time

What part of your job takes the most time? Are there some long, time-consuming jobs your people do that you wish you could shorten? If you study those long jobs, you may find a way to reduce the time it takes to do them.

How to Do It: Break the entire job up into its parts or components and look at each to see if it truly is necessary. What would happen if a step were shortened or omitted? Can two or more steps be combined so that they're done simultaneously? Continue searching until you find a step or two that you can do something about.

Review the work procedure to make sure the job isn't being done in a roundabout way simply because someone once started to do it that way. Are the steps of the work procedure in the best order? Don't be influenced by the fact that there hasn't been a change in a procedure for years. It's time now that you make a change to save time—and do a better job besides.

Successfully applied, work standards can increase worker effectiveness and work performance levels. This, in turn, saves the company a lot of money in cost of labor. But, you must be careful how you apply them.

Case-in-Point: Bob Spencer, a maintenance engineer I interviewed, said, "The first and most important step in instituting a standards program is to select the measurements. Make sure they are accurate and well-developed, based on fact and experience. If the standard allows too much time for a job to be completed, the efficiency of the craftsman is reduced. If not enough time is allowed, he will lose respect for and be frustrated by the system."

1.10 Three Ways to Save Time on Routine Jobs

Most supervisors have a lot of routine work to do every day. Generally, they have been handling it the same way for so long that they don't pay too much attention to the procedure. Are there ways they can get some of it done faster or more efficiently? Experienced supervisors save time on routine jobs in three ways. You should do the same.

1. Get into the habit of doing the same job at the same time each day. You'll adjust to the task much quicker, won't overlook a part of it, and will get it done fast. You are able to do this because habit takes over, letting you go through the motions automatically.

2. Concentrate on doing one thing at a time. Very few people can effectively carry out two thinking activities at the same time. With manual tasks, attempting to do two jobs simultaneously frequently results in mistakes. The time spent correcting them is usually more than what was saved.

3. Finish one job before you start another. Jumping back and forth on jobs causes you to waste time because you need "review" time on each occasion to pick up where you left off. Be aware of this when you assign work to your people. If you want to hear someone grumble about management inefficiency, tell a man to start a new job before he's finished the one he's working on.

1.11 Following Up to Assure Results

Some people think that a supervisor gets things done by simply asking someone to do them, that once an order is given all you need to do is sit back and wait for it to be carried out. A supervisor who gets much accomplished knows better. You just can't delegate a job to someone and forget it. You've got to follow up.

The successful supervisor also knows that there's a difference between ordinary jobs that can be followed up routinely and more difficult ones that require proper timing. The tough jobs need attention from time to time to keep them from bogging down.

If you want to get along well with a person, you must be aware that you can overdo your follow-up.

Case-in-Point: A detail-happy supervisor in a steel fabricating plant handed a job to a worker and immediately asked him how long it would take. "Four hours," the man replied, "if you stand over me, all day." The worker made a point which the supervisor may have needed to be reminded of. No one is an effective supervisor until he has learned how to give a job to someone and then get out of his way to let him do it.

The fact remains that you can't just give work to someone and then forget it. You need to follow through for best results. Sad to say, some otherwise capable supervisors fail at this. They may think and plan well, and also make good assignments. But then they relax, only to be surprised when things don't work out as they expected. Don't let yourself get in this position. You've got to follow up to assure good results.

1.12 Easy Ways of Following Up

The effective supervisor has a follow-up procedure which has become routine in carrying out the duties of his job. "I can't just *hope* that a job I've asked to be done is handled—I have to see or find out for myself," the supervisor will say.

How do you go about following up? Here are a few tips on how to become an expert at it:

1. Get around to the areas where your people are working. See if somebody needs help or has a question. By observing the progress of a job you can determine if the work is going well and when it probably will be finished.

2. When you ask for some work to be done in the future or want to do something yourself later, make a note of it. If you use a calendar for this purpose, put the information on the date when you should follow up.

3. Keep a list of jobs to be done and work to be completed. Refer to the list frequently to plan and decide priority of jobs.

4. Issue a progress report periodically. List work completed, work in progress, and work to be done later. Prepare your report from a previous one. If you do a thorough job of reporting, you'll have a valuable record which will enable you to become very proficient at following up.

2

Tested Supervisory Techniques
That Keep You in Control
of People and Events

Supervisors are leaders. To be successful they must be skilled in the techniques of working with people, directing them, guiding them, and helping them. Supervisors are also managers. With a management position goes the responsibility of decision making and execution of decisions. Since you are "the company" to your people, it is important that you know company policy, follow its rules and procedures, and implement good practices. Effective leaders promote safety and good housekeeping, and they keep in control of people and events.

In order to keep in control, you need to plan your work. This will enable you to get the optimum from your people, be prepared for contingencies, and stay on top of the job. Being in control requires that you be informed and aware, conditions you achieve through observing the work and learning how your people feel about it. The supervisor who is in control gets the best from employees, doesn't oversupervise, and is adept at handling complaints.

2.1 Proven Ways of Selling Company Policy

An employee who is proud to work for a company and thinks well of its products or services is likely to be very productive on the job. That person usually knows and readily accepts company policy also. But what about the person who cares little about the company and seemingly is interested only in the pay? How do you sell company policy to such a person?

You as a supervisor are responsible for carrying out company policy. You do this with the practices you follow and the rules you go by. If all employees are aware of the company's practices and rules and follow them, then everyone goes in the right direction, works together, and the company is a well-organized group.

One of the best ways of communicating with your people about company practices and rules is through a letter given to each individual. The letter should give specific information on starting and quitting times, lunch periods, rules on absenteeism and lateness, and standards of conduct. Safety and security matters are also frequently mentioned. Many companies issue separate booklets detailing fringe benefits that are granted employees. Notices on the bulletin boards, the company newspaper, and handouts in pay envelopes are other ways of informing employees about rules and regulations, company business, and recreational activities.

Despite the written information available to all employees, some of your people will have questions about company policy. You must be familiar with these matters so that you can provide intelligent answers. In addition, you should periodically remind an individual of proper conduct if the person is developing bad habits or violating company rules.

Unless your company is relatively new, its policies and practices have been developed over the years as the best ways and methods of operating. Nevertheless, if you discover a policy or practice which you feel should be changed, you should recommend that this be done to your superior.

2.2 Effective Use of Planning

Many supervisors have demonstrated to themselves and to their company that planning helps get more jobs done with better results and in less time. Planning is worthwhile for several reasons:

1. It enables you to set a course of action to achieve goals and reach objectives.

2. It helps you to solve your problems faster and easier.

3. It prepares you for what to do in case certain things happen, what to do under particular circumstances, and how you should react to future events.

4. It provides the steps for you to follow to improve yourself and get ahead.

When you plan you keep in control of people and events because planning involves getting information, facts, and data which enable you to make good decisions. The more knowledge and know-how you have, the better equipped you are to handle your job.

How do you go about planning? To illustrate what planning is all about, let's assume you are a production supervisor. You're expected to get out the product, and you have people, material, and equipment at your disposal.

When you plan, you decide which people you are going to assign to which jobs. You determine the material that will be needed and you make arrangements to have it available. You think about the machines and equipment which will be operated. You consider the time factor such as when the work will start, how long it will take, and when the job will be finished. You think about quality and quantity in regard to the product and how you will assure them. And throughout all this thinking and deciding, you have in mind safety, good housekeeping, minimum cost, and good human relations.

Successful supervisors are effective planners. They achieve optimum performance and results from people, material, and equipment through use of that skill.

2.3 Five Requirements of Good Plans

To get the most from your planning you must be careful how you plan. Experienced supervisors say that to make good plans you need to:

1. Be specific rather than general. The more explicit and clear your plan is, the less chance there is for it to be misunderstood or misapplied. Define your goals and objectives and indicate the means for attaining them.

2. Distinguish between the known and the unknown. Estimate the probable effects of the unknown. Make your planning more than just anticipation and reaction.

3. Make your plan as logical and practical as possible. The more facts it is based on, the better it is. Make reasonable judgments if facts are not available. Intelligent thinking should serve as the foundation for a plan.

4. Introduce flexibility and looseness so that the plan may readily be modified if circumstances require it. Recognize that no plan is infallible nor can

it cover all possible contingencies. Conditions under which a plan will be most effective change as do the variables and factors on which the plan is based.

5. Be sure the plan is consistent with the aims and goals of the company and the way it conducts its business. Formulate the plan to be acceptable to the people who will implement it and the persons who will be affected. Acceptable plans are more willingly adopted and carried out than ones which are objectionable in one or more respects.

2.4 How to Get the Best from Your People

You should always try to get the best from your people. By doing so you carry out the responsibilities of your job which include holding down costs, maintaining quality, and meeting production goals. When you accomplish these things, you also prove your worth as a supervisor as well as enjoy and get satisfaction from your work.

People on the job tend to live up to what is expected of them. If you treat them like mature, responsible individuals, most of them will act the part.

Having confidence in the abilities of your people to do their jobs will help you in motivating and persuading them to do their best. You will not be inclined to tell them exactly what to do nor to insist that things be done your way. You will discover sooner or later that some of your people will do a job better than you can. Knowing that your people will do good work will also deter you from watching them closely, something that most workers dislike.

Many workers will do their best when you give them the responsibility for getting the job done and don't interfere when they are doing it. They will also do their best if you show that you appreciate their efforts. Praise for a job well done is welcomed by everyone provided it is sincere and deserved.

The supervisor who shows an interest in people and their welfare is usually liked and respected. When people think well of their supervisor they are more likely to do their best on the job.

2.5 How to Avoid Oversupervising

By planning the work to be done supervisors can increase the productivity of their people. Knowing their people's likes, dislikes, and skills, and what they expect from their work enables supervisors to fit jobs to their people whenever possible. More cooperation and higher job satisfaction will result. However, you must be careful how you fit jobs and how you supervise those jobs.

Studies have shown that oversimplifying the job and oversupervising the worker can cause problems. Limiting someone to a single task leads to boredom and frustration, both of which may result in low productivity.

Oversupervising suggests to the worker that the supervisor questions or has doubts whether the worker can and will do the job satisfactorily. Too much supervision destroys morale and ambition leading to lower productivity. In turn, this brings on closer supervision which leads to still lower productivity. Everybody loses.

If a supervisor knows what a man expects from his work and his attitude toward it, the leader can apply the optimum level of supervision. So the problem boils down to knowing the man, his goals, and his outlook. It behooves the supervisor to sharpen his skill in observation and perception. Acquiring a high level of empathy also helps.

Most workers like to have a say about how they handle their jobs. They want to control various aspects of what they do. They want responsibilities that fit their skills and abilities.

Supervisors should give their people a chance to solve their own problems, learn new skills, and gain experience. Given such opportunities, employees can become more valuable to the company while at the same time raise their esteem and prestige. Putting a man on a job where he can see his accomplishments and contributions is bound to benefit both the man and the organization. If his deeds are also recognized through praise and rewards, he is further motivated to higher levels of productivity.

2.6 How to Handle Job Observation and Inspection

Getting ahead on the job is often related to the degree of awareness of the individual. Knowing what is going on in the area and seeing beyond the job itself are two major requirements of the person who wants to be an effective supervisor.

The successful supervisor uses his or her observation skill to suggest and adopt ways to improve operations in the office and on the production line. The skill comes in handy when equipment and facilities must be inspected for malfunctions, and it pays off in improved safety, lower cost of operation, and better quality of product or service.

You can learn to be a good observer. Here are several pointers to help you on the way:

Have an open mind. If you are determined to observe well, you'll do a better job of it. Decide to see more than just what you hope to see. Be aware that bias and prejudice can cause you to see things in a wrong light, while an open mind will enable you to reason and think about what you see. Think for yourself when observing rather than be influenced by others.

Be prepared. Decide what to look for and where you will look. Plan to have adequate time to see everything. You must be prepared both mentally and physically. The task will be more difficult if you are impatient, tired, or otherwise physically uncomfortable. A plan or checklist of things to look for will help you observe more quickly and also serve as a way to avoid overlooking something.

Beware of habit. You must be cautious with habit because it can blind you—you may walk right past something that needs attention and not see it. Another stumbling block is familiarity. Look again when you get the feeling that you've seen everything. Rule out past appearances by trying to look at something as if you were noticing it for the first time. Analyze a situation from all angles. Don't let habit tempt you to reach a hasty conclusion.

Take your time. You want to get more than just a general idea out of what you see. Look for details to give you a broader picture. Look for differences in the equipment, material, and procedures from that with which you are familiar. Take the time to look carefully for things which are not apparent at first glance.

Keep notes. Write down your observations while they are fresh in your mind. Getting things down on paper frees your mind for concentrating on what you are seeing by relieving it of also remembering. Try to use a system in your notes by grouping similar items. The picture will be clearer when you refer to your notes later.

2.7 Effective Methods of Promoting Safety

The safety of employees in business and industry places a tremendous responsibility on supervisors. It also presents a challenge for supervisors to show initiative in the prevention of accidents.

Safety can never be taken for granted. No organization attains a good safety record through luck or chance. Behind every good safety record that a company achieves you will find much planning and a great amount of hard work.

You promote and communicate safety by creating an awareness of it in the minds of your people. You accomplish this by setting up a safety program and carrying it out conscientiously and thoroughly.

You and other supervisors play key roles in your organization's safety program. Aside from the obvious demand of knowing the company's safety rules and setting a good example for your people, you must actively participate by instructing your people in safe work methods. You should also encourage workers to discuss accident prevention through anticipating unusual risks in the work areas and following up by providing safety equipment. When you see a hazard you must immediately do something about it. You must also investigate, analyze, and report every accident.

No job is so important or so urgent that time cannot be taken to do it in a safe manner. This means that you must always see that your people are performing their work safely and that they are not taking shortcuts that could lead to an accident or injury. Continuous training in safety is a requisite of an effective safety program.

Case-in-Point: At the Russellville, Ark. plant of Morton Frozen Foods Div., I.T.T. Continental Baking Co., hoses on the plant floor were getting run over, stepped on, and worst of all, tripped over. Glen Ray, a receiving supervisor, solved this problem with a hose reel. He put the reel and hose in a box, mounted it on wheels, and designed it with an inlet and coupling on the outside for quick hookup. Now floors are clear, hoses aren't damaged, and people aren't having tripping accidents.

2.8 How to Make an Accident Investigation

Supervisors rather than safety engineers or directors are expected to make accident investigations in most companies. The reason for this is that supervisors know the operations better, have the responsibility and authority to take whatever corrective action is necessary, and are looked upon as leaders. If you make a prompt and thorough investigation of an accident, you gain the trust and confidence of your people because they see you are looking out for their interest and are concerned with their safety. However, your investigation must be more than simply reporting the explanation of the individual who saw or had the accident. The report should include recommendations for corrective action.

Investigating an accident requires that you be patient and tactful in getting information about it. Talking to the person who was involved is the first thing to do. Try to put the person at ease. Point out that the purpose of the investigation is not to put the blame on anyone but only to prevent a similar accident from happening again, and that you need help to do this.

Go to the accident area, if possible, and also do your talking in private. The person involved will be more at ease if the two of you are alone; what you report will not be influenced by comments and opinions of others in the person's presence. Let the person describe what happened without interruption. If you don't understand something, ask about it later.

Avoid judging what happened or is said. You don't want to put the person on the defensive. Limit your questions to asking for facts rather than opinions, to learn what happened, what was done, and how it was done. "Why" questions may make the person defensive. Ask your questions in a friendly, helpful manner, and ask the type which cannot be answered with only a "yes" or "no."

It's a good idea to repeat the account of the accident to the person after you've heard and written it down. This will enable the person to correct any errors in your story as well as perhaps add something you omitted. Finish the investigation by discussing what should be done to prevent a similar accident. You thus confirm the purpose of your investigation and prove that you want to help.

2.9 The Painless Way of Staying Ahead on Housekeeping

Failure to practice good housekeeping is a major reason why accidents continue to happen in offices and plants. But, safety isn't the only reason for an organization wanting and needing to keep working areas picked up, neat, and orderly. Many companies have domonstrated that employee attitude and productivity are much better in a clean working place than in a dirty one.

Any organization that is sincere in wanting to stay ahead on housekeeping must have a plan of action and a follow-up procedure. Once an active program is adopted, good housekeeping can be relatively painless. Planning, inspecting, and enforcing are the steps that those in charge of a program must follow.

Planning involves deciding what needs to be done and how people, equipment, and materials fit as well as are dependent on each other. Responsibilities must then be established and tasks assigned. Some areas and equipment need attention more often than others. Waste and scrap pickup and disposal must be handled. A concerted effort of employees at housekeeping pays off.

Case-in-Point: Recently the Department of Labor conducted a follow-up inspection of Price Cabinet Shop, Huntsville, Alabama, and issued a citation charging repeated violation of an OSHA regulation on failure to practice good housekeeping. The compliance officer said he had found tripping hazards, like sawdust and scrap lumber, on the shop floor. The company argued that the floor had been cleaned, and that the debris had accumulated within minutes before the inspection. Moreover, said the company, since the previous inspection and citation for housekeeping violations, it had hired a new employee to keep the shop clean. To require that the company clean the shop floor every half hour or so would be unreasonable. The Review Commission Judge vacated the citation, ruling that the company had made adequate efforts to keep the shop clean.

You can keep ahead of housekeeping if you periodically inspect your office or plant and communicate your findings. But don't think that only a few key people should see your report. You must sell the necessity for good housekeeping to *all* employees. Everyone needs to cooperate in putting things in their place and keeping work areas neat. Organizations which have sold their people on this and gotten cooperation have reaped a side benefit—they have kept their janitorial labor cost low.

Control and enforcement are the backbones of a good housekeeping program. When you stress them, you make sure your program elements are handled and your goals achieved. Supervisors need to continually point out that housekeeping is part of the job and follow through to see that their people do not forget it.

2.10 Five Ways to Sell Good Housekeeping

You occasionally are going to meet with opposition when you tell someone to spend time housekeeping. For example, you might hear, "House-keeping? You must be kidding. I've got a job to do," or "That's not my job. We've got janitors for that type of work." How do you answer such people? How do you sell them on the importance and necessity of good housekeeping? Here are five ways to do it:

1. Point out that good housekeeping makes a job safer because it eliminates most of the major causes of accidents and fires. Safety is everybody's business and certainly everybody wants to be safe on the job.

2. Prove that good housekeeping has a positive effect on people in that work areas are more cheerful when they are neat and clean. Work is more fun. People feel better and get along better with each other.

3. Demonstrate that good housekeeping makes work less tiring. When you have all your work tools right at hand and don't need to search for materials and instructions, you don't suffer frustration or aggravation. Poor housekeeping brings on mental fatigue in that depressing surroundings can make the work seem more difficult and boring than it really is.

4. Show that good housekeeping helps in maintaining health and well-being. Dust and dirt never did anybody any good. Scrap and waste in the work area limit work space, lead to poor quality workmanship, and result in low or no satisfaction with job accomplishment.

5. Convince a person that good housekeeping is a personal thing—that nobody can expect someone else to do all of it—that a person on the job knows his or her work area better than anybody else—and that a person develops pride from being a good housekeeper.

2.11 How to Handle Employee Complaints

A complaint is always justified from the viewpoint of the person making it, and prompt handling of a complaint is always desirable. If you remember these two points about complaints you'll do a better job of handling them.

One of the poorest ways a supervisor can go about handling a complaint is to put the blame on someone such as upper management. Passing the buck only raises suspicions—it's like the supervisor saying, "It's not my fault, but I'll help you anyway." Instead of looking for excuses, ask the person, "What's wrong?" or "What happened?" That way, you attack the problem by concentrating on *what* went wrong rather than *who* is to blame. The two of you can then work together to get the complaint handled.

Many complaints that people have fit certain categories. For example, a lot of complaints can be classed under lack of information or misunderstanding of the facts. Complaints about the amount of employees' benefits, deductions from pay, or company procedures can usually be handled with a few questions and answers from you. If you don't have an answer at your fingertips, tell the person you will get it, and be sure to do so.

Poor communications are behind many complaints. You may have thought your instructions were very clear but they were not. If a job is done poorly or wrongly, the person responsible may gripe in anticipation of being criticized. The answer to this problem is to make sure you're understood. Get feedback from questions you ask the person or the person asks you before the job is started.

Some complaints are a transfer-of-anger type. The man who comes to work after a quarrel with his wife or has trouble with his car on the way may be in a poor frame of mind and looking for something to complain about. A few tactful questions put to him about how things are going in general will reveal the situation. Sympathy and empathy on your part often may be enough to handle the complaint; if not, offer to look into the matter and do so.

Handling a complaint is probably one of the toughest parts of a supervisor's job. You've got to put yourself in the complainer's position and realize how the person feels. Once you do that, it'll be much easier for you to offer your help. You and the complainer will both feel better besides.

2.12 Seven Rules for Handling Complaints

You can handle a complaint easily and effectively if you go about it in a definite manner. Also, the person complaining will feel much better about the complaint if you follow some rules in discussing it with him or her. Try the following the next time you must handle a complaint:

1. Agree that the person has a valid complaint, that you'd feel the same way if you were in such a situation. Say you're sorry that it has caused the person inconvenience.
2. Investigate by using questions to bring out details. Get the facts. Listen carefully.

3. Sympathize and commiserate with the person to further reduce negative emotions. Show your concern.

4. Take at least part of the blame for the mistake or error which led to the complaint.

5. Make the complainer feel important. Recognize position, responsibility, and involvement.

6. Save the complainer's face when explaining a situation or why circumstances are as they are.

7. Try to help solve the complaint. Tell the person promptly when you have done so.

2.13 Ways to Discipline Which Get Results

Discipline is effective when its application eliminates the need for it in the future. This is another way of saying that effective discipline gets results. You should never apply discipline without also giving an explanation and providing instruction on correct behavior.

For discipline to have a long-lasting effect, it must be acceptable to the person receiving it. Unacceptable discipline causes resentment and hostility, either of which may bring on feelings of wanting to get revenge. Poor discipline also results in creating a "don't care" attitude. Supervisors who have been successful at disciplining get results without making people angry. Here are the ways you can do the same:

1. Get all the facts before you say or do anything. Disciplining someone is a serious matter—you don't want to make the mistake of disciplining the wrong person or of taking unwarranted action.

2. Consider each incident separately. Circumstances vary and people are different in their thoughts, motives, and deeds. You may not be able to apply a standard type of discipline for the specific incident.

3. Maintain control. Don't lose your temper. Never attempt to discipline when there is a possibility that emotion rather than reason is controlling your thinking. You will be less likely to make the mistake of being unfair to both the person and the company.

4. Be consistent. Enforce the rules of behavior and conduct with the same degree of strictness in every case. Being rough with one person and gentle with another for the same infraction leads to nothing but displeasure and unrest. You may be accused of being unfair and prejudiced besides.

5. Have set rules concerning discipline for common incidents. When penalties for failure to comply with rules are made known to everyone, people know what to expect in the way of discipline. The person who is disciplined

knows also that no personal factor of the supervisor was involved in his or her discipline.

2.14 Three Key Features of an Effective Discipline Program

A discipline program can be effective only if it is uniform, corrective, and progressive. Each feature is of equal importance in getting results.

A uniform program prevents the imposition of different discipline for the same offense. Without a guideline, one supervisor might issue a written warning for fighting in the plant while another might suspend the guilty person for two or three days. A spelled-out, understood penalty for fighting prevents such inequities.

Corrective discipline defines what proper conduct is, thus giving a person the opportunity to correct his or her improper conduct. This discipline also warns other employees that improper conduct or the breaking of company rules will not be tolerated and will subject guilty individuals to disciplinary action.

The progressive feature of a discipline procedure provides for increasing the severity of the discipline with repeated offenses. Typical procedure might be oral warning for the first offense, written warning for the second, a one-day suspension for the third, a five-day suspension for the fourth, and discharge for the fifth.

2.15 How to Choose the Most Appropriate Discipline

Deciding what disciplinary action you should impose for breaking a rule may be difficult if your company has not established penalties for specific rule infractions. You must decide between discipline that is too severe to be fair and discipline that is too mild to be corrective. Here are six questions which when answered will help you choose the most appropriate action:

1. How serious was the rule infraction?
2. What were the circumstances?
3. How long has the person been employed by the company?
4. What is the person's past conduct record?
5. When was the last time the person required discipline?
6. What is the discipline usually administered for this rule infraction?

Making judgments: A common procedure today in companies which have severe personnel behavioral problems is to take a "cooling off" period before imposing discipline. Better decisions have resulted when time is taken for more investigation, reasoning, and thought before deciding the proper discipline.

3

Training and Development Know-Hows That Assure Results

People make a company. Their skills and abilities, their performance on the job, and their productivity determine the company's profitability and its growth. The better the people are at doing their work, the more successful the company is likely to be in selling its products or performing services.

Almost every person hired by an organization must be *trained* to do their work. Although they may be experienced to a degree from previous jobs they've held, they still must learn the company's policies, methods, and procedures and abide by its rules and regulations. To get satisfaction from their work, they must know how to do it efficiently. Moreover, these needs and requirements of employees are continuing matters because of the constant change which goes on and our rapid advance in technology.

Supervisors play key roles in training and developing employees from the day they are hired until they become skilled and productive on the job. How quickly they do and how adept they become depends on the abilities and know-hows of their trainers and supervisors. You as a supervisor are a greater asset to your company if you are a good teacher and trainer.

3.1 Handling the Job of Inducting and Orienting New Employees

The supervisor handles the job of inducting and orienting new employees best by communicating personally with them. Effective communicating paves the road for understanding and provides the basis for good relations between the employee and the company in the future. The time and personal attention that's given a new-hire during the first few days on the job is invaluable in making the employee feel wanted and important. Such contact gives the person a sense of security as well as demonstrating that the company is interested in the employee's future.

Introductions and a tour of the department and work area should be one of the first steps to make the employee familiar with people he or she will work with. Show the person what each employee does and how people work together in putting out the product or performing a service. Point out the company's facilities such as the restrooms, canteen or cafeteria, supply sources, and how the employee can find and talk to you.

Inducting and orienting a new employee includes discussing company rules, procedures, and policy, and also handing out manuals, safety, and job specifications relating to the work he or she will be doing. A supervisor should distribute the manuals in person to call attention to the employee that the supervisor is the person to go to for information and advice. You should inform the person also how the job will be learned and who will provide the training.

Motivation, attitude, and morale are greatly influenced with events which occur the first few days the new employee is on the job. You can help promote these by the kind of attention you give the person. Certainly, the employee will appreciate it. Regardless, your objective should not be forgotten—to have the company acquire a satisfied and productive employee.

3.2 Eight Principles of Effective Orientation of Employees

Getting a new employee off to a good start on the job is a responsibility of the supervisor which is important to the company and the employee. How you handle this responsibility may decide what the employee thinks of the company and the job as well as the quality and quantity of work he or she performs in the future.

You can do an effective job of orientation if you apply the following principles and act accordingly:

1. Make the person feel welcome. Try to allay any fears and anxiety which the person may have.

2. Recognize that a person has a big adjustment to make when starting a new job. Adjustments are not always easy or quickly made.

3. Give the person reasons for wanting to work for you and the company. First impressions are important.

4. Be friendly and helpful. Work at having the person like you.

5. Promote the person with other people and make friendly introductions. Do what you can to make it easy for the person to get along with other employees.

6. Point out the good features of the job; play down the poor ones. Sell the job, the department, and the company.

7. Enlist the help of one or more other employees to see that the person learns his way around. Be sure the person is not ignored.

8. Follow up frequently to answer questions which the person may have. Show interest and appreciation for the abilities and skills which the person develops.

3.3 How to Know When Training Is Needed

Supervisors are responsible for the development, progress, and performance of their people; training their people is the way to carry out this responsibility. But, how do supervisors know when training is needed? What are the signs that tell them people need training on the job?

The need for training should be considered when:

1. New methods or work procedures are started.

2. Production goals are not being met.

3. Employees lack a sense of purpose.

4. Costs of operations are increasing without apparent reason.

5. Quality of the product or service is declining.

6. Accidents are increasing.

7. Pride in the job is missing.

8. Complaints and grievances are excessive.

9. Workers are asking numerous questions about the job.

10. High turnover and absenteeism are prevalent.

This list is not complete since training needs and type vary with organizations. However, it serves as a guide for supervisors to determine when training is needed and where training efforts may need to be directed.

Case-in-Point: Tim Blackwell, a supervisor in a large South Carolina company, told me why he likes to see his company push training of the men who work for him. "Sure, training costs money," he said, "but it costs a lot more to slow down work or shut down an operation because someone's absent and you have no replacement person to step in."

3.4 Successful Ways of Selling People on Training

Although you are aware of the value of training and how it helps people with their work, you may need to convince some of your people of this. They may feel that training is a waste of time. You must show them how training pays off.

You can sell training most successfully by pointing out how it helped others to get ahead, how it brought them job security, and how it raised their income.

You can increase a person's interest in training by mentioning the advantage of being able to handle a job well. Training enables a person to learn the what, the how, and the why of a job. When a person knows these, the job becomes interesting and provides more satisfaction, with accomplishment besides.

Case-in-Point: Joe Serenka, Foreman of the Hammer Shop at the Pittsburgh Works of Jones & Laughlin Steel Corporation[1] completed the J & L Machinist Apprenticeship and worked his way up to his present position from which he supervises three other foremen and, through them, a total of 45 men. During his company service he studied in the company apprenticeship program as well as outside (Pittsburgh Institute of Technology, University of Pittsburgh).

"I don't know how anybody can downgrade training," Joe says. "It just makes good sense. Craftsmen on the job ten years or so should go back to school—to pick up new wrinkles. After all, if you can't update the material or the process—and often you can't—you can only update the *method*: and you do that by updating the man."

---

[1]From *Case Studies in Effective Training*, ICS Training for Business and Industry.

3.5 Five Easy Steps to Conducting a Training Program

Supervisors may train employees or may assist in setting up the company's training program. In either case, they should be aware of the steps involved. They are: defining the area where training is needed, planning the presentation, obtaining the training resources and media, recruiting the training personnel, and implementing the program.

Defining the area: Do the office workers need training in operating the machines or in office procedures? Do the men in the maintenance department need instruction in reading blueprints or in understanding hydraulics? The specific need of the employees should dictate the scope and range of the training program.

Planning the presentation: How will the instruction and training be provided? Who will conduct it? On the job or in a classroom? How will it be administered? How complete will it be? Factors such as these must be considered and decided.

Training resources and media: Many resources are available for training programs. The training departments of companies have learned that the best programs they can present include several training tools. Resources they use include: programmed instruction manuals, high school and college courses, vendor training sessions, on-the-job training, in-house training classes, seminars, and current literature.

Recruiting the trainer: Even though many of the resources and media include material and tools, individual personal attention is important to any training program. Some person or persons must be recruited to see that classes are conducted, to answer questions and provide assistance, to act as monitors, and to see that the training accomplishes its objectives.

Implementing the program: Dedication and hard work are behind successful training. If the preliminary steps have been carried out industriously and sincerely, this last step will go well and trainees will benefit. Training should not be delayed or postponed once a decision is made to do it. The sooner the program can be implemented, the sooner trainees will begin to improve their skills.

3.6 The Technique of On-the-Job Training

Supervisors usually are responsible for giving instruction when the performance of an employee falls below an acceptable standard. Such instruction is generally called on-the-job training.

With today's demand for greater productivity in business and industry, pressure is on management to improve the performance of both new and long-time employees. Whether it is called training, educating, or coaching, it basically consists of the supervisor helping the employee to be more productive. The ultimate goal of on-the-job training is to develop self-reliant employees.

On-the-job training is successful only when the supervisor/employee relationship has a foundation of mutual acceptance and trust. Employees who feel they are being judged rather than helped will not talk freely and when asked questions may defend their actions rather than change or agree to cooperate. Supervisors must recognize that employees are individuals with human emotions, and that they cannot be treated as machines. Employees often decide *what* they will hear and *how* they will respond.

Effective on-the-job training puts three requirements on the supervisor:

1. The supervisor must see the training as a joint effort. Both the supervisor and the employee must be willing to view their attitudes, feelings, and work problems constructively.

2. The supervisor must develop a trust relationship with the employee. Information is not shared in a threatening situation.

3. The supervisor must listen and accept what is said in a nonjudgmental manner. Listening with attention encourages employees to fully communicate and accept suggestions for improving their work.

3.7 Tips on Teaching and Training: Making Sure You're Understood

Successful teachers and trainers possess a skill which serves them well—their technique in communicating makes them easily understood. They are effective trainers because they constantly work at being simple, concise, and clear. Here are some tips for you on the technique:

1. Use an easygoing approach. This puts trainees more at ease and in a mood to learn.

2. Speak the language of your listeners. By using words they know and understand, you leave no doubt in their minds.

3. Prefer short words to long ones, simple words to complex ones, and short sentences to long ones. Being brief and concise helps you to be clear.

4. Keep emotion out of your style. Facts may be ignored when emotion is present. Emotional ideas may cloud the issue for some listeners.

5. Connect new ideas with old ones and modern procedures with outmoded ones. Learning is easier when the relationship to something familiar is pointed out.

6. Explain simple things first. Save the difficult ones for later when trainee's minds are better adjusted to learning.

7. Pause between steps of procedures and change of subjects to give trainees time to absorb the instructions. Let them think a bit—it helps learning.

8. Encourage feedback. Promote questions to determine if you are getting through and to find out what you should repeat and where you may need to place emphasis.

9. Avoid negative approaches to subjects. Attempt to put the record straight on negative comments from trainees. Your effectiveness as a trainer is always better when you stress the positive.

10. Limit the number of ideas or points covered at a single session. It's better to do a thorough job with a few ideas than an incomplete job with many. When time is short, be satisfied to get across one idea clearly and completely.

3.8 How to Train by the Four-Step Method of Instruction

A four-step method of instruction of new employees is a proven method of training today, particularly in the operation of machinery or equipment. To be effective at training your people on how to do a job, you should know and practice this method. Here's how to do it:

Step 1: *Get the person ready to learn.* Describe the job and find out what the person knows about it. Familiarize the person with the work area and the surroundings. Encourage and enthuse the trainee in doing good work.

Step: *Show how to do the job.* Give tools, material, and equipment their proper names. Demonstrate each step, describing it as you go. Emphasize the key points. Go slowly so that the trainee will not miss anything and gets the whole picture. Teach and instruct only as fast as you think you are being understood.

Step 3: *Let the person do the job.* Watch carefully and correct any mistakes, noting where the person needs more instruction. Ask the trainee to explain the key points of the job and where mistakes, if any, were made. Have the person do the job several times until you are sure he or she can handle it without help.

Step 4: *Turn the job over to the person.* Follow up frequently to see if the person has a problem or question. Give praise for a job well-done to encourage future good performance.

3.9 Answering How Much You Should Teach at One Time

The amount you should try to teach people at one time depends on how difficult the job is and how fast the trainees can learn. Each trainee on the job is different just like each student in school is different. Some learn fast while others learn slow. Set the amount you teach at one time to the learning rate of the slowest person being trained.

New employees usually are nervous and anxious to do well, adding to the difficulty of their learning a job. You need to be understanding and patient. Try to put them at ease. Compliment them when they make progress and do well. They will learn faster if you are not demanding or critical.

Always start teaching and training slowly to allow trainees to get accustomed to the job and their surroundings. Recognize that trainees may be under tension. They also don't want to look bad in the presence of others.

Make teaching the basics and the fundamentals your main objective. When people know the rudiments of a job it is easier for them to learn the refinements of it.

Avoid comparing the progress of one individual with that of another, remembering that each person is different in how fast a job is learned and how much is remembered. Give the slow learner more of your attention than the fast one.

3.10 Delegating: When and Why to Do It

Most successful supervisors are skilled in the art of delegating. In case you're undecided about your need to do it, be convinced if you frequently find yourself in one or more of the following situations:

1. Taking work home at night or working a lot of overtime.
2. Failing to give important jobs the amount of attention they deserve.
3. Getting important jobs done just on time or a day or two late.
4. Spending too much time on relatively unimportant jobs.
5. Finding that much of the work you're doing is very routine in nature.

You must certainly practice delegation if you have hopes of moving up in your organization. Your skill in delegating could be the deciding factor in whether you can handle greater responsibilities and a bigger job since a successful manager gets things done through others.

If you are hesitating to delegate because you are afraid of a subordinate moving up too fast or because you feel you must do a job yourself to have it done right, such arguments are false. A subordinate moving up fast shows your boss and others that you're ready for advancement—you've got a person ready to take your place. If you feel that your subordinate can't do a job as well as you can, consider whether it's really necessary that the job be done that well.

Unwillingness to delegate may be a psychological problem with some supervisors. They may fear that credit for the job being done will go to someone else, that it will become known that others know more about a particular job than they, or that someone may do the job better than they've been doing it. After they begin to delegate, these fears become inconsequential or disappear entirely. All supervisors have much more to gain than to lose by delegating.

3.11 Five Tested and Proven Steps to Successful Delegating

Nearly all supervisors today must delegate some duties at one time or another. You, therefore, should know how to delegate. Here are the steps you should follow to be successful at it:

1. Decide what part of your work you can delegate. One obvious choice is a job which another person can do as well or better than you can. Reserve for yourself those tasks which require the experience, skill, and training which only you possess.

2. Delegate to more than one person, if possible. Carefully select the person to whom you're going to delegate a specific task by suiting the task to the person. By spreading assignments among all your people, and especially those who have the ability and desire to get ahead, you enable each to demonstrate their potential as well as gain recognition for getting a job done.

3. Be clear and concise when delegating. Right from the beginning you must clarify what decisions you are delegating and what you are reserving for yourself. Delegating fails when the person to whom you have delegated a task fails to perform it or makes a decision beyond the scope of authority granted.

4. Tell other people in the department or company about your delegation. If you fail to let people know what and to whom you've delegated, you make it difficult for your helpers to get cooperation and to avoid resentment when making decisions.

5. Follow up on people and tasks. Even though you may have delegated some decision-making responsibility, you still have the total responsibility. You must keep up-to-date too, on what you have delegated. Stay on top of these things by asking that your people report to you from time to time.

Caution When you delegate your work you must be careful not to go overboard. Some of your duties and responsibilities should *not* be delegated. Management expects you to handle such matters as planning, scheduling, policy formation, coordinating, control, and supervision. If you give those away you might just as well start looking for another job—your company won't need you.

3.12 How to Recruit a Temporary Supervisor

You can't be on the job every day. Everybody takes a vacation now and then, and few people are not ill once in a while. Somebody is needed to handle your job in your absence. Since you know your people better than anyone else, it is logical that you be asked to recommend someone. Talk to your boss about this to get agreement on arranging for someone to replace you.

Although you would be pleased if all of your people would like to have your job, face the fact that not everyone wants the responsibility which goes with being a supervisor. Since you want the best qualified person for the job, look for qualities of leadership among your people. Note if the person who qualifies gets along well with other employees. Is he or she concerned with efficiency and cost? Quality and quantity of product or service? A desire to get the job done? When you find such a person among your people, talk to him or her saying that you think the person would make a good supervisor. Then ask if he or she would be interested in taking your place the next time you are absent.

If you meet with reluctance or refusal, point out that the experience would be good and that acting as a temporary supervisor is a step to a better job with the company. Also, suggest that the person try the job for only one or two days to start.

When you get acceptance, be considerate and understanding as you show the person how to do your work. How you help the person to handle the job as well as how you show confidence in his or her ability to do it may be a factor in how effective the person turns out to be.

Caution: When offering one of your people the opportunity to act as a temporary supervisor you may be tempted to pick the person with the most education. You could make a mistake in doing so. The three vital attributes a first-line supervisor must have are leadership, sensitivity, and initiative. Astute and knowledgeable managers know that the presence or absence of these attributes has nothing to do with a candidate's educational level. College graduates may lack them while up-from-the-ranks, practical-experienced individuals may have them in abundance.

4

Making
Your Point and
Making It Stick

You are a leader of people, and you get things done through people rather than doing them yourself. To be a successful leader you've got to make decisions, motivate people, direct them, and follow through on tasks which take skill energy, drive, and enthusiasm. Along the way you will run into obstacles and problems, both with people and things. Often, in working with people and to overcome these obstacles and problems you will need to make your point and make it stick.

In this chapter you'll find ways to be firm and forceful when you ask your people for something or give instructions on the job. People look to their supervisor for guidance. You provide that guidance when you make your point and make it stick. You have to know, of course, what your people want in order to communicate with them effectively.

4.1 How to Know What Your People Want

The supervisor who knows what his people want has a big jump on having good relations with them because he recognizes their needs and can do something about them. Making your point and making it stick are a lot simpler when you understand your people. Logically, people are more willing to cooperate when they know that their boss is looking out for them and is interested in their welfare.

There is no single answer to good supervisor-worker relations. However, aside from decent treatment and fair pay, all people want and need certain things from their jobs. Most employees, for example, need a sense of security. They want to know that they will still have their job tomorrow, next month, and next year. They want to feel secure within their group, to accept the people they work with, and to be fully accepted by them and their supervisor.

Employees like to feel that they belong, that they are part of a team. They want a sense of participation, a feeling of being "in" on things. When you tell your people, for example, that a new product is coming through that will require a change in procedure, make sure *all* are informed, not just the few that may be directly involved. When you announce the new hours for the cafeteria, tell *everyone* including those who usually don't eat their lunch there. If you start the use of a new tool, give *all* your people a chance to use it.

People on the job usually have a desire for challenging work. They look for opportunities to use all of their talents; therefore, they welcome assignments which require they do their best and, at the same time, enable them to discover abilities they didn't realize they possessed.

Case-in-Point: "Casey" Jones, supervisor of the pipefitters at an Ohio oil refinery, recognized the value of letting his craftsmen show their job skills. "Although most of our work is of a repair nature," he said, "we occasionally make some new installations such as putting in a heating system, an eye wash, or a safety shower. When I assign the fellows such a job, I don't give them all the details of how to do the job. Letting them figure out elevations, source of supply, and locations of valves, among other things, gives them some responsibility and makes their work more satisfying."

A number of surveys have been conducted in recent years among employees in which they were asked what they want and expect from their jobs, and the degree of importance of those things. The supervisors of these employees were also asked what they thought were important to the people they supervised.

Employees generally rated the human aspect of their jobs as being far more important than the tangible monetary factors. For example, people wanted "full appreciation of work done" and "help on personal problems." Shirley Combs wanted to be told that the department management appreciated the time and effort she put into tracing and expediting the shipment of forms the department needed. Bob Smith expected his supervisor to "hear him out" and express sympathy on his problems with his new car.

Supervisors thought that "good wages" and "job security" were most important to their people. They also minimized the human aspects of earning a living. Have you ever thought about how boring that job that Charley White does must be and how you might make it more interesting for him?

The surveys show that often we are incorrect in our assumptions of what we think is important to another person. They also show us that a problem exists when employees who think "full appreciation of work done" is important are being led by a supervisor who thinks this is relatively unimportant.

Get to know what your people want and you'll find that your job is more challenging, yet easier.

4.2 Proven Ways of Getting to Know People and Their Skills

People are like fingerprints in that no two are exactly alike. So the better you know them as individuals, the better job you can do of leading and supervising them. Your task of placing them on jobs suited to their abilities becomes much easier when you know more about them.

Case-in-Point: B.I. Anderson, maintenance supervisor for Pan American World Airways at the Seattle-Tacoma (Wash.) Airport,[1] expressed this axiom well when he said, "I've learned to search for each man's abilities and then zero in on them. It's as simple as using a screwdriver instead of a hammer. Men's skills vary, and it's up to the foreman to dig them out."

How to Do It: How can you determine when you really know your people? Because people change in how they think and feel from day to day, this is difficult. But you can test yourself by seeing if you can answer these questions about any one of your men:

1. How skilled is he on his job? Does he need training?
2. How is the quality and quantity of his work? Is he accurate? Does he make errors?
3. Does he show initiative? Is his judgment good?
4. Does he accept responsibility? Can he proceed on his own or does he continually need guidance?
5. Is he impulsive? Can he think out a problem?

---

[1]Reprinted from *Supervisor's Memory Jogger,* National Foremen's Institute, Jan. 1974. By permission of the publisher. Bureau of Business Practice, 24 Rope Ferry Road, Waterford, Connecticut 06386. Copyright, Bureau of Business Practice, Inc.

6. Does he work well with others? Is he a loner or a team member?

If you can answer most of these questions about each of your people, you probably know them well.

4.3 Successful Ways to Motivate and Inspire People

Personnel experts and industrial psychologists have learned that most of the good things a company may do to make working conditions pleasant and satisfying such as clean and safe work areas, fringe benefits, and good personnel relations, are soon taken for granted and cease to be ways to motivate people. In fact, these things may even become demotivators if they do not keep up with change.

Today, the job itself is the most important motivator. Workers want jobs that give them a sense of achievement, enable them to be recognized, and permit them to move up to something better after good performance. They are motivated by work that is meaningful, gives them responsibility, and lets them grow.

Case-in-Point: Two pipefitters in one of Akron, Ohio's rubber factories told their supervisor they were planning to go into business for themselves if the company couldn't provide them with more challenging work than they were then doing. One of the men expressed their feelings clearly when he said, "We get tired of the same uninteresting work of unplugging lines and fixing leaks day after day. We like construction work and installing new facilities—that's the type of work we'll do if we decide to leave the company."

How to Do It: You can help to motivate your people. Here are some of the ways you can do it:

1. Provide them opportunities for training which will result in their earning more money. This will help them meet their social needs.

2. Give them things to do that challenge and bring out the best in them. This will satisfy their ego needs.

3. Enable them to use more of their potential. This increases their sense of security.

4. Aid them to achieve more, to grow, and to develop. This will give them a sense of accomplishment and satisfaction.

Case-in-Point: The supervisor in the plant engineering division of Boeing Commercial Airplane Co.[2] in Seattle, Washington, Clifton F. Garrison, says

---

[2]From *Motivation as a Continuous In-House Program,* Southern Plant Engineering and Maintenance Conference, Nov., 1977.

that his company believes that trained and motivated personnel are one of its important assets. When talking about the company's pollution control program, he said, "Boeing has found that an effective program depends upon the awareness and commitment of all employees, but particularly the manufacturing and service personnel. Consequently, a great deal of effort is directed towards these people. They are on the firing line as far as pollution control is concerned, and their actions go a long way in preventing spills."

Another Approach: Benjamin M. Hines, director of personnel planning for some time for General Foods Corporation,[3] says that people are effectively and properly motivated when:

1. They are convinced that they are performing useful and challenging work.

2. They share a feeling of enthusiasm and optimism about the aims and capability of company management.

3. They respect the ability and understanding of their immediate supervisor.

4. They know the objectives, responsibilities, and standards of acceptable performance connected with their jobs.

5. They have a chance to take part in formulating goals, policies, and organizational procedures related to their own areas of activity.

6. They are free from fear of whimsical or capricious actions that will end their jobs.

7. They are provided with the possibility of advancement in salary and position if deserved.

4.4 Nine Principles of Effective Motivation

Of the many ways that workers may be motivated, a few stand out as basic in that they motivate while also satisfy the needs of individuals. The more these principles and conditions can be provided in the working atmosphere, the more people will respond productively:

1. Being a member of a "good bunch of fellows" is important for job satisfaction and good productivity.

2. Socialization on the job without influencing output negatively is desirable.

---

[3]From *Foremanship,* Dartnell, Jan., 1975.

3. Working conditions which make communication easy satisfy the worker's need for socialization.

4. Good compatibility of persons working together promotes good performance.

5. If a worker does not get satisfaction from the job, it is only an unpleasant interlude to the hours after work.

6. Supervisors should be viewed by workers as friendly helpers rather than drivers or dictators to be resisted as much as possible.

7. Supervisors should speak and act with authority. Appearing unsure causes anxiety and worry in the minds of their people.

8. Motivation of workers is at its best when supervisors are accepted, respected, and liked.

9. Supervisors should be as informal and down-to-earth in their relations with workers as management will permit.

4.5 Positive Result-Getters: Making People Feel Important

If you can make people feel important, they will be more willing to cooperate, do good work, and be pleased with their job. The psychology behind this is simple—feeling important makes you look at your work as worthwhile, necessary to the company, and something not everyone can do. When you don't feel important, it's natural not to be enthusiastic about your work or anxious to get it done.

Case-in-Point: James Twomey, liaison man for Consolidated Edison Co.[4] of New York, acknowledges that most jobs today are dull and routine. He suggests that one of a supervisor's responsibilities is to "humanize" them. The National Foremen's Institute reported how Twomey told them he had handled a difficult situation recently:

"A balky oldtimer refused to do a splicing job in an emergency. When the foreman asked him to do the job, he replied he couldn't do it. The foreman then called me.

"I knew I had to get through to the man. We'd worked together when I was a splicer, so I knew what he could do.

" 'John,' I said, 'I've seen you work and I know you. As an old friend, I'm asking you to do the job for us. This is an emergency.'

"That little bit of praise and a pat on the back was all it took to get him doing the work. We got a first class job done in jig-time."

---

[4]Reprinted from *Supervisor's Memory Jogger*, July, 1973. By permission of the publisher. Bureau of Business Practice, 24 Rope Ferry Road, Waterford, Connecticut 06386. Copyright, Bureau of Business Practice, Inc.

How to Do It: A good way to make a man feel important is to thank him for something he has accomplished, adding that not everybody could have done what he did. Pointing out that his skill, knowledge, and experience enabled him to do a good job is another way of telling him of his importance.

The most pleasant word to a man's ears is his own name. It makes him an individual distinct and unique from others. It adds identity. So, to make a man feel important, use his name when talking to him and when talking to others about him in his presence.

Alternate Action: You can motivate a man and also make him feel important by giving him responsibility. But you must do this carefully—it's not sufficient for you to simply ask a person to do a certain job for you. You have got to point out the importance of the job.

Case-in-Point: Jack Cramer, supervisor in a chemical manufacturing plant, received an order for some special chemicals. The order came from a company that the plant had been trying to sell for more than a year. Jack could have routinely turned over the job of filling the order to his clerk without mentioning its importance, but he saw an opportunity to motivate as well as raise the ego of Bill Willis, one of the order clerks. He approached him saying, "Bill, there's a special order coming through that I'd like you to personally handle. It could be a big factor in the plant's future business. I want to be sure the order is filled properly and also that it gets out on time, so I'm asking you to do this."

Jack accomplished his objective of making Bill feel important as evidenced by Bill's enthusiastic and careful handling of the job. And, of course, the order was given the special attention and consideration it deserved.

4.6 Six Ways to Inflate the Ego of People

Would you like to puff up your people and satisfy their need to feel appreciated? If you succeed at this they'll like their work more and do a better job besides.

How to Do It:

1. Give them your full attention and show interest when they communicate with you. They especially appreciate this when they know you are busy.

2. Keep them completely informed on all matters which concern them. You show that you're interested in them and their work.

3. Treat them with courtesy, dignity, and respect. Put them on your level or higher, if possible.

4. Provide them opportunities to do things they usually aren't privileged to do. Let them represent the department at a function, for example, or excuse them from work when they have a personal problem to handle.

5. Give them a chance to perform unusually well so they will look good in the eyes of others. Compliment them in the presence of their peers.

6. See that they get rewards for job accomplishment. A personal letter from management, recognition on the company bulletin board or in the company newspaper, or a personal gift are a few of the ways this can be done.

4.7 How to Keep Your People Busy

When operations are normal and when there is lots of work to be done, you probably have no problem with keeping your people busy (unless you have some goof-offs in your group, and that's another problem). But the story is different when things are slow, when equipment or material is causing trouble, or when schedules are not routine. At times like these you must beware of a "ho-hum" attitude taking over which adversely affects the group's productivity and the company's profits. The answer to the problem is to keep your people busy.

How to Do It: Motivational experts will tell you that one of the best ways to get performance from employees is to keep them active and interested. You can do this in several ways. One is by stockpiling new jobs. Keep a running list of projects and tasks as you learn of them, and assign them to your people at opportune times. The list will serve another purpose—you will not forget certain jobs which you have been asked to handle.

Another way you can keep up enthusiasm is by giving your people specific deadlines with each job. "The worker who goes home at night knowing he has a job to complete or a new project to start the next day, knows he's important to the company and will perform accordingly," says one management advisory service.

Other benefits derive from keeping your people busy. Active workers get more satisfaction from doing jobs and feel better at the end of the workday. High productivity can only be realized when work is accomplished with a minimum of manhours spent on it. Busy people also don't have time for goofing off and horseplay.

To keep people busy you must plan and schedule their work. Moreover, you must do this every day if you are to perform services on time or meet production schedules. Failure to keep people busy cause costs to rise, so it is an important part of your job.

Case-in-Point: Linda Nestor, supervisor of office operations in an insurance company in Philadelphia, has an answer to the problem of office efficiency. "I've seen times when my girls have seemingly caught up with their work and don't have anything to do. So now I keep a 'tickler' file of jobs which we can pick up and which make us more efficient when the workload is heavy. For example, one of these jobs is updating the files—removing cancelled policies. Another is searching out misfiles. You'd be surprised at how much smoother our work gets when we're not trying to find misplaced proposals, endorsements, and policies."

The idea of having a list of fill-in jobs is a boon in maintenance and job shop departments. Time-conscious supervisors can fit in small jobs at times when it isn't practical to begin large ones, such as before the lunch break or near the end of the workday. Why not take a look at your area to see where you can be more efficient as well as cut costs by keeping your people busy?

4.8 Solving the Problem of Placing Blame

It's natural when something goes wrong to look for someone to blame because everyone has a self-preservation instinct. Yet, more often than we care to admit, we, ourselves, are guilty. However, whether we are at fault or someone else is, how we undo a wrong or correct a mistake should be of more concern to us than placing blame.

How to Do It: When reprimanding an employee is necessary, you must be careful to avoid finding fault with the person's abilities. Although you may accuse a man of almost anything such as laziness, carelessness, forgetfulness, or negligence, and not damage his ego, if you call him "stupid," even indirectly, you hit that which he values most highly: his opinion of himself as a competent, above-average person.

Case-in-Point: Jack Martin, an impulsive, aggressive supervisor in a machine shop in Chicago, Ill., learned one day that a machinist working for him had made a serious error in the cutting of a shaft. Angrily, he approached the man at his machine, blurting out, "How could you have made such a stupid mistake? My eight-year-old son could have done this job and he doesn't know the first thing about machining."

When the man's face reddened, Jack realized he had said the wrong thing, but it was too late. Making matters worse, bystanders at other machines had heard him. Jack lost the respect of some of his people that day, and they didn't let him forget the incident quickly either. Weeks later, some of the men occasionally used the words "stupid mistake" when they sensed he could hear their conversation.

4.9 How You Can Be the Boss Without Being Obvious About It

With a few exceptions, most successful supervisors do not carry out their responsibilities by telling the world, "I am the boss. You do as I say." It takes an egotistical and commanding personality to behave in such manner. Few supervisors are built that way. Most effective supervisors have learned that they get along better and get more accomplished if they play down their position as "giver of orders."

Yet, there are times when you've got to make your point and make it stick. Being decisive will minimize the difficulty of getting through when there is no question of what should be done. A vigorous and confident approach to solving a problem also commands respect. The supervisor who is steady and consistent has no trouble in making his point and making it stick.

Your people, the ones who work for you, are well aware that you are their boss. Some people dislike taking orders from anyone. Then, too, consider the general feeling of many workers who want to have a voice in what they do and how they handle their job. The aware and perceptive supervisor realizes that his personnel relations stand to be better if he can be the boss without being obvious about it. Successful supervisors can be in the background yet make their point and make it stick.

Case-in-Point: "I like to keep out of the limelight when my department receives recognition for being safe on the job or keeping work areas neat and clean," reports Stan Weber, supervisor in the Acme Steel Products Company in Los Angeles. "After all, my people's efforts more than mine achieved these things—they should get the credit. And I sense that some of them feel that way, too. I'd be out of line in their eyes to act otherwise."

A few supervisors today believe that being inaccessible is the sign of a true leader; some even think it is a status symbol of their authority. They couldn't be more wrong. When someone who works for you wants to talk to you, it's only right that you be available. After all, you should know what the problem is and it shouldn't have to get worse before you hear about it. Being around and knowing what's going on makes you more a part of the team, as well as being an inconspicuous boss.

How to Do It: Your best way of knowing what's going on is to keep a close, friendly relationship with your people. If they see you are interested in what they are doing, they'll gladly talk. But if you are impatient, disinterested, or suggest you are not concerned, people are not going to consult you about anything until they absolutely have to.

Sharp supervisors make it easy for workers to get through to them because they know that being reachable enables them to stay on top of the job. Good supervisors also don't become angry or irritated when they get bad news. They know that if people find that their bosses become upset when things aren't going right, there's a reluctance to let them know when there's trouble.

If keeping you informed is not difficult for your people, they are more likely to do so. You won't need to continually ask or give the impression you are in charge and must make decisions. Follow up on job assignments after a reasonable length of time. You will get the reputation of being efficient as well as in control, both of which will enable you to make your orders stick. Keeping in touch makes it possible for you to be the boss without being obvious about it.

4.10 The Art of Saying "No" Diplomatically

All leaders occasionally have to say "no" to their people much as they may dislike doing so. Whether it's a request for time off, additional pay, or a simple suggestion relating to how work should be done, it still is a negative response you're making. Recognize that it is inevitable that you must now and then say "no" because every suggestion, idea, or request cannot be granted.

How to Do It: If your answer to a request is "no" don't hesitate to say so. Also, don't delay your refusal because you only make it harder to say later. Be aware, however, that many times it would be more satisfying to your listener and more to the advantage of yourself and your company if you would explain your decision. Give the reason for the refusal first, and then add, "I know this probably isn't the answer you'd like to hear, but for this reason you can understand why I am unable to say 'yes.'"

Although "no" is sometimes hard to take, you may be surprised how much your being frank and honest is appreciated. Also, your people will realize that your position requires you to sometimes make your point and make it stick.

Be careful, however, of the quick, emphatic "no" because it can cause trouble. Better that you discuss the reasons that will lead to your eventual negative answer. You will find that most people will convince themselves that they could not expect a positive answer and that they will reason "no" was a fair answer on your part.

4.11 How to Earn Respect Without Forcing It

Everyone needs to feel worthy and respected. Supervisors, especially, hope their people respect them because knowing this gives them confidence in carrying out their responsibilities. You should want to earn the respect of your people if you do not already have it. When you have respect you have no problem in difficult situations with making your point and making it stick.

How to Do It: One way you can gain respect is by admitting when you're wrong. It isn't true that admitting when you're wrong weakens your image and effectiveness on the job. Job holders don't expect their supervisor to be right all the time. They do, however, respect a supervisor who admits an error.

Face-to-face personal contact is always preferable to written communications when making a point and making it stick. Your expressions, voice inflection, comments, and manner of speaking all help to promote understanding and leave no doubt of your intentions.

The supervisor who lets his people know that he expects them to fulfill their job requirements will get respect and loyalty *provided* he also lets them know he is there to help them meet those requirements.

Case-in-Point: Wilbur A. Erskine, assistant treasurer, Cambridge (Mass.) Gas Co.,[5] says that, "The supervisor who has an honest concern for the well-being of his people will gain their respect and good will. He should take a sincere interest in their personal lives and do whatever he can to help them with their problems." He adds, "This will give them a feeling of kinship with the boss that will show in good work performance."

You can win respect of employees by being naturally friendly and by showing concern for human dignity. Avoid being biased or prejudiced. Give recognition to suggestions. People always respect honesty and sincerity. Moreover, they expect these qualities in their supervisors. They also look up to a leader who is strong, creative, and decisive.

Another way you can earn the respect of your people is to *not* prove to them that you can still do every job in your area as well or better than anyone else. You may not realize it, but your people know your capabilities and your skills—you don't have to remind anyone of them. Besides, it is wrong for you to do what is their work. Your job as supervisor is to help, advise, and suggest how work should be done. Your people will respect you more if you limit your activity to those things.

4.12 Five Ways to Avoid Discrimination

A tendency has been growing in personnel relations to put up with incompetence in order to avoid a charge of discrimination. For instance, you might approve the hiring of a worker that you would not have considered before, or you might put off the firing of a person who is performing unsatisfactorily and shows no inclination to change for the better.

Of course, you must never discriminate against people on the basis of color, race, sex, or creed, or for any reason that is immaterial or irrelevant to the job. Favoring a minority person over a more capable majority person—reverse discrimination—is just as bad. If business or industry discriminates at

---

[5]Reprinted from *Supervisor's Memory Jogger*, Sept. 1969. By permission of the publisher. Bureau of Business Practice, 24 Rope Ferry Road, Waterford, Connecticut 06386. Copyright, Bureau of Business Practice, Inc.

all with employees, it must be only on the basis of skill, ability, or performance.

How to Do It: As a supervisor, you don't need to put up with poor performance. In fact, you should do something about it. But how do you avoid charges of discrimination after you take action? Here are five ways to protect yourself:

1. Set standards and rules of conduct and performance for your people. Make sure everyone is aware of them. A proven way of assuring this is to give each person a letter listing the rules and what the company expects from its employees.

2. Let people know about unsatisfactory behavior and performance. Warn them. Although you may give a man time to learn and change his ways, there is a limit to how far you can go with this.

3. Conduct performance appraisals periodically making a written record of each interview. A history of such personnel information in your files will enable you to determine if an individual's performance is changing for the worse or the better. The records will serve as justification if you must apply discipline or take drastic action.

4. Give people who perform unsatisfactorily a second and even a third chance if you see improvement. But treat people alike in this respect in that you are not more lenient with a minority than a majority person.

5. Discuss termination with the personnel department if this route appears to be the best course to follow. Make sure your reasons are justified and your records are complete.

5

How Successful Supervisors Use Persuasion

Supervisors are managers—they get work done through other people. Their success at this depends on how effectively they communicate in suggesting, asking, and requesting. Problems sometimes arise since the communications between supervisors and their people are not in one direction only. People have their own ideas about why a job is necessary and how and when it should be done. Their thinking on these matters may differ from that of their supervisors. They may see things differently and they may not want to go along with what they are asked to do. They may need to be persuaded.

Successful supervisors are skilled in the art of persuasion. They persuade in different ways depending on the circumstances and the people involved. It pays to learn and know how they do it.

5.1 How to Get People to Want to Do Something

Simply urging people to do something will often cause them to respond, but you can't count on this to get results day after day. You've got to come up with more than this to realize continuous agreement with you and good performance. What you need to achieve is have *them* see for themselves what is needed, have *them* want to do something, and have *them* decide what they'll do.

The trick behind successful persuasion is getting people to make decisions on their own. Most people prefer that *they* rather than *you* decide how to reach a goal. Doing and reaching it their way gives them some responsibility and makes them feel they are more than just order-takers.

Your ability to persuade is put to the test when you ask your people to make a change in their way of doing things or to stop doing one thing and begin doing another. Naturally, you would like to have them go along with you with a minimum of grumbling, complaining, and objecting. How do you do it? Here are the ways to effectively go about persuading them:

1. When you explain something, do a complete job of it including the bad with the good. Since the facts will eventually be known anyway, see that the information comes from you. But, play up the good. It makes acceptance easier.

2. Avoid overselling. Although it's expected you will praise something you're in favor of, don't go too far. People have good memories when it comes to promises and predictions you make. You could be embarrassed later if things don't work out right.

3. Be careful not to exaggerate. Don't lead people to think you're going all out when actually you plan to make only a small change, or that a complete new way of doing a job is coming up when you're changing only one step.

4. Introduce change slowly. Don't spring a new way of doing things suddenly and without warning. Prepare people for change by talking about it beforehand, saying what you're thinking about doing and why it's necessary.

5. Be timely. Clear the way for something new before announcing it to make sure you aren't faced with a postponement before you get started. Pick the opportune time for a change that greatly affects people. Be ready to follow through on a proposal once you make it.

6. Ask for comments and suggestions when you are considering a change. Show that you want everyone to know what you are proposing, that you are concerned with their acceptance, and that you want their approval. People will go along with you more readily if they are permitted to have their say.

5.2 Eight Tried-and-Tested Principles of the Art of Persuasion

If you can get people to willingly do something extra or go out of their way for you, you probably are good at persuading. Skill in persuading is invaluable when working with and leading people.

You can acquire the skill of getting people to agree with you, accept your thinking, and willingly cooperate. Here are eight principles of the art of persuasion you should practice to become adept at it:

How to Do It:

1. Be honest and sincere. Say why you want something. Never conceal the fact when *you* have something to gain from what you're proposing. Practice "telling it like it is" to bolster and maintain your credibility.

2. Soft-pedal your approach. Recognize that you may be asking people to agree that you know more than they do, or that you are right and they are wrong. Expect to run into resistance occasionally and be prepared to counter it tactfully and discreetly.

3. Be logical and practical. State the facts that prompted your request rather than expect your listeners to be aware of those facts and reach the same conclusions from them. A methodical manner of attacking a problem shows that you are in command of the situation.

4. Stress the positive consequences of your requests. Point out how your listeners will benefit from what you propose. Call attention to the fact that good results will come from doing the right thing and bad results from doing the wrong thing.

5. Act as expected of a leader. People are more easily persuaded by a person who has led and directed projects before, who knows the ropes, and who has a reputation for success as a leader.

6. Be patient. Give people time to think about what you are saying or suggesting, especially when you are selling a new idea or a different way of doing a job. Agreement or compliance reached slowly is better than none at all.

7. Avoid a demanding and assertive tone. It puts people on the defensive. You do not want people to feel that they are being forced into something or that they have little choice in the matter.

8. Recognize emotion and its importance. Concede before you contend. Listen before you talk. People are more easily persuaded after they have had a chance to have their say and get things off their chests. Allow time for emotion to drain away before you try to persuade with reason and logic.

5.3 Listen if You Want to Persuade

You will be much better at persuasion if you are a good listener. The supervisor who knows his or her people—their worries, ambitions, habits, and touchy points—comes to appreciate why they behave as they do and what motives stir them. The best and fastest way to know them is to encourage them to talk freely, without fear of ridicule or disapproval, and be a good listener. Listening to people enables you to understand how they feel on a subject, whether or not you feel the same way. Never dominate a conversation or meeting by doing all the talking yourself if you want to find out where your people stand. When you understand people you know the best way to go about persuading them.

Listening is a key step when you have a problem to solve and need to sell people on its solution.

How-to-Do-It: Present and discuss the problem with the people who will be involved. *Listen* to the pros and cons until someone suggests the answer that you had reached when you first became aware of the problem. "That sounds good," you say, "but how do we go about it?" Lead them to the answer you've already reached, letting them think it's *their* idea. They'll make it work, and you will have done an excellent job of persuasion unbeknown to them.

5.4 How to Set an Example as a Means of Persuading

Your persuasion will carry more impact if you are already doing what you're asking of someone else. The following of company rules and procedures, for example, should always be your policy.

How-to-Do-It: If company rules limit coffee breaks to just two a day, be sure that you never exceed that. Wear your safety glasses in the work areas where you expect and ask your people to do so. Never run, even when you are being called, for long distance phone calls. And don't smoke in the no-smoking areas.

You can set an example in many ways to help you persuade people to do or not do something. Having a good attitude undoubtedly has an effect on people and helps when the workload is heavy and pressure is on to get things done. Attitude, like enthusiasm, tends to rub off and influence how people think and act. If people know you are honest, sincere, and always try to do the right thing, they take this into consideration when you ask for something. If you are cooperative and friendly, people will find it difficult to treat you otherwise.

Optimists are usually winners, and this is generally recognized. People are more easily persuaded by someone who looks at things positively, sees opportunity, and isn't easily discouraged. If you set and live up to high standards for your organization, your people are more likely to follow your good example.

5.5 Making Your Presence Do Things for You

Despite your skill at motivation and your dedication to increasing the productivity of your people, you will now and then find that some of them are not doing their best work or the amount they're capable of. In addition, you will frequently be faced with the problem of how to get some people to reduce their idle time and work more efficiently.

Discussing their inadequate performance with them should be your first step to getting them to change for the better. In many cases you may be successful with this, but the better performance may last only a short time. You need to do something else to solve the problem.

Successful supervisors have learned that their presence is often all that is needed to keep people on the job and not abuse personal time allowances. The way to do this most effectively is to faithfully and frequently visit the work areas. You'll be showing an interest in your people, keeping up-to-date on job progress, and quickly getting a jump on problems which arise with the work. The supervisor who sits in the office much of the time can't stay on top of the job and know that his people are getting out the work.

5.6 How to Refuse Tactfully

Although you know you may be better accepted and that people will probably like you more if you always agree with them, you simply cannot do that. A supervisor often has to say no to a simple request, turn down a suggestion, or refuse an offer.

People do not like to be refused or told they cannot do something. Everyone believes they are right in their thinking and that what they ask for is not unreasonable. They expect a yes answer and are disappointed when they don't get it. They may be argumentative when you say no, so you must try to soften your refusal. You can refuse someone tactfully if you try.

How-to-Do-It: The best way to handle a refusal is to give it with honesty and understanding, using the kindest words you know. Never let someone leave you with your no answer without learning exactly why you felt you had to give it. Explain your feeling and your position.

Try to leave a way out for the person you're refusing. Acknowledge the good thinking behind it, and agree that it is reasonable to feel the way the person does. Offer to help by looking for a solution to the problem. Perhaps someone else can do what is being asked of you.

It never pays to trample a person with a flat no. Everyone has some dignity which should be considered. Be kind and wear a smile when you must say no.

5.7 Disagreeing Agreeably: How the "Pros" Do It

The ability to disagree agreeably—that is without offending, irritating, or disturbing—is a valuable attribute to managers and supervisors who have to periodically disagree with people yet retain their interest and cooperation. You can learn how to disagree pleasantly. Here's how the "pros" do it:

1. Avoid words that show you are strongly of the opposite opinion or that the other person is wrong. Such words often cause people to defend themselves vehemently and become angry. Simply state the person's viewpoint accurately and fairly while you contrast it with your own.

2. After careful listening, agree to the other person's logic. Point out the areas where you agree. You can probably accept at least part of a person's thinking—mention that. If you elaborate on areas of disagreement, you promote antagonism and appear to be argumentative.

3. Appeal to the facts. Go over those which led to your position and thinking. Bring to light as much evidence as possible to back you up.

4. Stick with the issue at hand. Never bring up previous disagreements, past mistakes, or personalities.

5. Maintain your composure and keep your cool. Smile when you discuss the issue. Avoid giving an impression of being demanding or stubborn.

6. Bring up indirection. Suggest another use for the person's idea or how the person's suggestion would be good for solving a different problem.

Case-in-Point: One of my supervisors early in my career was a whiz at turning down my suggestions without discouraging me. Harry Viergutz, Chief Chemist for The Milwaukee Road, would answer, for example, "That's good thinking. We can probably do that with the study we're going to make on that new steel we intend to use on axles. I don't think the idea will work on this study because..." Another comment I remember him making was, "I bet the boys in the research lab could use your idea."

7. Admit you could be wrong but ask the other person to go along with you just this one time.

5.8 Proven Ways of Developing Credibility

Supervisors who are effective at persuasion usually are reliable and dependable. They have also acquired a following of people who work with and for them. In a few words: they have credibility. Since they are respected and admired, they are easily able to persuade people to their way of thinking.

To be effective on the job you must have credibility. Top-notch supervisors acquire it over a period of time on the job. You can do it too.

How-to-Do-It:

1. Be consistent in how you treat people and predictable in what you do and say. People like to know that you will act and respond today the same as you did yesterday.

2. Show stability and a capability of controlling your emotions. Especially hold your temper in check. Be steady and constant in your efforts.

3. Be loyal to your people and your company. Carry out your promises by doing things when and how you said you would. Follow through on your plans and programs, particularly those that concern your people.

4. Recognize obstacles and work out ways to overcome them. Solve problems in a realistic and practical manner. Have convictions and face the truth. Don't hedge when you're on the spot.

5. Make yourself available for advice and help. Be aware of people and their feelings. Communicate this to them. Show empathy and sympathy. Be a friend.

6. Maintain your health and your appearance. Have clean thoughts and a high standard of decency and morals. Show faith and trust. Be a model of integrity.

Supervisors with credibility have an easy time on the job because they get along well with almost everyone. They seldom have a problem persuading others to agree with them or to do something.

5.9 Tested Answers to the Problem of Procrastinating

People procrastinate most often when they are faced with a difficult decision or have an unpleasant job to do. All of us are guilty of it to some degree at one time or another. Supervisors are no exception, nor are people on the job.

You can overcome the problem of procrastination by taking pride in your work and developing confidence in your abilities. Realizing that many situations are not as bad as they may seem also helps to beat procrastination. Decide early that you cannot continue to put something off indefinitely.

Although getting started on a distasteful job is no easy matter, your best bet is to go after the job when you are fresh and in a good mood. Once you start, stay with it until you finish. This saves facing the unpleasantness a second time.

A new approach to the problem is to apply self-psychology. Imagine yourself doing the job and succeeding without difficulty. Such thinking can inflate your ego so that your fear of failing or running into trouble is much less. You can literally talk yourself into starting the job.

What about solving the procrastination problem of other people? Effective supervisors have found three ways to go about this: minimize the distastefulness or difficulty of the job, calm their fear of failure, and bolster their confidence in themselves. Asking a person who is procrastinating if you can help will sometimes also get action.

5.10 How to Give Compliments

People who receive compliments on their achievements are more enthusiastic about their work. They are also more easily persuaded to do more and to go out of their way to help. Everyone likes to hear that they've been noticed and that they're appreciated. Compliments encourage people to continue to do good work.

But compliments must be sincere. An insincere compliment can do more harm than good. You must also be sure a person deserves your kind words or you may raise suspicions of your motive for giving them. A person knows when he or she has done a good job and a compliment is appropriate.

Be sure of the facts concerning the deed or accomplishment before you do your complimenting. Also, give your full attention to the person. By so doing you show that you have evaluated the act and decided it is deserving of praise. In addition, you do not give an impression that you are carrying out one of your duties with the compliment.

A word of caution about compliments: you can overdo them. For example, complimenting a person frequently for something that has become routine in performance with the person wears thin after a time. If you space out your praise to once a week or month, it will have a greater impact and mean more to the individual.

It's better to be generous than tight with compliments however. People appreciate a "thank you" even though they may have been complimented. Compliments leave a good taste in the mouth of the person giving them too, so the recipient of your praise isn't the only one who benefits from such words.

5.11 Techniques That Work on Raising Enthusiasm

The company that has enthusiastic employees, people who like their work and are interested in what they are doing, has an advantage over other companies whose employees don't feel this way about their jobs. Supervisors can motivate and increase the enthusiasm of employees by the way they communicate with them. However, supervisors must be enthusiastic themselves. You cannot sell something effectively if you haven't first sold yourself.

One of the ways a supervisor can get a person interested and enthused about a job or undertaking is to recount a success story of another person under similar circumstances or in a similar situation. Evangelists use this technique in their teaching with much success.

Enthusiasm for something new can be promoted if you can assure a resumption of present practice if the new procedure does not work out to one's satisfaction. If a person can be convinced that nothing will be lost (and something probably can be gained) through a change, reluctance to change can often be overcome.

Since fear is often behind a person's lack of enthusiasm, try eliminating it. People have many fears about the future and the unknown, such as fear of suffering a loss, and fear of being harmed. If you can answer such fears and minimize risks in their eyes, you can expect more cooperation and more willingness to accept change. The supervisor's support in allaying fears is essential for security needs of employees.

Creating fear rather than eliminating it is a different approach to solving the problem of lack of interest. Fear of bad publicity, for example, can cause people to change their thinking about their behavior and also motivate them to action. In situations where an organization has not been able to get people to follow the rules, management may threaten to make public the offenders' names.

Case-in-Point: Parking scoff-laws in Buffalo, N.Y. could at one time look forward to seeing their names in the local newspaper. The Parking Violations Bureau of the city published a list of 56 violators who owed the city a total of $95,318. Each person on the list owed a minimum of $1,200 in fines according to the bureau director. Understandably, the city expected that other violators with less severe records would pay up rather than risk seeing their names in the paper.

Lack of enthusiasm on the part of individuals often stems from the fact that nobody will listen to them. They begin to feel that they are not understood, that nobody cares, and that they must watch out for themselves. If you would listen to their ideas, their opinions, and their thinking, they would have more confidence in themselves and their abilities. A person can be enthusiastic when he or she has confidence, but it is difficult to be enthusiastic without it.

6

How Effective
Supervisors
Handle
People

Experienced supervisors know that they need to be accepted by their people in order to be successful. They work with and treat their people accordingly, recognizing that each person they communicate with is different and responds differently to their direction.

You must know people and how they think if you expect to be able to handle them. A knowledge of emotion, how to recognize it, and what to do about it are requisites to getting along well with others. Being tactful pays off, and if you are also adept at promoting morale, you should be effective in handling people.

Everyone makes a mistake now and then. Supervisors who are skilled in remedying them as well as learning from them can reduce the number of mistakes that are made and their seriousness.

Criticism may be called for and should be given when an employee's work is not satisfactory or adequate. Effective supervisors are able to handle this unpleasant task without difficulty proving that adeptness in the art of criticizing is a valuable asset when handling people

6.1 Understanding People: Why They Act as They Do

Your job is easier if you understand people because you know how they feel and what to expect of them. You can be prepared to handle most of the people problems that face you on the job. Thus, a supervisor who knows a bit about human relations and psychology usually gets along better with people than someone who hasn't had such education. Understanding what makes people tick can be learned outside the classroom. Here is some insight on why people act as they do.

If you wonder why a person sometimes acts strangely or doesn't do what you expect, look for the results of the person's action for the answer. People act the way they think they should act in a particular situation at that time. Their upbringing and their previous experiences account for much of what they say and do.

People usually will not try harder on a job unless they feel they are accomplishing something. If the job is difficult, they are more likely to become frustrated or discouraged than motivated to greater effort. Search for the incentive in what they are trying to do. If it is weak or nonexistent, you can expect the task will be difficult and not easily accomplished.

Praise for what has been accomplished helps to motivate people to further accomplishment. Criticism tends to demotivate, unless it is constructive and encouraging. Discipline is similar to criticism in that the way it is administered determines the effect it has. When people know they are appreciated they tend to justify that appreciation.

People are usually perceptive in knowing what you expect of them and how you think they will do on the job. If you expect them to do well they most likely will. If you don't have confidence in them, they will not try as hard.

Case-in-Point: Years ago a personnel manager told me about an incident involving two workers whom he transferred to a new department because they became surplus in the department where a process was discontinued. The foreman losing the men praised them to their new foreman, saying "You're getting two good workers, Clark and Jackson. They have good attitudes and don't shirk on the job." As a result, their new foreman welcomed them and by his treatment of them the first few days in the department, led them to believe that he thought highly of them and expected them to be good workers. Confirming his expectation, they did very well on their new jobs.

When the two foremen met at a social function with the personnel manager a year later, the subject of how Clark and Jackson were doing came up. The first foreman then admitted that he had sensed reluctance of the second foreman to accept Clark and Jackson so had made up the story of their good performance. The two men had been far from outstanding in the work they had done for him but he didn't want them to lose their jobs with the company.

6.2 Guidelines to How to Get People to Accept You

The most successful supervisors have the confidence of their people because people on the job generally do better when they respect and accept their leaders. When you are accepted, people go along and cooperate with you.

You cannot force people to accept you—you earn acceptance. The way you work with people, the things you say and do, determine how much you are accepted.

Here are six guidelines to how to get acceptance:

1. Make people feel they are working *with* you rather than *for* you. You can do this by *asking* for help rather than by *demanding* it, by acting as a member of the team and contributing your share.

2. Give people the best break you can on work assignments. If you have a choice of several ways of getting a job done, pick the one which the people involved would prefer. Look for human rather than material answers to problems. Plan work projects to make them easy on people.

3. Be fair and tolerant. Avoid favoritism when assigning work. Show that you are not biased or prejudiced by treating people equally.

4. Have high morals and follow the rules. Know right from wrong and behave accordingly. Be loyal. Put the interest of your people and your company ahead of your own.

5. Always keep your promises. Be reliable. People will learn that they can depend on you to correct a bad situation or solve a problem if it's possible for you to do so.

6. Avoid being cold and aloof. Show that you like people. Become knowledgeable in their interests. Join in conversations. Don't be all business all of the time.

Caution: Telling people they are doing fine when they really are not doesn't help you or them. You mislead people if you don't express your true feelings. Worse, when people realize that you don't always mean what you say, they soon doubt everything you say no matter how you say it. You've got to be honest with people.

6.3 Sure-Fire Ways to Bring About Better Employee Performance

Supervisors play key roles in how employees work and the quantity of their output. This is to be expected since supervisors participate in training and instructing, assigning jobs, and guiding.

Successful supervisors get good performance from their people because they know the best ways to treat them, some of which are simply application of common sense. Good human relations and a cooperative approach to the work promote interest and reduce tension, both of which help people to do their work without taking shortcuts or being careless. Then, too, people are just naturally more conscientious and efficient if they feel their company represented by the supervisor is interested in their welfare and job satisfaction.

Case-in-Point: The Eastern Central Motor Carriers Association, with offices in Cuyahoga Falls, Ohio, does well in this respect. Don Leyland, office manager, says, "We don't have a set time for coffee breaks, so people have a lot of freedom. The company furnishes coffee-making facilities and a refrigerator for soft drinks. An office committee handles ordering supplies, paying for them, and preparing the coffee. Payments are made on the honor system, and the profits from the operation go toward an employee picnic in the summer."

Companies which try to have their employees get satisfaction from their work usually get better performance from them. For example, it pays for a company to renovate and remodel its work areas periodically if only to achieve better morale. Although industrial engineers knowledgeable in material handling and process flow can achieve higher production rates by making changes and modernizing the plant or office, much of the better performance of employees is psychologically rather than physically related to the change because employees see that management is concerned with their comfort and ease of performing the work. High lumen lighting helps avoid eyestrain, especially when the lights are placed so there are no shadows. The liberal use of colors, particularly the pastels, also contributes to efficiency. Color makes people more alert to their surroundings as well as less fatigued after several hours on the job.

Supervisors can promote efficiency and reduce frustration by pushing their people on housekeeping and cleaning of work areas, and the putting of tools and supplies in their places. A well-designed office has an adequate number of files and cabinets. Supervisors should see that their people use them rather than leave work material on desks and tables.

Case-in-Point: "Retrieval of records is faster and easier when they are properly filed," says Lynn Thompson, supervisor in an insurance office in Chicago. "We had one girl in the communications department who frequently left dockets on her desk at the end of the day. After the processing people had trouble finding specific dockets the next day, we talked to the girl about it. We seldom fail to be able to put our hands on a specific docket at any time now."

6.4 Tactfulness Pays Off in Handling People

A successful supervisor understands people and knows how to get along with them. If you want to do the same, you must be perceptive to the feelings of people and be skillful in what you say to them. This specific skill is referred to as being tactful.

Being tactful enables you to talk and deal with people without offending them or turning them off. Although you may always try to be tactful, you may not always be completely successful. For example, highly educated and technically trained people may neglect this personal factor in their zeal and drive toward a group objective. Their failing to be tactful shows when they are abrupt or critical and when they have little if any patience with others who haven't their education or training. If you sense that you may have that problem, at least with some people, decide now on a self-improvement program.

How-to-Do-It: Ask your boss for help and advice. He or she will level with you and help you to come across better with people. Your problem may be as simple as an annoying mannerism which you are not aware of.

You can practice tact on the job in many ways. Here are a few manners you can adopt to your advantage if you haven't already done so.

Put yourself in the other fellow's place when you ask for something. Will the fellow benefit from doing what you ask? Look for how and mention it. Is the fellow interested and concerned about the outcome? If you explain and give reasons for your request you may create an interest.

Requests to do something are always better than orders to do so. Orders should be given only in emergencies or when immediate action is needed. Asking for volunteers is even better and avoids putting a burden on someone who particularly dislikes doing what you're asking for.

Be slow to criticize or find fault—avoid doing it at all, if possible. If you must speak about an error or omission, find out what happened and how it can be prevented from happening again rather than placing blame on someone.

A positive and optimistic attitude helps in being tactful, especially when you talk with people about jobs and their work. Knowing people's likes and dislikes also makes it easier to be kind and considerate. Recognize that people think and act differently, one from another. Expect people to have different opinions than yours so that you are not surprised when you hear them and are at a loss as to what to say.

A tactful person makes good use of the words *please* and *thank you*. Add them to your vocabulary and watch for the effect they have on people.

6.5 Ten Ways to Promote Good Morale on the Job

Since the morale of people on the job affects their performance, supervisors must constantly try to maintain and improve it. Good morale means a healthy, optimistic, and positive attitude toward the job, the company, and life in general. When employees have good morale the quality and quantity of their work meets or exceeds their supervisor's expectations.

"Good morale should begin with management, and one of the best ways to get it is to give every employee a feeling of participation in what's going on," says Earl G. Dobbins, water and sewer administrator, city of Savannah, Ga. Effective supervisors promote and sustain the morale of their people.

Here are ten ways in which they do it:

1. Treat each person as an individual distinct from others. Call each person by his or her name and provide each with the maximum rank and status possible.

2. Make it easy for people to communicate. Have them feel they can talk to you about their problems and troubles at any time. Keep people informed. Speak to them as you would want them to speak to you.

3. Fight constantly against monotony. Boredom results from a dull routine. Vary people's assignments if you can, and show them something new occasionally.

4. Be sure people have all the information they need to do a good job. Let them know of changes that may affect them. Answer rumors quickly.

Case-in-Point: When the Pentagon announced an Air Force budget cut a few years ago, employees at one plant in the industry began to worry about their jobs. To handle the problem, the company president set up two bulletin boards in the work area. One board he labeled RUMOR, the other FACT. On the RUMOR board anyone could write down the current gossip and the President would promptly print the facts concerning it on the FACT board. Within two months the President had answered 100 questions; tension dropped and morale climbed.

5. Recognize good effort and achievement. Let people know how they are doing but avoid comparing their performance with others. Appraise frequently—being ignored is worse than being criticized.

6. Encourage talent and skill. Promote suggestions and creativity. Show an interest in people and their work. Compliment good performance and extra effort. Use words that show respect.

7. Be tactful and kind when correcting or criticizing. Be considerate. Work at having your words accepted. Avoid harsh, caustic remarks.

8. Provide good working conditions. Strive for efficient work methods. Try to eliminate unpleasant tasks and drudgery. Be concerned with the safety and health of people. Assume responsibility for what happens to them.

9. Give as much authority and responsibility as positions and skills permit. Pay fairly, consistent with output and accomplishment, and reward for extra contribution.

10. Promote enthusiasm. Maintain a cheerful, friendly atmosphere to make work less stressful.

6.6 The Problem of Emotion: Proven Answers to It

In working with people you will frequently find that emotion rather than reason is behind a person's action. If you hope to change a decision or get cooperation on a matter with an emotional person you'll have to allow for the emotion in what you say and do.

Supervisors with many years of experience usually have learned how to work with emotional people. They know what words they should and shouldn't use when trying to persuade a person, and they know how to talk to someone without causing resentment or anger. In a nutshell, they know how to "handle" people.

You will find that most of the expressed emotions of people are minor in nature and easily dealt with. Once you are aware of them, you can act and talk accordingly. For example, some workers object to their supervisor *telling* them to do something rather than asking them to do it. Others don't want to hear, "*I* want it done this way." If the supervisors would say *we* rather than *I*, the worker would be more willing to cooperate.

If you overgeneralize or exaggerate you may irritate some individuals. Words like, "You *always* do things the hard way," or "You drinking coffee *again*?" tend to make people resentful. Being specific when referring to acts and deeds is a better way to get your point across.

It's wise also to avoid extremes in words. Seldom is something all bad or all good, all black or all white; people are not completely satisfied or completely dissatisfied. Between extremes lies a large area, one where most conditions are found. If you are moderate in the words you use, you are less likely to be challenged.

Try to separate facts from opinions when getting into discussions. Also, be slow to respond if you are not sure of a person's meaning. Heated discussions usually develop when people are quick to contradict or disagree, when they don't take time to think and consider the other person's viewpoint.

Occasionally a supervisor is faced with working with a person who displays extreme emotions. How to get along with such a person is answered in Chapter 17.

6.7 How to Recognize Emotion

You have to recognize emotion in order to do a good job of contending with it. If you are aware of an emotional state of someone you can either avoid a confrontation with the person or, if that's not possible, be very careful with what you say. Various signals an emotional person sends out can alert you of the need to be patient, tolerant, and understanding. Here are a few such signals. Be wary if a person:

1. Is restless and undecided about what to do. No way seems right, consequently nothing is done. When a person is in such a state of mind, span of attention is usually short and movement from one activity to another is rapid.

2. Complains about matters which previously were of no concern, or notices for the first time a condition which has long existed. The person looks for and comments about a negative turn of events and shows displeasure with the way things are going. Such subjects are talked about at great length.

3. Tends to respond negatively to almost everything which is said. You can sense the motion of the head signifying "no" before you finish talking as if saying, "I'm not going to agree regardless of what you suggest or request."

4. Is quick to take the opposite side in a discussion and wishes to argue. Very voluble. Gives many reasons for an opposing viewpoint; the reasons may be weak but they are strongly expressed.

5. Who usually appears cheerful has a turned down mouth, a wrinkled brow, or a clenched fist. These forms of body communication can indicate displeasure, worry, or anger. Watch out for a curled lip on someone who is about to speak to you. You can expect a critical or derogatory remark, and if it remains after being said, there is more to come.

6.8 How to Criticize Constructively

Criticizing is one of the most unenjoyable tasks a supervisor has to perform. Nobody likes to be criticized and few people enjoy criticizing others. Supervisors should know how to criticize constructively to save hurting people and to have them benefit from it.

Getting all the facts is a prerequisite to criticizing. If you ask for facts and listen instead of talk, you are more likely to get the information you need to do the job right as well as avoid giving criticism which may not be justified.

To criticize constructively, the criticism should be directed at the task, not the person. Constructive criticism builds and instructs. It does not tear down. The trick to doing a good job of criticizing is not to belittle but to improve.

Criticism should be given without offending and in a manner which *you* would accept if *you* were being criticized. The person you criticize should feel that you are trying to help. If you do it properly, you will not cause hurt nor will the person feel you are overstepping your bounds. Criticizing a person for a failure is permissible, and even wise, *if equal consideration is given to the person's success*. This may be the only way the person knows he is being recognized.

Caution: Criticism should be directed at employees who have the ability and potential to do better. Don't waste your time criticizing a person whose performance is hopeless. Look for another job for that person.

6.9 Expert Insight on the Art of Criticizing

Most people know when they deserve criticism. Often a person expects to be criticized and is surprised if it doesn't happen. But whether or not a person expects it, you must be the one to decide how and when to do it. Above all, you must be sure that it is necessary or you should not do it.

Successful supervisors are skilled in the art of criticizing. If you asked for their insight and advice on how to do it, here's what they would tell you:

1. Your effectiveness is determined by your manner. Losing your temper, being sarcastic, and acting disgusted are crude ways of criticizing. Never lower yourself to such levels. Criticize without being emotional. A calm, helping tone softens criticism and gets a better response besides.

2. Always criticize in private to avoid embarrassment. Everyone has some pride; you accomplish nothing by attacking it. The people you criticize will be thankful to you if you show respect and consideration for them and their feelings.

3. Give reasons why a person's actions or deeds are unacceptable. Suggest correct and better ways to do things and offer to help the person learn them. Say that you know the person can do better.

4. Be positive with your admonition and advice. Stress the value of the right way of doing things.

5. Say something friendly and in an uplifting manner after you have criticized. Leave the person feeling that he or she has been helped.

6.10 Effective Ways to Handle On-the-Job Mistakes

Anyone who has a job to do is going to occasionally make a mistake. Making errors and mistakes is a human trait and happens to everyone. Although you can expect the people who work for you to make mistakes, what you do about those mistakes should be your main concern. You have some control over the frequency and severity of mistakes if you deal properly with them.

Supervisors are effective in dealing with mistakes when they adopt techniques which enable themselves and their people to learn from such errors. As a result, fewer and less serious mistakes are made in the future. You should investigate a mistake as soon after it occurs as possible because you may still be able to limit the loss or damage by corrective action. Determine a mistake's importance and significance first. You will then see how much time and effort you should put into contending with it. Plan to investigate every mistake you learn about; this is the only way to assure that something is done toward preventing reoccurrences.

Don't jump to conclusions when investigating. You may not learn the cause if you do. It's difficult, if not impossible, to take corrective action if you don't know the cause.

Always maintain your composure by being careful to not show resentment against a person who made an error. Remember that everybody makes mistakes. If you discuss the mistake with the person at fault, be sure your comments are constructive and also given in private. Avoid belittling or ridiculing.

The most important step of handling on-the-job mistakes is what you do after investigating them. Take positive steps to prevent reoccurrences.

6.11 How to Investigate a Mistake

There's a right way and a wrong way to investigate a mistake. Doing it the right way gives you a far better chance of learning the reason why the mistake was made and also avoids hard feelings.

The right way is to forgo personal references to the incident. Simply ask, "What happened?" This approach takes attention away from the person involved and directs it to the mistake itself.

How-to-Do-It: In the plant you might say, "This is the first accident we've had in this area—what happened?" In the office you might ask when investigating a misrouted order, "Are the address files up to date?" and then, "What happened?"

Facts alone should tell you what the problem is. Since many of the facts you need can be supplied only by the person who made the mistake, try to get them from him or her with the least friction.

Case-in-Point: Linda Ellis, office supervisor for Acme Products in Camden, N.J., says "I'm always very careful about my girls' feelings when I check out a mistake. I know that the person who made the mistake is embarrassed and nervous, so I try to be calm, sympathetic, and reassuring in what I say. The girls know this, so they seldom try to cover up an error and I can easily get the facts. As a result we can usually do something to prevent the mistake being made again.

Caution: Mistakes are serious matters. Even though you may treat them as inevitable, never be flippant about them. If you let down on investigating mistakes you may give the impression that you are also willing to accept other breaches of performance of people on the job.

6.12 Making the Best Out of Mistakes

Everyone is embarrassed when a mistake is made. But that shouldn't keep a person from doing something about it afterward. You may as well make the best out of a mistake.

It's wise to be quick to admit a mistake if you actually made it. People learn about a mistake sooner or later, and they don't readily accept evasion on such matters.

Try to remedy the mistake quickly, even if you have to put aside something else you're doing. Correct the mistake now, not tomorrow. You can show your concern by apologizing to the person who is affected, whether or not you are guilty. Trying to do something for the person to make up for the mistake is also a good gesture on your part.

A supervisor should maintain prestige and reputation by treating mistakes as rare occurrences when talking about them with other people. Putting up a good front can psychologically help to prevent mistakes by assuring people they are capable of performing error-free work.

7

Supervisory Decisionmaking: How the "Pros" Do It

Being decisive is a valuable attribute of a supervisor. When making decisions, he or she carries out the leadership responsibility of the job, while at the same time providing assurance and confidence to employees to go ahead with their work without fear. Motivation to action is behind any decision. Procrastination must be overcome and the skill of making decisions under pressure developed if the supervisor is to be effective on the job.

To be decisive you need insight and determination. You must want to solve problems and have the confidence to do so. Knowing how and when decisions should be made is basic to the art. Along with being familiar with the theory of making judgments, a decision maker must be aware of the many factors which influence decisions and their relative importance. But, most of all, you need facts and information to work with.

What distinguishes a good decision from a bad one? What are the causes of poor decisions? How do you resolve a bad one? When supervisors know the answers to such questions they are better qualified to make good decisions.

7.1 Being Decisive: Tips on How to Go About It

Reluctance to make a decision can handicap a supervisor. People on the job expect their leaders to be decisive and in control. Workers become fearful, uneasy, and even unwilling to proceed when they sense that the supervisor is unsure of what direction to go or what move to make. A decisive supervisor commands respect and gets action.

You can learn to be decisive by being definite in how you handle your responsibilities. Once you get into the swing of it, you'll find it easy to hold to the pattern.

The ways to go about it are as follows:

1. Make minor decisions promptly. Disposing of them as quickly as possible gives you more time to devote to matters that are really important.

2. Be solid and firm when you make a decision. Don't be half-sure or leave any doubt of your intentions.

3. Forget the alternatives once you make a decision. Don't waste time thinking about what you could or should have done.

4. Dispel any thoughts that you might make a mistake. Such thinking weakens your resolution to be decisive.

5. Carry out your decisions. Until you take action nothing happens and you aren't decisive.

7.2 The Need for Facts to Make Good Decisions

Successful decision makers thrive on facts—they can't make decisions without them. This is a good point to remember the next time you are faced with an important decision. What do you need to know? What's been the practice with this type of problem? Who is involved? When must the decision be made? To make good decisions you must have the answers to questions such as these.

Case-in-Point: Rapidly increasing costs have caused managers' and supervisors' attention to be focused on maintenance activities in many of today's plants, particularly in the process industries where maintenance is a large variable in product cost. As a result, researchers at Louisiana State University,[1] Baton Rouge, decided to evolve a management system for

---

[1]From *Maintenance Engineering*, Dec., 1975.

maintenance to assist all levels of management in decision making. The initial objectives of this system, which were widely applicable to many types and sizes of process industries, included:

- Keeping historical records of all maintenance activities and accumulating labor and material costs for each facility.
- Providing schedules to initiate work orders for all requirements.
- Generating management reports describing costs, labor performance, resource utilization, and, in general, all other control reports which would aid in the management of a maintenance system.

The management system which resulted from the researchers' work helps managers and supervisors in maintenance departments to make good decisions. Supervisors often have trouble making decisions because their people throw problems at them without the facts. With little or no information to work with, a supervisor must dig and look into a problem at length before he or she can make a judgment. A midwestern manufacturing manager wasn't pleased with the amount of time he had to spend this way and also felt he might overlook some facts relevant to a specific problem. His approach: he requires assistants to report *why* something is wrong in addition to *what*—and to suggest at least two possible solutions. With sufficient facts then available, he is able to initiate immediate and appropriate action or recognize the need for delay.

7.3 Insight to When and How Decisions Should Be Made

How can a supervisor decide when to act and when to leave a condition well enough alone? Even though a major responsibility of your job is to make decisions, often the best decision you can make is to take no action.

Experienced supervisors have learned to distinguish between a real problem that requires action and a condition or situation that merely rubs them the wrong way. Before they act they consider a situation from several angles realizing that they can make better decisions through insight. You should follow such practices.

For example, make sure a problem is yours before you try to handle it— you might be assuming a responsibility that belongs to someone else. Approach a problem with the attitude of what you can do and how you can help, not how you're going to use your authority to get matters straightened out.

Resist being impulsive—give your insight power a chance to work. Refrain from a startling or radical decision—save it for an emergency or crisis situation. If you feel you must act on a matter, direct your attention to prevention rather than cure—work on the cause of a problem rather than the correction of it.

Insight will help you to avoid making important decisions when you're under pressure or stress; with insight, you'll be aware that you can make the best decision when you are calm and have time to think.

Supervisors who are good at making decisions have certain attributes which help to make them successful. You can acquire those attributes through a program of self-discipline and using insight.

Here is what you should do:

1. Be active in seeking out problems rather than waiting for them to come to you. Develop an insight to conditions and situations which should be changed.

2. Be knowledgeable and informed about your department, company, and industry. Know what the standard procedure is for handling certain problems.

3. Be adept at setting priorities. Understand the relationship between planning, scheduling, and implementing. Know your people and their capabilities.

4. Be creative and innovative. Find new and unique solutions to problems.

5. Be skilled at persuading and motivating people. See that your decisions are acted upon and carried out. Do a good job of following up.

7.4 Four Basic Steps to Making Decisions

You needn't have the experience of similar problems in order to make good decisions. You can make good decisions if you are not too hasty to act, get the facts, and take the time to think. Four basic steps are involved in making decisions.

First, be sure you understand the problem. Writing it down often helps to define it. The experts at problem solving say you have gone most of the way to a decision if you have been able to clearly state the problem and what decision you have to make.

Second, look for all alternative answers. Get information and data. Talk to people to get their opinions and recommendations. Check the records. Examine the facts related to the problem and weigh them as to their importance.

Third, look at the good points and the bad points of each alternative. Will each alternative actually solve the problem? Are risks involved with some? What's wrong with what appears to be the best choice? An alternative which has a high degree of permanency as a characteristic may have the advantage of preventing a reoccurrence of the same or a similar problem.

Fourth, pick the best alternative as your decision. Take action and follow up to observe the results so that you have the experience to handle a similar problem in the future.

7.5 Decision Factors: Keys to Good Decisions

Experienced executives and managers know that many factors must be considered when making a decision. They have learned that the soundness of their decisions depends on whether they have given the proper weight to each of the factors they have considered.

What are the important factors when making decisions? You can be more sure of making a good decision if you go over the following checklist before you act.

1. Is the decision clear and to the point? Does it leave any questions unanswered?
2. Does the decision consider the risk involved and allow for it?
3. If there are several steps to be taken, are they in the right order?
4. Is the decision compatible with company rules and regulations?
5. Has timing been considered? Is it optimum?
6. Have authorized and interested personnel participated in the decision? Are they in agreement?
7. Is the decision based on experience and history? Does it deviate from past practice?
8. Will the expected results of the decision be acceptable to those who must carry it out?

If you find that your analysis of the problem doesn't include one or more of these factors, you would be well advised to reconsider before you take action.

Case-in-Point: Bob Burke, supervisor at Inland Steel in Indiana, deals with some rough-and-tough workers in his department. He feels that he must be especially careful in making disciplinary decisions. He said that before he does anything, he always asks himself three questions about his proposed decision. They are:

1. Have I made a decision based upon my best judgment or based upon the authority I have?
2. Will this particular decision be good as a general rule for everyone? Would I even want it applied to myself?

3. Would I make this same decision if I knew it would be publicized around the company? In other words, would I be willing to defend the decision in another department?

7.6 Understanding Decision Making: Causes of Poor Decisions

Understanding what's involved in making decisions is of value to you because it will lessen the pressure on you when you must make a decision. By knowing the factors which affect decision making you can also improve your skill at supervising. To learn the reasons why some supervisors are unable to consistently make good decisions, I consulted some industrial executives and managers. They told me that you, as a supervisor, can get in trouble with decisions because of one or more of the following:

1. Insufficient or poor information to work with. Lack of information leads to guessing—you may guess wrong. Bad information leads to false conclusions—you decide wrongly.

2. Not enough time to decide. If you have more time to get facts and consider them, you increase your chance to make a wise decision.

3. Fear of the situation and the consequence of the decision. If you are scared and lack confidence your decisions may be adversely affected.

4. Concern with risk. You may be overcautious when the risk is great.

5. Not enough authority. Responsibility without authority leads to weak, unenforceable decisions.

6. Low importance. If you consider a matter not serious, you may not give it enough attention or ignore it entirely.

7. Emotion. Emotions are behind bias and prejudice. Poor decisions often result when emotion rather than reason dictates.

7.7 How to Stay on Top of Problems

It's understandable that you might become upset if you are continually faced with problems, but remember that problems don't affect or interrupt your work—they *are* your work. If you didn't have problems, you wouldn't be needed as a supervisor.

Supervisors who stay on top of problems are skilled in overcoming trouble, delays, and the various roadblocks that prevent jobs from running smoothly.

To follow in their footsteps, *here's what to do:*

1. Handle problems as promptly as possible. Any delay on your part simply aggravates matters, upsets people, and increases costs.

2. Know when and where your presence is likely needed. Try to be there. Learn to supervise several jobs at the same time.

3. Split your attention among your people so that none are neglected for long. If any person runs into a problem you will soon know about it.

4. Practice preventive action by doing things which avoid problems. Anticipate trouble and take steps to prevent it. You will have fewer problems and more time to work on those you have.

Case-in-Point: Dick Ryan, plant engineer at Hamilton Standard in Windsor Locks,[2] CT, says, "When it comes to decision making on plant equipment design and layout, the maintenance factor has too often been left out. The first opportunity the maintenance people have to see the extent of a project—construction or simple installations of new or redesigned units—is usually after all decisions have been made. Then they are 'stuck' with fixing any problems which occur and learning new systems without knowing the designer's background data or intentions." Think how much easier Dick Ryan's job could be if maintenance people were consulted during the design stage of engineering projects at his plant.

7.8 Tips on Being Logical When Solving Problems

Supervisors should always try to be logical when solving problems. Being logical means not letting bias, prejudice, habit, or instinct be a basis for thinking and judging. Although this may be easier said than done because people usually are not aware they are being influenced, letting facts alone be controlling will result in better decisions.

To be logical in making a decision you must follow a plan and watch your steps along the way. You must test the facts on which you base your decision and not let emotions, hopes, desires, and fears be a part of your thought pattern.

Avoid the urge to come up with a quick answer such as the first one that comes to mind. Be able to trace how you reason. Consider all the facts which could have a bearing on a problem and be unwilling to discard a fact without giving it more than a cursory glance. Doing some tangential thinking is good in that it helps to deter impulsiveness while at the same time possibly exposes an alternative solution.

Caution: Examine carefully any solution which very much pleases you or which you feel you were expected to come up with. In the same vein, beware if the solution to a problem seems too easy.

---

[2]From *Maintenance Engineering*, Dec., 1975.

In a last analysis, be willing to accept a solution based on facts alone even though the conclusion may be unpleasant or disagreeable.

Case-in-Point: Periodically supervisors may be told by their superiors that they've got to cut costs on their operations. "You can't argue about something like that," said a supervisor to me a few years ago. "The word came down from my boss that my labor costs were too high. He had the figures for comparing my labor costs with those of another department doing similar work. Upper management suggested to him that a cut of 10 percent be made in the number of people in my department. Well, I tried to find other areas where I could reduce our costs, but we had already gone over that a few months before. I finally had to sit down with my boss and decide which two people in my department would have to leave."

7.9 Guidelines to the Level at Which a Decision Should Be Made

Supervisors are usually required to make several decisions during a day on the job. At times they may question whether a particular decision is their's to make, whether it shouldn't be made at a higher level of management. They need guidelines to help them with this problem.

When determining the specific level of management at which a decision should be made, two principles should be followed:

1. The decision should be made at the lowest level in the organization consistent with the functions of management positions. If the problem requiring a decision fits into the normal, everyday duties and responsibilities of the supervisor, he or she should make the decision.

2. The decision should be made at a level high enough to include consideration of all characteristics that affect it. If the decision is unusual, may have a great impact, involves qualitative factors, may be difficult to reverse, or has a high degree of permanency, a management person at a level higher than the supervisor should make the decision.

Case-in-Point #1: Complaints and grievances of employees should be handled as close to their source as possible because supervision and employees involved are the people most familiar with existing conditions. When a complaint or grievance is settled between the parties involved, it seldom leaves after-effects or lasting animosity.

Case-in-Point #2: An employee's request for a leave of absence at a time when the employee's help is sorely needed should be answered by a management person at a level higher than the supervisor. The request, if granted, could have an impact on the quantity or quality of the department output as well as bring up a question of management control of operations and personnel.

7.10 The Psychology Behind Decisions: How to Use It to Advantage

There's more to making a decision than just deciding. Most decisions that supervisors make involve people. You've got to consider their feelings and their reactions. Timing is another matter which should be thought out. One time to announce a decision or take action may be much better than another.

Successful supervisors use psychology in making decisions. They also check their hunches and intuitions; they hesitate to make a decision if they instinctively feel it isn't right. Their decisions are better and more readily accepted because of these practices.

Always consider the people involved in your decisions. Is your decision good from their viewpoint? Could you do better for them? Are you going to have an enforcement problem? If people can participate in your decision you will probably have better acceptance.

Wait, if possible, for the occasion when you are rested and relaxed when making an important decision. Realize that you are unable to think and reason well when you are tired or depressed.

Don't let other people force your decisions. There's a good chance they may be working for their benefit, not yours. Besides, you must feel that you are making the decision, not them.

If you must make a quick decision, continue to investigate the facts afterward. You will be prepared if you have to reverse the decision and be protecting yourself from unforeseen consequences.

Don't feel that you must announce a decision just because you have it made. Pick the best time and place for that. Doing this will give you a little extra time for second thoughts and to make arrangements for steps which will follow the announcement.

7.11 How to Resolve a Bad Decision

It's inevitable that at some time you're going to make a bad decision. Even the most experienced and successful supervisors do it. Although having to reverse or change your decision may be distasteful and also leave you feeling weak, you must do what you can to correct your mistake.

An important matter to be concerned about is that you don't make another bad decision when correcting the first one. Put forth extra effort and spend additional time, if necessary, to be sure this doesn't happen.

When you are considering reversing a decision, get some help and advice. Talk to the person or persons who were involved or played a part in it originally. Do they agree that complete reversal would be wise? Do they have an alternative course to follow? Get an opinion also from someone you consider knowledgeable and experienced but who was not involved.

Decide what would be best for you to do. Before you act, however, explain to your boss what has happened and what's on your mind. Although your boss will probably back you, you show that you respect his or her advice and you demonstrate that you consider it important to keep him or her informed.

7.12 Reacting to a Bad Decision: How to Handle Yourself

People expect something from you after they learn that you made a bad decision. They want to see how you react and they are interested in hearing what you have to say. Your credibility, reputation, and prestige are at stake. You show what type of person you are by what you do in this awkward and sometimes embarrassing situation.

Effective supervisors handle themselves well and don't lose the respect or admiration of their people. You should adopt their behavior pattern by explaining briefly and simply the reasons behind your decision to the people involved. But, don't go too far with this or you risk sounding defensive.

Avoid apologizing for a bad decision. If it caused some inconvenience, a short, sincere comment of regret is enough. Never, of course, try to place the blame on someone else. Everyone knows it was your decision—own up to it.

Be sure to inform people quickly of a new decision if you make one, and explain it. Show that you are confident that it is a good one.

Case-in-Point: Bill Trent, supervisor in a meat packing plant in Ohio, is quick to act when he learns that he made a bad decision. "I immediately get out in the plant to the fellows involved and say something like, 'Hey, fellow, I goofed,' and then proceed to explain. I usually see a few smiles and seldom get a derogatory comment, so I guess they take it right in stride, which they should. Everybody makes mistakes, you know." Trent's philosophy on his and his people's reaction to a bad decision shows why he is an effective supervisor.

7.13 Answers to Having to Make Quick Decisions

Few people are not bothered by having to make a decision quickly or under pressure. You can be more sure of making a good decision if you can take the time to get facts, consider them, and choose between alternatives. Supervisors frequently are faced with making decisions with little time to think about them. How they handle such problems often decides how fast they grow on the job and move up in the company to positions of greater responsibility.

It's easy to lose sight of your objective when you're under pressure. Since time is usually the reason for pressure, your best bet is to try for as much as you can get. Look over the situation to determine if you really must come up with a decision quickly or if only the person presenting the problem to you feels that you must. A problem sometimes appears worse than it is; inexperienced people and people not familiar with a condition may view it with unwarranted alarm. Then, too, many people are impatient when things are not going their way.

Case-in-Point: Bob Tully, a 55-year-old supervisor in a General Motors[3] assembly line plant in Michigan, has been under pressure many times in his career. His advice: "I used to take the short-range view. To get people out of my hair I was inclined to make decisions in favor of the man who complained the loudest. I learned the hard way that in trying to get rid of one problem I created three or four." Tully points out that you must keep in mind the big picture. Avoid putting a lot of effort into solving a problem-of-the-moment at the expense of the overall job.

When you find yourself in a position where you must make a quick decision and you're not prepared to do so, look for an answer that can temporarily take care of matters. You can profit at least two ways with this move: 1) you buy yourself time for further investigation, and 2) you let events take place which might change the situation, making your decision easier.

If you cannot find a for-the-moment out, you must, of course, make the best decision you are capable of. At least, however, give yourself a few moments to collect your thoughts before you act.

Case-in-Point: Charles Beamer, personnel manager at Plant 5 of the Goodyear Tire and Rubber Company in Akron, Ohio confided to me a few years ago about how he valued his pipe and tobacco at a meeting with the Union. When he found himself in a tight situation calling for an immediate decision or for the proper words to forestall one, he gained himself a few valuable seconds to maintain his composure and think by loading, tamping, and lighting up his pipe. While this little act may have caused some irritation among impatient participants at the meeting, it still served its purpose to the manager in helping him to make good and acceptable rulings.

7.14 What to Do When Your Decision Is Challenged

Not all of your decisions are going to be readily accepted because people have their own opinions, think differently than you, and may know something that you don't. Questions will be asked by your superiors, peers, or subordinates. You must be able to answer such questions and defend your decisions.

Successful supervisors do not become emotional when their decisions are questioned, regardless of how sure they feel they are right. Highly emotional behavior indicates a lack of stability and personal control which supervisors must have if they are to be effective on the job.

---

[3]Reprinted by permission from *Supervision Magazine,* July, 1973. Copyright 1973 by the National Research Bureau, Inc., 424 N. 3rd Street, Burlington, Iowa 52601.

The proper way to respond is to calmly say that you may be wrong, that the person has a right to his or her opinion, and that you would like to discuss it. Then, ask why it is felt that your decision is not good. Recognize all the while that you may have made a bad one.

Case-in-Point: Once a supervisor, now a production superintendent, George Sanders told me, "One of the best ways to handle objections to your idea or decision is to listen to them. Not only will this help you to fully understand the objection, but, if a man's objections are weak, he may discover this for himself if he's allowed to talk freely."

In most cases your decision may be challenged because people do not understand it or why you made it. It's a matter of communication—people were not informed of something concerning them—you must now do that. When you explain, they often will be satisfied. If you've made a good decision you should have no trouble with this.

It stands to reason that a person will sometimes have a valid and logical reason for challenging your decision. If this is evident, say the person has made a good point and that you will reconsider. Be sure to compliment the person for recognizing the questionable decision; also thank him or her for telling you about it. Re-evaluate the decision as soon as possible.

It pays to personally keep the person who challenges a decision informed when you reconsider it, whether you make a new decision or not. You show that you recognize and value the person's suggestions and that you hope he or she approves what you decide. If you reverse or make a new decision, go out of your way to see that the person is informed of this ahead of other individuals.

7.15 How to Contend with Procrastination

Procrastination is nothing more than putting off doing something. All of us are guilty of it to some degree at one time or another. You procrastinate most often when you are faced with a difficult decision or have an unpleasant job to do. The job may be more disagreeable if you are not convinced of the need for doing it. Procrastination sometimes leads to a decision not to do a job at all.

Case-in-Point: Supervisors sometimes have jobs that would require considerable work and time to handle. They may feel that the direct effect of handling a particular job does not justify the effort. As a result, they put it aside. Management consultants say it's dangerous to look only at the direct results. If supervisors handle jobs such as these and solve even minor problems they show employees that management is concerned with poor situations and won't tolerate something that shouldn't be happening, even if it takes more work than many people think it is worth.

You can overcome the problem of procrastination if you set your mind to do so.

How-to-Do-It: Develop a positive, optimistic attitude about your job and duties. Realize that conditions usually are not as bad as they may seem. Decide early that you cannot continue to put off something indefinitely.

While getting started on a distasteful job is no easy matter, your best bet is to go after the job when you are fresh and in a good frame of mind. Once you start, keep at it until you finish. This saves facing it a second time.

Procrastination itself isn't all that bad. You theoretically aren't procrastinating if you believe that not taking action is your decision. The mature, experienced supervisor may be doing the best thing when he or she decides to do nothing for the moment even though it appears that action of some sort should be taken.

Case-in-Point: It has become common practice in business and industry today to take a "cooling off" period before making judgments on personnel behavioral problems. Better decisions on discipline have resulted when time is taken for investigation because emotions are not as likely to be an influence.

8

How to Handle Problems of Communication

Getting through to people is the most difficult part of the job for many supervisors. The matter cannot be taken lightly because no single aspect of the supervisor's job can contribute to career success as much as being an effective communicator. Since communication on the job is so important, it should be promoted and encouraged at every opportunity. To do so, supervisors should be aware of the barriers and how to overcome them. They must continually seek and practice ways to keep communication channels open. Being informal and available to discuss almost any problem has proven to be of value.

Supervisors need to know the answers to the many problems of communicating on the job, such as how to promote upward communication, what to do when you aren't being informed, how to handle the situation of the boss being bypassed, and how much people should be told. Rumors should not be ignored; they require positive action by the supervisor. The grapevine can be a good communication tool if handled properly. And most important, supervisors need to be good listeners.

8.1 Keys to Effective Supervisor-Employee Communication

Two findings of a Bureau of National Affairs survey of 219 big and small manufacturers and other businesses were: the most effective employee communication techniques are verbal, and the first-line supervisor is the key link in the communication process. The survey also revealed that among downward communications techniques, the bulletin board is used by nearly all companies. Then comes supervisor's meetings, followed by company publications and meetings of employees in small groups.

Supervisors communicate with their people to inform them, to influence them, and to support them. Successful communicators have learned, however, that it isn't wise to try to do more than one of these at a time. Doing so weakens the transmission of the message and also dampens its impact.

Good communication is simply effective passing of information by the most suitable means available. The result is more important than how it is done. The communicator must give some thought to communicating and not just trust it to chance. Although the keys to effective employee communication are simple, they are very purposeful. When you communicate you must:

1. Have the receiver's attention. The receiver must be interested in you and what you have to say.

2. Have the receiver understand you. You accomplish this by using simple words, short sentences, and avoiding jargon.

3. Have the receiver accept your message. You succeed through reason, logic, and persuasion.

8.2 How to Communicate Information About the Company

By giving employees information and facts about their company, you can develop their interest and their loyalty. If they are not given any information, they may draw their own conclusions from what they already knew or heard elsewhere. If they have false information they may develop a poor opinion, a feeling which doesn't bode well for the company.

Your company makes quality products or performs a good service—it would not be able to stay in business if it didn't. Pointing this out to your people helps them to develop pride in their jobs and their company. Surveys have shown that many employees do not know much about their company's products or service. If this is true of your people, you should make an effort to change it.

Always take advantage of opportunities to tell people when the company receives honors and awards, or makes a contribution towards a community effort. Similarly, when one of your people makes the news, see that other workers know about it. The easiest way to do this is to put the item on the bulletin board.

A company should tell employees of its plans when acquiring and installing new equipment. The company should explain that the new equipment is being installed not only to cut costs but also to increase production and to boost sales which will probably increase jobs in the long run.

What about news about the company which isn't good? While it may not be wise to go out of your way to talk about things which make your company look bad, you still shouldn't hesitate to give bad news. Better that people hear it from you than from someone else.

If you are perceptive, you will be able to anticipate when you are going to get reactions from your people on announcements. Offer an explanation when you see that a company rule or policy is going to be unpopular. Although you may have to do a selling job, there is usually a good reason for rules such as prohibiting use of company refrigerators or ovens for handling food. If you explain such rules, you will find that people will go along with them better because they will see that the rules were made for their benefit.

Communicating information about the company prevents fears from arising about jobs and possible changes in working conditions. You'll find also that fewer rumors crop up when employees know what is going on.

Case-in-Point: Management of Tool Steel Gear and Pinion Company in Cincinnati, Ohio[1] believes in keeping its employees posted. "Of most importance to our employees is the number of orders we receive," is the way they put it. Every day, daily order sheets that list all orders received the previous day are put up on various bulletin boards around the plant. In this way, the company says, it gives its employees a feeling of security by keeping them informed of upcoming work. A member of management says, "It lets them know they'll have a job tomorrow."

8.3 How to Promote Upward Communication

Your job of supervising is much easier if your people keep you informed. You will have the facts that will help you make decisions, and you will be able to foresee problems that could arise. For these and other reasons it is to your advantage to promote upward communication from your people at every opportunity.

---

[1]Reprinted from *Supervisor's Bulletin*, Issue No. 347. By permission of the publisher. Bureau of Business Practice, 24 Rope Ferry Road, Waterford, Connecticut 06386. Copyright. Bureau of Business Practice, Inc.

How does a supervisor promote upward communication? The best way is to always be available and receptive to people who want to talk. Listen to all your people's ideas, regardless of how illogical or impractical they may sound. Listen also to their complaints, and answer them.

When people learn that you respect their opinion and are interested in their welfare, they will not hesitate to give you information, particularly if you show you appreciate it and tell them so. If they learn also that you are fair and honest, they will not hold back on telling you about mistakes rather than trying to cover them up.

To most workers the supervisor will always be the boss, and it behooves them to say what the boss likes to hear and to do what the boss wants them to do. It may be to some workers' interests to withhold certain information lest it be used against them or against others in the same work group. This psychological barrier to upward communication is simply fear. Successful supervisors do something about it by continually working toward ways to eliminate or reduce that fear.

How-to-Do-It: Be decisive on the job and confident that what you say and do is right. People usually have few fears when their leaders are positive in giving orders and directing work. When workers know that they are doing their work correctly and to their supervisor's liking, rapport improves and teamwork is given a boost. People just naturally communicate more when they feel secure.

Supervisors who want upward communication from their people to be good must keep up the morale. They must place a high value on the three strong desires of people: 1) to be recognized and given appreciation for work done, 2) to be kept informed so they are "in" on things, and 3) to receive friendly, sympathetic advice on personal problems. Understanding and willingness on the part of supervisors to meet these needs of their people will reduce communication fears and promote upward communication.

8.4 Ten Positive Ways to Avoid Creating Communication Barriers

Successful leaders are aware of the various barriers to communication that prevent understanding among people that work together. Here are several of the most serious ones. Experienced supervisors have learned to avoid them. To do the same, you must not be guilty of:

1. Failing to keep people informed. Supervisors may assume that because *they* saw something or heard something, *their* people also saw or heard it. Few people will admit that they do not know that they have not been informed. Instead they tend to bluff, pretend, or just sit back and wait. Withholding

information that people need to do a job robs them of dignity. Without knowing why, they not only lose contact, but also lose faith in the supervisor and the company.

2. Jumping to conclusions without evidence. People hesitate to communicate with a boss who jumps to conclusions without having the facts. They despair of the boss's ability to reason, decide, and solve problems. And they fear being blamed for something they didn't do.

3. Overlooking the impact of words. Taking a strong stand on a subject or making announcements which people take as threats may bring on severe reactions with communications suffering as a result. Be careful in your choice of words when talking with people. Avoid being too positive if you want them to respond without fear.

4. Forgetting that how something is said may be as important as what is said. Your tone of voice may say more than your words. Voices can show irritation, hostility, and insincerity without the words suggesting these things. Body communication may also give a strong message. Whatever, how a supervisor acts when communicating may tell others that this is the time to be silent, with the result that communication suffers.

5. Failing to admit a mistake. People who feel that it is wrong to admit a mistake do not believe there is power in accepting blame for errors and strength in offering apologies for wrongs which involve other people. It is just about impossible to have any true communication with a person who looks for mistakes in everyone but himself or herself.

6. Preferring performance to people. A supervisor who gives the impression that all that counts are profit, production, and getting the job done fails to give credit to people. As a result, people will shy away from communicating with such a person on matters which do not apply to those things.

7. Being unprepared. Communication suffers when you try to discuss an important matter with people without having facts or information to offer. You look bad and you make others look bad by not being clear on what you're talking about, what you're trying to achieve, and what you expect from them.

8. Distorting ideas. Being overly pessimistic or optimistic solely for the effect that you think it will have on your people usually doesn't work because reality is always a matter for personal interpretation. Such tactics are recognized for what they are and simply discounted. But a damper is put on communication because of them.

9. Forgetting the importance of experience. A supervisor who is unrealistic in his or her demands hinders the inexperienced employee who needs help. When a supervisor expects immediate results, perfection, and no excuses, that is asking too much of inexperienced people.

10. Resisting change. If you are for maintaining things as they are you

probably stand in the way of good communication with creative people. They may hold back their ideas to avoid a confrontation with you. Everyone loses when there is no communication.

8.5 Evaluation: A Major Barrier to Communication

One of the major barriers to effective communication is a person's natural tendency to evaluate, judge, and approve or disapprove a statement of another person. Although evaluating is common in almost all interchange of thoughts, it is much greater in situations where feelings and emotions are involved. The stronger the feelings, the more likely it is there will be no mutual agreement of two persons in their communication with each other. There will simply be two viewpoints, two feelings, and two judgments, with no agreement.

Case-in-Point: On more than one accasion I have listened to a heated discussion between two individuals in which both expressed strong feelings about a matter. After the two individuals had left each other without reaching an agreement, I thought a bit about the discussion and realized that they weren't talking about the same thing. Each was making a judgment from his own frame of reference. There was really nothing which could be called communication in their meeting since neither accepted the other's points.

If some time you sense that you are in a discussion which is not going to turn out in agreement, stop for a moment to consider your position. Do you see and understand the other person's view? Are you giving the person credit for it? Could you compromise the issue in some way? Try to reach at least one point of agreement before you leave each other. Your future communications will probably be better if you do.

8.6 Answers to How Much People on the Job Should Be Told

Today's employees want to know how what they do on the job contributes to the whole of their company. They also want to know what people in other departments are doing. And they like to be "in" on things whether or not they are involved.

Most people in management positions recognize that knowledge is a good motivator and morale builder. Still, the question remains of how much people on the job should be told. While everyone agrees that communication is good, it takes a lot of time, and time is money.

You can't tell everybody everything. It's not necessary to give people a lot of unwanted details. Information can be put into three categories when deciding what to pass on to your people.

1. That which they should have to properly do their work, such as how machines function, where supplies are, what forms should be used, when jobs must be completed, and similar information which relates to their specific job.

2. That which they should know because they might be affected, such as an expansion in the department or company, a rearrangement of work areas, or an increase in a production quota.

3. That which they would find helpful in relating to their position and contribution to the organization, such as information about the company's goals and achievements, sales, new products, and profits.

Generally, supervisors should see that their people are given information in the first two categories. The amount of information of the third category which should be told depends on the interests of the individuals. Those who are creative and innovative, such as research and development people, would welcome news about new products or services the company offers. Almost everyone should want to know how the company is doing profitwise and what the future looks like. Most employees are more interested in their company than their supervisors suspect.

Case-in-Point: In a personal interview with Richard Hammons, factory manager, J. Strickland and Company, Memphis, Tenn.,[2] he said, "Complete, constant, and thorough communications with every one of our personnel, all the way down the chain of command and all the way back up that chain, are the keys to loyalty of personnel and efficiency of production of our big line of toiletries and cosmetics. Those communications are particularly important because we are turning out more than 150 products (including sizes), and the sales department so often calls for different quantities of items as demands fluctuate, making frequent rescheduling necessary on the production lines.

"When some change in procedures is indicated, or when a new product is added to those to be produced, we not only tell each employee concerned with the change what is needed, but also discuss with them our planning for production, tell them what they are expected to accomplish—what quantities of inventories are required at the start and also later on.

"We find that this complete openness keeps morale high. The employees appreciate it."

Case-in-Point: Several years ago, the chemical division of a large rubber company undertook a waste control program in an effort to reduce raw material cost and thereby improve profits. The cost of individual chemicals were posted in the various process areas of the plant. Signs were posted also asking workers to avoid spills and use care in handling these materials. In some areas the

---

[2]From *Supervision Magazine,* Jan., 1972.

installation cost of new equipment and facilities was also spelled out to tell employees what it took in the way of investment by the company to run the plant.

Over a period of months there were no significant signs of less waste or carelessness on the part of employees, nor were employees impressed to the extent that their treatment of facilities improved. Should the company have reached the conclusion that employees felt the company could afford small material losses? Did the profit information that was published in the company newspaper tell the employees that the company had plenty of money for new equipment?

The company did not continue its cost information program after that experience, one reason being given that cost and profit information isn't understood by most employees.

8.7 Withholding Information: Why It's Sometimes Necessary

Although much communication between supervisors and their people is a sign of good management, there are times when information should be withheld and not made public. A supervisor should not pass along everything he or she knows when the following conditions exist:

1. Management has not finalized its plans. Rumors may be rampant when management is thinking about an expansion, a cutback, or a merger. Yet, the change may never go through. Usually management does not want information on such matters made public until its plans are finalized or close to it.

2. Information must be passed through regular channels. People involved in a change should be told before those not involved. Also, disclosing facts or change too soon to too many people may interfere with management's plans for publicity and promotion.

3. The information is related to security. Contracts or negotiations with the government, for example, often require secrecy. Other matters of security which are not discussed are those which involve the police such as property damage and theft investigations.

4. Revealing the information may hurt the company. Formulas, designs, and new procedures not protected by patents must be kept secret to prevent competitors from taking advantage of such information.

8.8 What to Do When You Aren't Being Informed

No executive or manager of a business wants to hear, "Why didn't you tell me?" from one of the employees. The question is a tip-off that a misfortune has occurred such as a lost sale, production delay, or customer complaint which might have been prevented with better communication.

Supervisors seldom complain about being given too much information. To the contrary, many of them feel that they are not being kept informed of matters which they should know about. The problem is a serious one with supervisors who work night shifts and are out of close touch with their superiors.

If you need more information to do your job satisfactorily, ask for it. If you don't receive it, then you have a real problem and had better look into your relationship with your boss. Before you do, however, think a bit about your situation.

Is your boss really at fault, or are you, perhaps, not reading all the memos sent you, listening carefully when the boss talks, and keeping your eyes open? If you decide that you are not at fault, let your boss know, doing it in a way that has impact and should get results.

How-to-Do-It: Discuss with your boss one or more recent problems or events that did not turn out well. Point out that if you had been informed, you could have handled them to his or her and the company's advantage. After hearing this, the boss will certainly take steps to see that you are kept up-to-date on matters in which you could become involved.

Case-in-Point: Effective communication with and between maintenance personnel is an essential ingredient for the successful maintenance program at the Globe Battery Division of Globe Union Inc., Milwaukee, Wisconsin.[3] Clyde Cheney, Maintenance Programs Coordinator, confirmed this when he said, "Too often, sophisticated systems which appear flawless from an 'ivory tower' standpoint fail miserably because we didn't get all the people who could do something about problems involved. To 'get the word' to our maintenance people in our 13 Globe-Union battery manufacturing plants, we now use an inexpensive and well-received *Maintenance Memo*. The frequency of an issue is tied to anticipated usefulness and the need as a practical consideration, instead of adherence to a rigid schedule. This permits us to get timely information to the reader quickly. After 33 issues, we are firmly convinced that our *Maintenance Memo* is here to stay as an effective but inexpensive communication device."

8.9 Being Informal: An Effective Way to Promote Communication

If you are impressed with your job title you are probably too formal with your people. Being formal hinders communications. It also tends to set you off as an individual who may be difficult to see or get along with. The supervisor

---

[3]From *Maintenance Engineering,* April, 1976.

who acts informally on the job usually knows more about what's happening in the office or plant.

Case-in-Point: "Allowing people to call me by my first name doesn't take away any of the dignity of my position," says Don Smith, supervisor in a west coast electronics plant. "If someone comes to talk to me, they're sometimes reluctant to ask, 'Mr. Smith, may I speak to you?' They tend to open up more when we're on a first-name basis."

Being informal on the job promotes teamwork also, since it plays down differences in job level and responsibility. People like to feel equal or better than other people in as many ways as they can. Being on a first-name basis with the boss is one way of doing it.

8.10 How to Handle the Situation When Your Boss Is Bypassed

You may be flattered and feel important when someone communicates with you on a matter which should be handled with your boss. Suppress your ego if this happens because you have been put in a delicate situation.

Such an act makes your boss very uncomfortable and even resentful, especially if he or she has felt insecure on the job or has a lot of pride. You must do what you can to help your boss in this situation.

How-to-Do-It: The proper way to go about it is to immediately bring the boss up-to-date. Inform him or her of exactly what has happened and ask what you should do. Usually you will be told to proceed as if the communication had come from the boss direct. You can be assured that the boss will appreciate your prompt discussion of the matter and your asking for guidance.

You may be tempted at times to bypass your boss on communications in any one of many matters for various reasons. You will be better off to avoid this. Or you may unavoidably do it when the boss's superior asks you for information or your opinion. Always let your boss know about it as soon as possible if such things happen. The position of supervisor in the hierarchy of management positions today calls for the supervisor to communicate directly with his or her superior in preference to all others. It is always to your best interest that you do so.

8.11 Four Tips on Using the Company Grapevine

Employees like to have information that relates to their work, their company, and the people who manage it. They particularly want to know about company plans and proposed changes that could affect their economic status. They will get this information one way or another.

If they receive it from official company sources, they will get facts and reliable information. But, if the company doesn't keep them informed, they will turn to the grapevine or rumors. Unfortunately, the latter may provide them partial truths, distortions, and misinterpretations.

Some authorities say that a supervisor must never use the grapevine either to disseminate information or receive it. They claim that "the grapevine, so often rife with rumors and lies, seldom carries the exact truth, although it sometimes carries enough of the truth to be quite believable and attract widespread attention." They say that the supervisor who uses the grapevine is asking for trouble.

Other authorities aren't so contrary about it. They say that the grapevine, properly used, can be an aid to communications. Clever supervisors can get things done and get touchy matters handled simply by planting information in appropriate areas. Of course, such means of communicating are not always sure-fire, but if you can't get a job done through usual channels you might try it. If you are so inclined, here are four tips on using the grapevine as a means of communication:

1. Never try to use the grapevine to gain an advantage over someone. If you don't have trust, you won't get communication. You could also lose your credibility.

2. Make sure you understand the situation, have the facts, and know the people involved. Don't try it if there's a big unknown matter which could disrupt everything.

3. Avoid letting the grapevine dictate to you. Be sure your people don't use it to convert you to their thinking on some matter on which you have a different opinion than they.

4. Learn who the talkers are and how they spread the news. Realize that there may be more than one way of getting the word around.

Caution: Be wary of an upper level grapevine. A grapevine in top management circles can be complex and vicious.

8.12 What to Do About Rumors

Since one of your responsibilities is to keep your people informed, dealing with rumors is one of your jobs. If rumors are ignored they can hurt morale, cause hard feelings, and result in foolish behavior of gullible individuals. You must do something when you suspect you've heard a rumor.

Here is what you should do:

1. Learn more about the rumor by asking your people what they've heard and where. If you can find out where the rumor started it will be easier to do something about it.

2. Tell people that you're checking. Suggest that they not be concerned until you get the facts.

3. Talk to your boss about the matter. He or she may know the truth or, if the rumor is true, why no statement has officially been made.

4. If you are unable to learn anything from your boss, begin checking with authorities. Ask them for guidance on what you can tell your people.

5. Give your people the facts. If there is no truth to the rumor, say so. If you have no information, tell them that. The most important thing you can do is to show that you care and that you want to do all you can to keep them informed.

8.13 Listening: The Communication Tool That Also Motivates

To motivate your people, you must develop in them a spirit of wanting to work and wanting to do a better job each day. A way to do this is to listen to them when they talk about their jobs and their problems. For proof of this, look at the persons in your group who have come up with ideas and suggestions. You'll find in most cases that innovations and improvements came from persons on the job who were encouraged and listened to.

People who work for the old-style, autocratic type supervisor seldom offer suggestions or are motivated to improve themselves. The autocratic type supervisor *tells* people what should be done, *how* it should be done, and *when* it should be done. Although the job gets done, it rarely, if ever, is in a manner better than the supervisor could do it. Individuality, originality, and initiative are stifled because the supervisor is mostly telling and seldom listening.

The democratic supervisor believes that people can and will make intelligent suggestions and decisions if they are permitted to do so. This happens if the supervisor trains them, helps them to develop, and listens to them.

Case-in-Point: John Sisty, Chief, Engineering Division, Veterans Administration Hospital at Oteen, North Carolina is a strong advocate of listening. At a recent Plant Engineering Conference[4] he said, "When I first took over our Engineering Division, my people came in a steady stream to present their problems. It was almost painful to watch their reaction when I would ask for their recommendations. They had very few answers to their problems because they had never been asked before. The ones they had were generally poor, but I listened. Within three weeks they had answers. I kept listening and their answers kept getting better and better. When they knew they would be asked, and their answers *listened to,* they started to study. A year later, 25 percent fewer men were doing 30 percent more work.

"As the men continued to improve themselves, I became enthused,

---

[4]From 1971 International Plant Eng. Conference, Anaheim, Cal., Sept., 1971.

continued to listen, started to study motivation, and developed the following practical guidelines. I say practical because they worked. Later, I learned from the experts and the psychologists why they worked. Here they are: To motivate your men, listen to them and convince them:

1. That they are important members of your team, that their job is important, and that it is important that they do a good job.

2. That you are interested in them personally.

3. That you recognize their years of experience as valuable assets to your organization.

4. That their ideas and suggestions are wanted and welcome, that they can come to you with their ideas, and that you will listen to them and help them put their ideas into practice.

5. That you will back them up, support their interest, fight for them if necessary, and praise them."

8.14 Proven Ways to Develop Good Listening Habits

Supervisors must be good listeners. Active listening on their part encourages workers to speak freely and explore problems. When employees see they are listened to by their supervisors they are more likely to listen more carefully themselves. This makes the supervisor's job of giving instructions and explaining work situations much easier.

Good listening habits can be acquired with practice. Here are the ways to go about it:

1. Listen with an open mind. Try to avoid mental blocks based on emotions. Hold off making comments until you've heard everything about a situation and had time to think about it.

2. Avoid interrupting anyone. Be an advocate of the doctrine that big people monopolize the listening and small people monopolize the talking.

3. Learn how to screen out noise and distraction so that you can concentrate on what is being said. When someone speaks to you, give the impression that what he or she has to say to you is very interesting and you want to hear more. It will make you listen more closely.

4. File away in the back of your mind the important points of what is being said while the other person talks.

5. Don't let highly charged or emotional words bother you. Keep your mind on the facts.

6. Avoid appearing and acting overly knowledgeable. You may turn off the speaker. Besides, you may miss something of value if you listen with the feeling that you already know what is being said.

9

Proven Techniques
That Make
Giving Orders Easy

Supervisors communicate with their people when instructing, training, and giving orders. Although all three functions require special skills, giving orders is the most important from the viewpoint of what is accomplished on the job. Supervisors who are adept at giving orders are better accepted by their people, and their people make fewer mistakes. Being aware of the pitfalls to avoid and the technique to follow makes the job of giving orders easier and simpler.

There's only one right way to put across management's decisions to employees and that is to give them as if they were your own. You strengthen your position as part of management and you demonstrate your ability to take on responsibility when you do this.

Avoiding misunderstandings is the major problem to be concerned with when giving orders. You can adopt proven practices to help you with this, one of which is to get feedback. Verbal orders have many advantages over other types but some orders should be put in writing. The well-rounded supervisor knows also how to write letters and memos that are effective.

9.1 Seven Tried-and-Proven Pointers on Giving Instructions

Supervisors manage and direct people in being productive and doing work in the proper manner. Even enthusiastic and efficient people need guidance if the maximum is to be realized from their efforts. How much gets done is usually up to the supervisors and the effectiveness of their instructions.

When supervisors are skilled in giving instructions, jobs are handled promptly, work is done correctly, and people get satisfaction from accomplishment. Here are some pointers on the art:

1. Decide beforehand who you are going to ask to carry out your instructions. Think about how you're going to explain them to the person. Consider the timing—one time may be poor while another very appropriate. Decide where the job should be done, and determine if tools and materials are available.

2. Promote receptiveness for your instructions with preliminary remarks. Put your listener in a good frame of mind by first talking about things other than the job such as the person's hobby or a mutual interest. By asking a question or two you can determine the person's attitude and emotional state. Knowing this helps in choosing your tone and deciding what words to use.

3. Be clear and specific. Use simple words and talk at a speed which gives your listener time to understand. Break up complicated and lengthy instructions into small steps and put them in logical order. Be consistent—if you call something by a certain name at one time, use the same name when you refer to it later.

4. Emphasize the positive. Tell a person the *right* way to do a job rather than *not* to do it the *wrong* way. When you instruct positively you are more convincing and persuasive—what you say is more credible and authoritative. Positive instructions are more readily accepted than negative ones.

5. Favor optimism. Show that you are confident your instructions are good and easily carried out. Indicate that you know your listeners have the capability and want to do the job. Wear a smile instead of a frown. Be interested instead of indifferent to how people feel.

6. Present ideas. When you instruct with ideas you ask for opinions and you appeal to your listener's knowledge and judgment. Ideas make your instructions more interesting and cause people to think, thus promoting understanding as well as acceptability.

7. Point out benefits. Talk about gains to show listeners what's in it for them. Do this by mentioning their benefits and the company's in the same statement. For example, tell people they will be safer, the quality of the product will be better, and the work will be easier if they use the right tools. Stating benefits results in better attitude, more cooperation, and higher productivity.

9.2 Mood and Temperament: Factors That Affect Your Receptiveness

You will be more effective in giving instructions and orders when you are in a good frame of mind because your mood and temperament show in your words and actions. Conversely, you must be careful if you wish your orders to be accepted willingly and without question when you're not at your best. Here are a few precautions to help you handle your mood whatever it might be.

Although you might be charged up with energy and ambition, recognize that other people may not feel this way at the same time. Be considerate and reasonable in what you expect someone to do for you. Requesting a large amount of work to be done in a short period of time may cause people to think you unfair. It's better to challenge someone to do a bit more with occasional encouragement and praise for what has been done. The unreasonable approach can result in gripes, complaints, and even slowups in work performance.

Avoid being sarcastic. Your listener may not understand why you are in this mood and may also resent such treatment, feeling that it is unjustified. Sarcasm certainly will not cause a person to do a better job—if anything, it will only cause hard feelings.

Losing your temper does not help to get things done either. It may make the other fellow lose his and result in an argument. Angry people don't get jobs done. Besides, the instructions you give when you are angry will not be your best. People misunderstand the meaning of words said in anger.

Being sympathetic, considerate, enthusiastic, and cheerful influences people to be that way themselves. When you wish to stress the importance of your instructions, you can convey the point by being concerned, serious, and earnest. Remember, though, that your listener will perceive and accept your intentions only if you are sincere and honest.

Case-in-Point: Tom Gordon, electrical supervisor at The Goodyear Tire and Rubber Co., Akron, Ohio, told me, "A friendly and confident 'I know you can do it' comment on my part gets my instructions accepted and carried out faster than a sour 'this is probably too tough for you' remark. My men seem to sense how I feel about their capability to get a job done. Along the same line, I've noticed that a smile instead of a frown, and patience rather than anxiety will get things done faster in the long run. You've got to be interested instead of indifferent to how your people feel. And always remember, it shows."

9.3 Tips on How to Give Orders

Supervisors are constantly communicating with their people on what's to be done and who is to do it. The more adept they are at doing this, the more they get done. However, they can be highly successful day after day only if they have people who willingly cooperate. How supervisors give orders often determines how much cooperation they get.

A good supervisor seldom should have to command someone to do a job. The message can be put across by asking that the work be done. Sometimes a supervisor can present a problem, discuss it, and then suggest that someone "take care of it." Another discreet way to ask for a job to be done is to suggest an action "we" should take, thus implying that other people are involved, even though the employee alone does the job. Ideally, the supervisor should help people analyze a situation in such a way that the situation itself dictates the order.

Managers at all levels should try to get subordinates to feel that they have the right to make suggestions and express their views on the ways jobs are to be done. People on the job are closer to the work than anyone. Over a period of time they get to know what a machine will do or how something can be simply accomplished. It pays to take advantage of such knowledge and experience.

Most people prefer not to be told to do something. Taking an order puts them beneath the person giving the order. The more you can put yourself on an equal level with your people, the more success you'll have in getting their help and cooperation.

Supervisors should realize that orders can be given in many ways, and that the best way depends on the specific situation and the individual involved. Experienced supervisors usually follow a procedure of first trying for agreement on what is to be done. If this doesn't work, they try suggesting. Failing at this, they try asking. As a last resort, they issue a direct command.

Case-in-Point: "I may give orders to do a job a certain way and have one of my men come up with an idea he thinks would do the job quicker and better," says John Chase, line superintendent with the Bangor (Maine) Hydro-Electric Co.[1] "A man in a supervisory position must have an open mind and be ready to accept ideas, even if they may be contrary to his thinking," he added.

9.4 Tested Steps Which Make Giving Orders Easy

Giving orders that are always clear and completely understood doesn't come naturally to most supervisors, primarily because they are not aware of what is required to do so. Several factors affect understanding for one thing.

---

[1]Reprinted from *Supervisor's Memory Jogger,* Jan. 1967. By permission of the publisher. Bureau of Business Practice, 24 Rope Ferry Road, Waterford, Connecticut 06386. Copyright, Bureau of Business Practice, Inc.

For example, how much is taken for granted by the people who give orders? Do the receivers of the orders see things the same or differently? Do personal feelings get in the way when giving orders? Successful supervisors take such factors into consideration. To contend with them they give orders in three steps.

First, they present organized facts about a situation or condition before they give an order. Doing this enables them to eliminate assumptions. Then they say what they want done.

Second, they explain the reason why they are asking for something and why they want it done in a certain way. Doing this makes clear the necessity for the work and how they see it should be done.

Third, they check for understanding. Doing this enables them to learn if their message got through and to probe for feelings and reactions.

Successful supervisors always follow up to see if their orders were carried out. They learn if their requests were clear and understood, and if the work was done correctly. If something went awry, they investigate so they can avoid a reoccurrence.

9.5 Pitfalls the "Pros" Avoid in Giving Orders

Because the "pros" know the ins and outs of giving orders, they stay out of trouble which less experienced order-givers get into. Here are a few of the most troublesome pitfalls they avoid.

1. Giving conflicting instructions. Telling your people to do something that isn't standard practice or against company rules can get you and your people in real trouble. The same advice applies to telling one person to do a job a certain way and the next person a different way.

2. Being inconsistent. You can't be wishy-washy one day and stubborn the next. If you are easygoing one time and tough another, you cause uncertainty and anxiety among the people who work for you.

3. Acting important. Inexperienced supervisors may try to show their authority to get jobs done. The "pros" know they can gain their people's respect and compliance without coming down hard on them.

4. Showing favoritism. You must distribute the work fairly and not give the easiest work to the same people. Also, be sure the difficult-to-handle people get their share of the tough jobs.

5. Giving too many orders. Too many orders or too many details at one time confuse people. Limit your orders and make them short and specific.

6. Assuming understanding. Get the person to ask questions about the order or repeat it back to you in different words. You cannot assume anything.

7. Being offhand. Give your orders in a serious manner if you expect your people to take them seriously. Every order you give should be important.

9.6 How to Improve Your Order-Giving Technique

Although telling your people to do something seems simple enough, there is more to the art than is apparent. If you are an expert at giving orders, you probably are also skilled in planning, motivating, and persuading because those endeavors are prerequisites to giving good orders. Since giving orders is one of your main responsibilities, your success as a supervisor is measured by how skilled you are at it. You can improve your technique by adopting the following suggestions:

1. Promote team effort when you give orders. Point out that the person's contribution is part of a total effort in which other people also contribute. Explain how what the person does will benefit other people and why his or her cooperation is needed. Say that it takes people working together to reach the company's goals, and illustrate your statement by giving examples of it in your own department.

2. Make your order appropriate for the person and the situation. Use different approaches depending on the workload, the mood of the individual, the importance of the order, and the urgency with which it should be carried out. A request is always better than a command because it makes the person feel that cooperation is being asked for rather than demanded.

The suggestion is another type of order which is usually effective. Its success depends on the initiative and cooperative attitude of people. Although the order is implied, it brings a positive response from conscientious individuals.

Because of its demanding and authoritative tone you should seldom use a direct order. Limit its use to times of emergency to indicate the urgency of the situation, or when working with people who don't respond to any other type of order.

3. Make your order clear and complete. Keep it as simple as possible, but be sure it includes all the information needed for it to be carried out quickly and efficiently. If more than one person is involved, clarify who is responsible for doing what. If time is a factor, say when the job should be started.

Check for understanding of your order by asking that it be repeated back to you. Go over how the most difficult part of the job will be handled. Confirm that you have provided the information needed.

4. Give your order at the opportune time, such as when the receiver is most receptive. Avoid giving an order when the person is very busy or engrossed in another matter. If an order is complex or detailed, give it when the person is fresh and alert—there will be less chance of misunderstanding. Be aware that an order given just before lunch or at quitting time might be forgotten when the person resumes work.

Deciding when to issue an order can be just as critical as the order itself, especially if the order involves a major change. Experienced supervisors analyze the timing of their orders as to whether the greater risk lies in waiting or in acting immediately; they consider the probable outcome in each case and act accordingly. But, they also recognize that many things take time and that mistakes are likely if they're impatient. Impatient people often make poor decisions in trying to settle matters quickly.

Case-in-Point: "Any damn fool can give orders," says Jean Richer, manager of the Champlain Area for Canadian National Railways (Montreal). "A good supervisor coordinates the work. He gets the work done through others by picking the right man for the right job and by giving encouragement and support to his people to do a good job."

9.7 The Right Way to Put Across Management's Decisions

The supervisor who is skilled in giving orders has a great advantage over one who doesn't have that ability. The skilled person issues orders which are easily understood and don't result in hard feelings or resentment. Such a leader also does not use a higher authority's name in order to gain acceptance and compliance.

To put across management's decisions properly you must give and be responsible for them as if they were your own, whether you wholeheartedly agree with them or not. A weak supervisor says, *"The boss* would like you to...." A strong supervisor says, *"I* would like you to...."

Case-in-Point: "Although I didn't agree with upper management's decision on what we were going to ask the operators of the new machines to do, I knew that, being a member of management, I had to follow the procedure we had agreed to and not let my people know how I felt." So spoke John Teller, supervisor in a fabric mill in Alabama, when telling me about how a new process was running. "The plant manager was right, as he usually is. I would have looked bad if I hadn't given him my support. Besides, we have a much stronger management team when we are in agreement on our policies and procedures. We do our darnest to make things work the best way possible."

9.8 How to Avoid Misunderstandings

We would be much more efficient and make fewer mistakes if we didn't have misunderstandings. Unfortunately, there are many ways that misunderstandings occur and conditions often are such to make them likely. The best way to avoid them is to recognize a situation where you might have a misunderstanding, and take steps to prevent it. Here are some tips on how to avoid misunderstanding, both on your own and your listener's part.

A common kind of misunderstanding results when you assume a person attaches the same meaning to certain words that you do. The way such misunderstanding can be avoided is for the listener to repeat the message in different words, asking if that is what is meant. Another way is to ask a question pertaining to the message.

Misunderstandings also occur when someone simply doesn't hear certain words. Failure to hear *not,* for example, can cause a person to do something by mistake. It pays to repeat a message of this type using different words but emphasizing the *not*.

Many misunderstandings result from a person's poor choice of words. The words that you use in giving an order to someone may be taken as mandatory or discretionary. *Shall, will, is to,* and *must* are words which order action, while words such as *may, recommend,* and *suggest* do not require action. The word *should* may be interpreted either way.

You can make your message clear and help a person to better understand it if you come right to the point when you start talking. If you begin by asking a question which the listener doesn't know the reason for, you put the listener at a disadvantage. It's better to start by saying what you want or why you've come to talk.

When people don't speak the same language in the terms they use to describe something, they are very prone to have a misunderstanding. Make sure when you talk about a quantity or use numbers that your listener really understands. Use a written note if you have any doubts.

Case-in-Point: A supervisor in a small machine shop in Canton, Ohio told me of a misunderstanding that embarrassed him. One of his machinists had told him that the last box of a special fastener was used from the storeroom and that more should be ordered. The supervisor asked the company buyer to order "a box" of the fasteners knowing they were packed 12 to a box and there were few calls for them. The buyer, accustomed to ordering material of this type in gross lots, placed the order with the supplier for "a gross." The shop still had many boxes of the item in the storeroom several years later.

Case-in-Point: A supervisor in a plant in Chicago was involved in the loss of 200 gallons of a high cost chemical a few years ago through a misunderstanding. He had phoned a pipefitter to "remove the bottom valve on #60 tank so it could be flushed out." The pipefitter understood the supervisor to say #16 tank, and the spill resulted. Shortly after this incident the company adopted the use of A.V.O. (Avoid Verbal Orders) forms for transmitting such instructions.

9.9 Feedback: The Sure-Fire Way of Assuring Understanding

Since communication between people sometimes is a stumbling block in putting a plan or order into action, effective leaders have devised a way to check that the information and instructions they give are understood. They need to because many employees do not let their supervisors know of their ignorance by asking questions or by saying they do not understand.

Feedback has been proven to be the best way to assure understanding of your instructions or message. You get it by asking your listener to repeat your message back to you. You get it also by asking questions and listening.

Case-in-Point: At the Chemigum Plant of the Goodyear Tire and Rubber Company, Akron, Ohio, supervisors use a questionnaire to get feedback on safety. "We have a group of general questions which we ask a man after he has become familiar with the plant, his job, and the Safe Practice Manual," reports John Haynes, maintenance foreman. "If he can't answer the questions, we know that he needs more training on safety. We try to see that he gets the information and learns the safety rules."

Feedback takes place between a supervisor and his or her superior when the superior requests reports on the status and progress of work projects. The superior learns from the report if management's decisions are being carried out and if agreed upon procedures are being followed by the supervisor.

If you want to feel more certain that your instructions and orders to your people are understood, get feedback from them in one form or another.

9.10 When to Put Your Orders in Writing

It's much easier to give instructions and orders orally than in writing. Face-to-face communication is faster, more direct, and often more clear since you can add tone and feeling to your message. However, some orders are better put in writing. Here are a few examples of such cases.

If an order must be carried out in steps and the sequence is important, put the order in writing. The person carrying it out can refer to the order as the job progresses. Similarly, if an order is complex and includes quantities, having it in writing will help to prevent omissions and mistakes.

Whenever you change an order that was in writing, put the new order also in writing. If an order must be passed from one person to another, such as from one work shift to another, it's a good idea to have it in writing. Put it in the department log book or in a memo to be passed on to the people.

If your order has a high degree of permanence to it and may need to be referred to in the future, having it in writing will expedite and facilitate that.

Caution: Written communications have a big weakness—the reader can't ask questions. Consequently, a written message which is unclear, incomplete, or poorly written for some other reason may not accomplish its objective. When you write an order, read it back as if you were the reader to make certain that it conveys the request or information you intended.

9.11 How to Write Letters and Memos That Are Effective

Supervisors occasionally need to write a business letter to communicate with someone outside the company. More frequently, perhaps, they write memorandums (memos) to people within the company. Letters are written to request information or appointments, and when soliciting sales. Memos are written for communication between departments and when a supervisor writes to his or her boss.

The letter and the memo are similar in several respects. Both provide information or request it. Both are used when the subject matter or issue, while important, is not immediately urgent, and both may be retained in record files. Both should be as brief, concise, and clear as you can make them.

There are no unimportant letters. In addition to being a useful way to communicate, each provides you the opportunity to make a good impression. Although some may lead nowhere, others may produce unexpected, fruitful results. The company which takes advantage of these opportunities for making friends and influencing people favorably is bound to prosper and grow more than the company which fails to do so.

You can write effective letters and memos by following a definite procedure. It pays to do a good job on them since they reflect your initiative, capabilities, and business skill. Here's how to write ones that are effective as well as complimentary to you:

- Think about and organize what you want to say before you start to write. If your missive is to be complex or long, make a rough outline of the key points and their sequence; then write from it.

- Limit the length of your message. Unless important information would be sacrificed, try to hold your writing to one page. Your most important consideration should be to provide the necessary basic information—you can't assume the recipient to be as familiar with the subject as you are.

- Use simple language and short sentences. Avoid trite expressions and wordy business clichés in letters, and jargon in memos. A supervisor in the Customer Service Department of a large mail order company told me, "Business conversation is not as stilted and formal as it used to be.

It's much more friendly and informal now. Business letters should sound that way too."

A good writer can convey almost any message—even an unpleasant one—in a friendly, courteous way by using words that won't hurt the reader's feelings yet be unmistakably clear. It isn't so much *what* you say as *how* you say it. It's the tone of your note that counts.

9.12 Recordkeeping: A Vital Means of Control

Keeping records is one of the responsibilities of people who make decisions and give orders. Supervisors must not only document most of their work but also see that much of the data gets into the files. Maintaining an up-to-date set of records is the only way to keep track of production operations, maintenance, service, and procedural changes of a business.

Most supervisors dislike paperwork, preferring instead to spend their time with their people to see that problems are solved and work accomplished. Yet records must be made and kept if costs are to be controlled, operations conducted at optimum efficiency, and the business properly managed.

Although some supervisors may have relatively few duties involving records, the ones they do have are vital. Unless the department has a clerk, they are responsible for the time spent by their people on the job and records of absenteeism. In the office a supervisor may be expected to see that accounting records of various types are kept including purchase orders, invoices, insurance and tax documents, wages and salaries, and the many fringe benefits which companies give their employees. In the plant a supervisor may need to keep records of machines, parts, equipment capacity and rating, preventive maintenance, raw materials, finished stock, inspections, accidents, and the various process data relating to the products manufactured or the service the company performs.

Accurate data and records are a "must" in today's business and industrial operations for several reasons. Data is needed for making management decisions and to measure operating efficiency. Good records are needed to support proposals for capital expenditures or for improvements in existing systems. Records are also needed to supply the various local, state, and federal governments the many types of information and data they want.

The best way to handle records on the job is to keep up with them as you create them. Postponing making a record can lead to stress to do it later when you may be busy with other matters. There is always the risk, too, that you will forget to make the record. This can lead to criticism as well as frustration when the information is needed later.

10

Guaranteed Methods for Getting Cooperation

Since cooperation of people makes work easier and gets more done, supervisors should continually be looking for how to get it, both from their people on the job and from their peers. Fortunately, there are many ways to promote cooperation and bring about good employee performance. Successful supervisors do it by building a close rapport with people, keeping them informed, helping them with their problems, and showing appreciation for good work, among other ways.

Supervisors must be aware of the roadblocks to getting cooperation. A major pitfall is attitude. Effective supervisors have the right attitude toward their people and the job to be done. They are able to influence the attitude of their people also.

Cooperation from people on the job must be augmented with cooperation from peers in order to maximize productivity. Communication plays a big part in getting along with other supervisors in solving problems and reaching goals. Meetings provide the setting for supervisors to show responsibility and cooperation.

10.1 What People Like About Their Supervisors

Surveys of people on the job reveal that liking the supervisor is one of the reasons most frequently mentioned for liking the job. This finding explains why a person may do a good job for one supervisor and a poor one for another.

Workers can give you many reasons why they prefer one supervisor to another and why they respect one and not another. If you want to be in the select group, you should think about some of the characteristics that people like to see in their supervisor.

Case-in-Point: John Chance, warehousing manager of Diana Stores Corp., North Bergen, N.J., says that without respect a supervisor might as well "pack in the job." "Being a boss means giving, receiving, even demanding respect of the people you supervise. And when you give it, there's no doubt you'll receive it," is the way he puts it.

Today's workers are good judges of their leaders. Workers hope that their supervisors:

1. Show a concern more with them than their output. Workers want their supervisors to be friends, not bosses who threaten them or demand work from them.

2. Do different work than their people. Supervisors should be planners and organizers. They should guide and train, investigate problems, and improve working conditions.

3. Show people how to do a job correctly when they've done it wrong. They should not bawl out people who make mistakes nor should they demand obedience.

4. Have trust and confidence that their people can do the work. Supervisors should give their people authority and responsibility as well as freedom in how to do a job.

5. Act and talk positively. Good leaders praise and compliment people for their accomplishments. They also boost morale and promote teamwork.

Caution: Although being friendly with your people can gain you their cooperation on the job, if you extend the friendliness off the job, you could be in for trouble. "A supervisor must be careful in his social dealings with his men," says John P. Butler, Dover Division line supervisor, Public Service Co.

of New Hampshire.[1] "Too much socializing can create on-the-job problems that can affect the supervisor's control and hurt his effectiveness. I don't think a man in my position can socialize with a man one minute, then expect him not to think he can't have special considerations the next just because he's close to the boss." Butler's observations might be summarized as: be friendly, but discreet.

10.2 Getting Cooperation by Asking Questions

When you ask one of your people for help, you inflate the person's ego because you indicate that he or she has the capability to help or the knowledge which is of value to you and the company. Asking for help, therefore, is a good way to compliment someone.

You have three objectives when you ask a person a question: to get information, to tell the person of your needs, and to get cooperation. Here are some examples of how to use questions to gain these benefits. Ask them to:

1. Concentrate attention. You ask what goal the team is shooting for, or why a procedure isn't working right.

2. Get agreement. You ask if everybody feels the same about what should be done or if somebody has doubts or disagrees.

3. Provide reasons. You ask why a job has been done a certain way when searching for a better way.

4. Receive suggestions. You ask for ideas to solve problems or to do a job safer or faster.

5. Promote thinking. You ask if the cause of a condition or situation is known as an approach to doing something about it.

Caution: Once you ask for suggestions, ideas, or help, you must be ready to accept these things and adopt them. If you establish a pattern of not doing this, you take the risk of not getting them in the future.

10.3 How to Use Self-Interest to Advantage

Psychologists tell us that people spend more than 90 percent of their thinking time speculating about themselves. Sharp supervisors take advantage of this fact to get cooperation from their people. You can do it too.

---

[1]Reprinted from *Supervisor's Memory Jogger*, Jan. 1967. By permission of the publisher. Bureau of Business Practice, 24 Rope Ferry Road, Waterford, Connecticut 06386. Copyright, Bureau of Business Practice, Inc.

How-to-Do-It: Before issuing instructions or giving an order, ask yourself how a person can gain by doing what you want. Then put your instructions or orders in terms of what's in it for him or her. Here are a few examples of the words to use with this technique:

"You won't risk getting the dangerous chemical in your eyes if you wear your goggles whenever you handle it."

"By getting that dirty job done today you won't have to put those clothes back on again tomorrow."

"If you'll help me with this work today, you can take off early tomorrow."

Try this technique for getting cooperation. You'll find many opportunities where you can use it. And the good thing about it is that it usually works.

10.4 Ten Sure-Fire Ways to Win People's Cooperation

Good supervision is the art of getting others to do what you want, when you want it and how you want it. But such response from people doesn't come automatically to a supervisor. You've got to build up your relations with people and earn their cooperation. Here are ten ways to promote and kindle their feelings to the point where they will willingly cooperate with you:

1. Stress team effort when you communicate; use the word "we" frequently.

2. Make an effort to reward people who do more than you ask of them.

3. Set practical and realistic goals for your people; discuss the goals, making sure they understand and accept them.

4. Praise maximally and criticize minimally; never embarrass a person in front of others.

5. Supervise by persuasion rather than by force or pressure.

6. Help people when they need it; respond to their desires and needs.

7. Be honest about problems and issues; show that you have people's best interests at heart.

8. Give people a chance to express their opinions; let them participate in problem solving and decision making.

9. Sponsor and promote training and development programs.

10. Demonstrate by what you say and do that you consider loyalty and integrity to be important virtues.

10.5 Roadblocks to Getting Cooperation

Most people on the job react adversely to weak leadership. They do it by failing to cooperate. Such people also are critical of poor managing. If you supervise in a manner they don't think is right, you create roadblocks to gaining their cooperation. Here are some supervisory actions which disappoint people and turn them off:

1. Not recognizing extra effort. When people go that extra mile, they expect you to notice and give them credit for it. If you ignore a special effort, you may not receive it again.

2. Being fair in judgment. When you make a statement that shows you overlook both incompetence and superior performance, you suggest that whatever people do makes no real difference to you. To be fair with people you should give criticism as well as compliments when they are due.

3. Passing off your own importance. Being meek and humble doesn't fit your position. Your people know you are in charge and have the authority to make decisions. Pretending that you are not important for any reason weakens your credibility and attacks the intelligence of your people who know better.

4. Being indecisive. If you aren't sure whether you want or don't want something, you cause confusion. When people don't know what you really want, they may suspect you are trapping them and will try to play it safe.

5. Using fear and intimidation. People don't work willingly for someone they fear. When people respect their supervisors they plan and discuss problems with them. They go along with their supervisors, not fearing them or looking for ways to betray or defeat them.

10.6 Making People Defensive: A Major Barrier to Cooperation

Supervisors must be careful to avoid making their people defensive if they want to have their cooperation. When people are on the defensive they are concerned with avoiding blame, being uncommitted, not getting involved, and just "watching out for themselves." In your relations with your people you should try to put them at ease.

How-to-Do-It: You can overcome this barrier with empathy and sympathy for people and their problems, by showing respect, and by recognizing that people have a right to their opinions.

People don't go on the defensive when they are shown consideration. Take time to talk with them, especially when they have problems or are making mistakes. They will usually feel better and try harder. Idle people are usually ignored people.

Case-in-Point: A few years ago the Martin-Decker Co. started Operation GIT[2] (Get It Together), in their main plant. This is a positive action program to reduce error and boost production. Anytime any employee spots an error in equipment assembly, calibration, instructions, specifications, or simple written communications, the person tags the mistake with a GIT sticker. By concentrating on fixing the problem, not fixing the blame, the company eliminates "finger pointing" and encourages cooperation between workers.

10.7 Six Pitfalls to Avoid when Seeking Cooperation

Since cooperation among people on the job is so important today, supervisors need to be constantly alert to combat anything which discourages it. The experts in human relations say there are six major behavioral characteristics which inhibit cooperation. I've listed them in a special way to make them easy to remember. Watch out for and try not to be guilty of these *P's:*

1. Prejudice—Having a preconceived opinion resulting from past experience. People and issues should be evaluated on their own merits. Keep an open mind to avoid being biased.

2. Preoccupation—Being so busy with other matters that you don't devote enough time to people. You've got to listen to people and show an interest in them if you want them to cooperate.

3. Premature judgment—Accepting first impressions or incomplete information. Obtain more data before you criticize, condemn, or reach a conclusion on a person's behavior.

4. Predisposition—Hearing what you want to hear and seeing what you want to see. Avoid making up your mind and then looking for evidence to support it.

5. Projection—Attributing your motives and faults to others. If you tend to be slow and need motivation, don't think that other people are necessarily also that way.

6. Poor appreciation—Lacking respect for others' views. Look at things and events as other people see them. Put yourself in their positions to understand their actions and feelings.

10.8 Three Ways to Bring About Better Employee Performance

If employees always willingly did their work to the best of their ability, supervisors would have a much easier job. Unfortunately, all people don't have

---

[2]From *Maintenance Engineering*, October, 1975.

this temperament. Some need to be motivated and others need to be encouraged. Some need close supervision while others go ahead well on their own. Successful supervisors have learned that they need to give of themselves if they expect to get good performance from their people. Although there may be several ways they can do this, three are especially effective. You should practice them to get the best from your people.

Most people like to be in on things. They like to know what's going on, and even more, they like to have a voice in decisions about their work and the job. If you give them a chance to participate in these matters, they're more likely to do a better job. Even if you don't adopt every one of their suggestions, they appreciate it when you give them the opportunity to discuss a matter and when you listen to them. Keep them informed. Let them know what's expected of them and why. Most people want to help but they need to know how they can.

Along the same lines, if you let people work out rules and regulations, they'll abide by them more. People are often more strict in this role than you would be. What's more they'll make it rough on anyone who gets out of line. Be warm and friendly in your approach to people. Avoid trying to push them. Talk *with* them rather than *at* them.

One of the best ways to bring about better employee performance is to treat people as individuals and to give them everything possible to show your appreciation for their efforts and achievements. If you can make them feel they are working *with* you rather than *for* you, you stand to get a maximum of cooperation. Give them recognition. Tell them that you consider them important and you depend on them.

An expert's comment: Phil Ensor, Director of Employee Relations at the Goodyear Tire and Rubber Co., recently wrote a paper on in-plant communications. He said, "The type of relationship which exists between the management group and the employees cannot be overlooked with respect to the extent communications will change organizational effectiveness. If the relationship is rigid, authoritative, and adversary, messages passed downward from 'the bosses' will be viewed as propaganda and will be for all practical purposes *disregarded*. None of us have a tendency to pay close attention to individuals and groups when little or no basis has been formulated for mutual trust and concern."

10.9 Advice for the "Do-It-Yourself" Supervisor

If you are singlehandedly trying to conquer all the challenges thrown your way, you're overlooking the major responsibility of your job as a supervisor. As a member of management, you are expected to get work done through others. Although a do-it-yourself supervisor may have good intentions, he or she should realize that a person has limitations, and that the company doesn't expect a supervisor to work alone. The supervisor who tries to handle a job without help may get only half the facts about a situation and consequently correct only part of a problem.

Today's total business needs are met best by a concerted team effort. Industrial supervisors, in particular, almost always have available to them staff support, both technical and administrative, to help work out problems. Office supervisors also have such support and can consult with department managers, their superiors, and officers of the company. When supervisors are faced with other than routine problems they should ask for this help.

If you are a do-it-yourself supervisor you are jeopardizing your future with the company because your actions suggest that you do not know how to delegate. When you can successfully delegate, you demonstrate that you are capable of moving up the management ladder to a better job.

10.10 Tips on Getting Along with Other Supervisors

Getting off on the right foot with other supervisors is like taking out insurance policies because you some time may need to look to them for help in the future. If you keep to yourself and aren't interested in your fellow supervisors, they will see no reason for offering advice or help when you could use it.

Even though your work and the job may seem to demand your full time, you must devote part of it to talking and socializing with your peers. Through such rapport you become part of the management team. When you share your thoughts on general plant or office problems you show that you are interested in your company. You also indicate that you are willing to help a supervisor when he needs it and that you will cooperate on a mutual problem.

Case-in-Point: One of the supervisors I knew in a rubber glove manufacturing plant showed his interest in his fellow supervisors and developed lasting friendships by occasionally asking them questions about their hobbies. Steve Kepler's questions usually were on fine or technical points which only an expert or well-experienced person in the art could answer. Steve thus was easily able to inflate the ego of a person. I noticed that Steve never failed to get advice or help on a supervisory problem from these people when he was troubled and wasn't sure how to proceed.

Among any group, including supervisors, you'll always find one or two persons who don't have much to say because they are shy or inexperienced. Sadly, they often are shunned by their peers. You can gain some good friends by working with such people and discussing supervisory problems because they are not accustomed to receiving such attention. The good relationships you thus develop will make your job of getting cooperation from people much easier.

10.11 The Importance of Talking Positively About Peers

The supervisor who always speaks positively or complimentarily about another supervisor finds it easy to get along well with them and with other company people. The temptation to criticize or blame someone at your level to promote yourself is often hard to resist, but you're better off if you absolutely avoid it. People on the job don't get ahead by tearing someone else down.

Disparaging remarks about a person's dress, manner, or behavior gain nothing and only make you appear biased and prejudiced. People are different, have different viewpoints, and different standards. Simply because you see things differently is no reason for you to condemn or ridicule people who look and act differently than you.

Saying a good word for another supervisor when you have the opportunity shows that you recognize the capabilities and attitudes of other people, that you are not self-centered, and that you give credit when it is due. You'll find that it also gains you cooperation from the person you compliment.

10.12 How to Keep Communication Channels Open with Other Supervisors

Mistakes and failures to get jobs handled in the plant or office can sometimes be traced to lack of cooperation between supervisors. The situation may be difficult to remedy when the company operates with two or three shifts. Management needs to take steps to improve communications among its supervisors in such situations.

You can do something about the problem by upgrading your relations with your fellow supervisors. Get to know those people on other shifts and in departments with which you work. Make friends with them and take time to discuss mutual problems. The rapport you have with your peers will help to improve business communications.

Don't assume that other supervisors know something about a job or work in progress simply because you know it. Ask them if they know about it. If you must report on a plant or office problem to a supervisor on the next shift, use a notebook or the department log book. That prevents you from forgetting to mention it at shift change.

Consider other supervisors' points of view. Don't get so involved in your own problems that you forget ones that they may have. They may need some of the information you have to do their job. Adapt your communication style to the needs of the supervisors involved, allowing for their experience, knowledge, and capabilities. If details are necessary in your communications, by all means provide them.

Never pass the buck or blame something on a supervisor of another shift. You may get out of trouble for the moment, but you'll lose the trust and respect of people for the long term. Show appreciation for help received. Be quick to thank people for information which they didn't need to give you.

Avoid indifference and lack of interest when working on problems which other supervisors could solve. To keep the communication channels open often takes patience, persistence, and tact. Be sure you're long rather than short on these things if you want to get cooperation from your peers.

10.13 Five Guaranteed Ways to Gain the Cooperation of Your Peers

Any supervisor who attempts to run a department without working with other supervisors is likely to get in trouble. Teamwork is necessary to solve today's personnel and labor problems, keep up with technology, and control costs. All these things must be properly managed if a company is to be profitable and grow.

Effective teamwork in the department and among other departments of the company requires good communication among supervisors and a willingness to cooperate in working toward goals. You can help to develop cooperation with your peers by improving your communications and by adopting a spirit of understanding. Here are five ways of doing this:

1. Consider how your actions affect the operation of other departments. Make decisions that will benefit rather than hinder them.

2. Recognize that other supervisors have goals to meet and commitments to honor, and realize they have problems just as you do. Treat them as partners rather than opponents. Offer to help whenever you have an opportunity.

3. Do everything you can to eliminate friction between your people and other supervisor's people. Promote friendly relations. Compromise, if necessary, on differences in order to achieve compatibility.

4. Explain and give reasons when you ask another supervisor to do something for you. Point out benefits from going along with your request.

5. Distinguish the difference between cooperation and interference when it comes to the performance and behavior of other supervisor's people. Try to always deal with supervisors rather than their people when you want help.

Case-in-Point: John Beers, supervisor in the Roger Mills Co. in Alabama, found two people smoking in the cotton stores area one afternoon when he was checking inventory. One of the men was his utility man, the other a warehouse man from the shipping and receiving department. Beers reported the incident to the Plant Safety Director and then told his own superior how he handled the problem as follows: "I was first concerned with the danger of fire in this 'no smoking' area so I stopped that. Then I told my man to get back to work and that I would talk to him later. Lastly, I spoke to the other worker's supervisor about the violation because I realized that it was up to the warehouse supervisor, not me, to discipline that man." Beers was complimented by his superior on how he handled the incident on both communication and cooperation with other management people.

10.14 Tips on Meetings: How to Handle Yourself

Since supervisors have the responsibility of getting work done and are accustomed to "being where the action is," many of them tend to feel that meetings don't accomplish much and are a waste of time. They may also tend to shy away from meetings because they feel uncomfortable in the presence of superiors or executives in addition to thinking that they won't make a good showing.

If you feel this way about meetings you should learn more about them and how to handle yourself at them. It's a sure thing that if you haven't already participated at meetings with your superiors, you will be asked to do so in the future. Here are some tips on what you should do and say to contribute and also benefit from meetings you are asked to attend.

The most important matter for you to be concerned with is that you come prepared. When you are invited you will be told the subject to be discussed. The wise supervisor gets facts and information about the subject before the meeting as well as trying to anticipate what may be asked of him or her.

If seating is optional, don't choose a place on the outskirts. Sit near your superior or near the influential people. You will be more a part of the meeting if you are associated with the decision makers.

To help you project the best image go light on humor. You want to appear responsible and businesslike. Do not treat a company meeting as a social event, yet be relaxed and friendly.

Be positive in your remarks and contributions. If it is necessary for you to criticize a proposal, have an alternate to offer. Never make any disagreement sound personal. Show that you want to do the best thing for the company.

Be prepared to defend your ideas or proposals. Keep calm regardless of what is said and don't take an attack as a personal matter. Instead of telling someone they are wrong, say you see what they mean but there are some facts they may not be aware of. Try to be cooperative and agreeable. Go along with decisions that the group makes and show your support.

Perfecting your skill in handling meetings may not get you a quick promotion, but it will enable you to contribute to the team effort and justify your position of responsibility with the company.

10.15 How to Hold Meetings That Count

In your career you will probably attend some meetings which will be a waste of time. Successful supervisors are seldom guilty of calling unnecessary meetings. If you hold a meeting, you should have a good reason for it to justify taking busy people from their work. And you must also be sure to conduct it properly to get the most from it. Meetings are good for identifying and recognizing problems. They are not good for trying to solve them.

The people who should be invited to the meeting is a matter for the person calling the meeting to decide. Obvious choices are those who will be asked to contribute to reaching the meeting's objective. People who will be affected by decisions made in the meeting are others who you may want to be present.

If you are to lead the meeting you should have as much information as you can gather to facilitate the discussion. To enable the participants to also come prepared, notify them sometime in advance of the meeting time. You can help matters by including a brief explanation of what the meeting will cover in your notification.

The first matter you should handle at the meeting is to state the reason for getting together and what you hope to accomplish. Resist any attempt of people to confuse the objectives or to broaden them, even though this may introduce complications since the participants will be looking out for their best interests. People at meetings usually try to be constructive but their motives may lead them to obstruct as well as introduce side issues.

To conduct an efficient meeting you must see that the discussion stays on the subject. Do this by immediately interjecting a question or statement relative to it whenever someone starts to stray. Another control you should exert is to exclude matters of implementation from the discussion until what has to be done has been decided.

Problems often encountered in a meeting are those concerning when and what decisions should be made. Members usually have several courses of action available to them, any one of which probably would lead to the desired objective. In such situations, it is better to select one and go ahead with it rather than continue the discussion in hopes of finding a perfect answer.

Try to keep the meeting moving along so that you don't lose the interest of the members and also that you cover all items you planned to discuss. One hour or less is an ideal time for the meeting to last. It's better to have a second meeting than to go beyond two hours.

When to close a meeting is another matter for you to decide. If you have an agenda to work from, you simply adjourn after you've handled the last item. Without an agenda, it's not so easy because people are inclined to go on until the leader announces that the meeting is over. You can signify the end by saying, "That's all I have to discuss today. Thank's for coming."

11

Positive Techniques for Maintaining Control of Quality

To control quality you must master the factors that affect it: materials, tools, and workmanship. All are equally important. Each by itself can be the cause of a poor quality product or service. Control of quality is maintained through the use of standards which the three factors must meet. Supervisors must be concerned with quality to the extent of checking for deviations from the standards, determining the reasons for the variances, and taking corrective action. This is no easy task when you realize that people with all their differences decide and control the quality of the products they turn out or the service they perform.

The supervisor who can get people interested in and enthusiastic about quality is in the best position for controlling it. Materials, tools, and equipment must constantly be inspected for meeting specifications and being in good condition. Workmanship problems can be solved in many ways, but you must also be able to combat excuses for poor quality. The supervisor who is effective at quality control knows the pitfalls to avoid on the job and where to get help when difficult problems arise.

11.1 How to Handle Quality Control: The Three Problem Areas

What is a supervisor involved with when he or she has the responsibility of quality control? Quality control means the continuous check, test, and mastery of the factors which affect quality. In manufacturing as well as service, the factors are the inputs to the job: materials, tools, and workmanship.

Control of materials requires you to know when any deviation from standard occurs so that you can either reject the nonstandard materials before they get into production or adjust the work process to handle their variances.

If tools and equipment are poorly maintained or out of adjustment, they may produce defective products. Also, if new or different tools are put in use, people must be trained and be knowledgeable in how to use them properly.

Workmanship is the human input into the company's product or service. Although attitude and skill affect the level of workmanship, quality may still be hard to maintain if materials vary or tools and equipment are difficult to use. To control workmanship you must set standards of performance and see that your people meet them. Workmanship problems are the most prevalent and difficult ones for supervisors to solve in quality control.

11.2 Using Standards as a Means of Control

Regardless of what department you supervise, your company has quality standards set up for the products you manufacture or the service you perform. In some companies these standards are referred to as specifications. They include and consist of weights, sizes, compositions, and times to perform jobs among others on which limits and tolerances are set. One of your job responsibilities is to check for deviations from the standards, determine the reasons for the variances, and correct them. This is no easy task when you consider that it is people with all their differences in performance who are required to meet those standards.

If you question why standards are necessary, be assured that they are. For one thing, people want to measure their performance against a mark or level. If people feel there are no standards, then they will set their own because they can't be comfortable without some means of pacing themselves. This truism applies to both quality and quantity of performance.

When people are left to set their own quality and pace level, trouble develops because the self-chosen standards will vary from person to person.

Depending on the person and the requirements of the work group, the standards can be too tight or too lax, resulting in conflicts. This can cause more trouble than it takes for the company to set standards and insist that they be met.

The company needs to set standards on quality and quantity as a means of control. Control of product quality would be difficult if not impossible without them. Supervisors play a major role in seeing that their people meet the standards.

11.3 The Importance of Maintaining High Standards

Only a small amount of attention and effort by a supervisor to improve the performance of workers can have tremendous effects on quality. For example, consider the worker who produces top quality work 95 percent of the time. One product out of 20 is defective—the other 19 are good. If the individual can raise his or her quality 4 percent, only one product out of 100 would be defective.

Of course, the supervisor must be aware of the reverse effect of poor performance on quality. If a person's quality output drops only slightly, the number of defective products increases very quickly. All of which means that once you have a person performing at a high percent of good quality you must do your utmost to keep that performance up.

Supervisors must maintain high standards of workmanship of individuals for another reason. The more people who work on a product, the greater the likelihood for defects and the greater the impact of poor workmanship. If three people, for example, contribute to the manufacture of a product, and each does quality work 95 percent of the time, the total reliability or quality output of the three is only 85.7 percent (95 X 95 X 95 = 85.7).

Although today's assembly line method of production enables people to turn out a large number of products, control of quality of those products is difficult. For this reason, it is important that you maintain high standards of workmanship at all times.

11.4 Four Ways to Stay on Top of Quality Control

Quality control is an everyday effort for a supervisor. You can never relax and feel that it will take care of itself. To do a good job on it you need to be able to pinpoint quality problems and know how to solve them. The experts on quality control tell us you can do this by becoming proficient in the following techniques:

1. Develop a sense of awareness of the constant need for quality and an intuition which enables you to know where to look for the cause of poor quality.

Studies have revealed that supervisors who are concerned with quality and try hard to maintain it have success records much above average.

2. Become an expert on quality and its control. Build a reputation for solving quality problems. Admittedly, this takes study and dedication, but it's worth it. People automatically do better work when they know they're working for an expert because they know the expert can spot poor quality as well as appreciate good quality.

3. Stay on top of quality by using your knowledge and know-how fully and sincerely. You can do this by analyzing inspection reports to determine where problems exist and where you should spend your time. Other ways are to inspect equipment regularly, see that maintenance work is completed promptly, and constantly check the quality of raw materials.

4. Keep in touch with workmanship. Recognize that skills and aptitudes vary from person to person. Some people need close supervision in order for them to consistently turn out high quality work. Others need to be checked only periodically. Some people adjust easily to unusual conditions. Others find strange situations difficult to contend with and need help.

11.5 Positive Ways to Get Workers Concerned with Quality

You can't control quality all by yourself—you need the help of every person on the job. If your people don't seem interested in quality, you must tackle the job of selling them on its importance.

To make people conscious of the importance of quality you must stress it on their first day on the job and bring it to their attention frequently afterward. Explain what good quality is and what the company strives for with its products or service. Show what kind of work is acceptable and what does not meet specifications.

Another way to impress upon employees the necessity of doing quality work is to convince them that their failure to do so makes problems for other employees, their fellow workers, and eventually the customers. When people know the reasons for doing their jobs a certain way, they are more likely to be quality-minded than if they are told only how to do their jobs.

You can get people to be concerned with quality by talking about the cost of poor quality and how quality actually is the determining factor of whether the company is profitable and stays in business. When you tell people their jobs are at stake you hit home with your selling of the importance of quality.

Perhaps the best way to sell quality is to point out the benefits of it. You can tell people, for example, that quality:

1. Reduces cost of rework as well as waste of time and material.

2. Meets competition and increases sales of products and services.

3. Builds pride in workmanship and satisfaction in accomplishment.

4. Gains recognition and enhances job security.

A Personal Viewpoint: Irving Bluestone, Vice President of the United Automobile, Aerospace and Agricultural Implement Workers of America (UAW), recently made some statements about quality to UAW local unions in the General Motors[1] section of his union. He said, "Good quality isn't the concern of General Motors alone. It's important to us workers, too! It can affect the security of the workers. Poor quality cuts down sales. Then it cuts down jobs. So good quality enhances the product—and the job security of the workers who produce it.

"We have always insisted that GM must recognize the interrelationship between quality performance and work pace. An overloaded worker can't give quality performance. Workers want to produce quality products. They must be given the time and the opportunity to do so. Workers want to take pride in the jobs they do.

"We urge each worker to pay close attention to the quality of his work. For when quality workmanship is the rule, the job security of workers is strengthened. Workers and their families benefit."

11.6 How to Build Enthusiasm for Quality Performance

Every supervisor wants high quality products or service to come from company employees. Quality workmanship is vital to a smooth-running department and plant. But all employees are not quality-minded. You need to motivate some people and you must create enthusiasm for quality performance with others. Companies through their supervisors practice several ways of doing these things.

One way they do it is to conduct a program or contest to name the "Employee of the Month," the person in the department or plant who contributes the most to quality for that period. To get people interested you must provide an incentive such as a bonus, time off with pay, or some other inducement. Although praise for doing good work on the company bulletin board or in the newspaper spurs some individuals, most people want both praise and money.

Taking time to discuss quality with each employee is another way to get across its importance. When you spend your time doing this and are sincere about it, the employee will see that the company puts high quality workmanship high on the list of the responsibilities of his or her job.

Since liking one's work and getting satisfaction from it shows in the

---

[1]From *Supervision Magazine*, July, 1973.

quality of one's performance, supervisors should try to match their people's skills and preferences to their jobs. If a person expresses repeated interest in another job or department, the company and the person will probably gain if a switch is made. A supervisor may not want to lose a good worker to another department, but if the change increases the quality of the person's workmanship, it's worthwhile. The supervisor who is flexible in this respect promotes and gets better quality performance from employees.

11.7 How to Make It Easy to Control Quality

One of the skills of successful supervisors is their ability to consistently keep up the quality of the products or service of their department. Part of their success with this can be attributed to the way they promote workmanship of their people. You can follow their lead on your job.

How-to-Do-It: Set up work procedures that make it easy for people to do good quality work. Then *recognize* and *comment* on the good quality work when they do it.

Most people like to feel that they are on top of their job and that what they do helps the company. You can boost this feeling and promote its continuance by not letting their efforts to meet or exceed the standards of the work go unnoticed. Tell your people you appreciate it when they do a good job.

All employees must accept the responsibility for controlling quality and meeting standards. Quality control isn't only a management function. Control requires detecting signs of poor quality and taking corrective steps immediately. You can't wait until the product or service drops below an acceptable level or specified standard. The way to keep in control of quality is to constantly stay on top of it. You do it by reacting as soon as you become aware of a downward trend in the condition of material, tools and equipment, or workmanship. A major deterioration in any one of these elements can cancel the satisfactory character of the other two.

Case-in-Point: The operator of a packaging machine in an office supply house noticed that the glue used by the machine was not resulting in complete closures—some of the packages were coming open after leaving the machine. His immediate response was to increase the amount of glue applied by the machine. He then notified his supervisor of the situation and both of them observed the operation to see if this adjustment corrected the problem. The supervisor also began to look for other causes such as misalignment of the glue applicator or poor quality glue. With both people working on this quality problem, it was soon solved. The packages sent out by the company continued to be tight and neat in appearance.

11.8 Personal Control: Key to Good Job Performance

Some of your people may feel that they are working for an impersonal company which has no control over the quality of their work, and that it's your job to make sure they do a good job. You should point out to these people that they are *employed* by "the company" the same as you, but they are *working* for you and responsible to you. With this approach you can develop personal control and achieve better performance from them.

You can accomplish this by letting them know they are people you respect and depend on. An employee who responds to your personal appeal will see a difference between letting "the company" down and letting you down. A person's pride in turning out quality work is reflected in your recognition and appreciation of his or her skills. But, in the same manner, a person who turns out poor quality work fails you as one who is depending on him or her.

By displaying personal interest and control you can develop a close relationship with your people. You can also make the need for quality a challenge to people to create personal pride in their efforts.

Case-in-Point: "I think a healthy pride in the work we are doing is very important," Ruth Berkey tells all her new employees. Berkey is office manager in a large chemical firm.

"Pride, the right kind of pride, increases our mental and physical powers, and keeps building up our self-confidence. Of course, pride in our work can come only with experience and skill. But if we do our work in a don't-care, slovenly manner, we'll never enjoy the benefits of pride."

11.9 How to Get Help on Quality Problems

Companies who are concerned with the quality of their products or service go to the trouble of learning what their customers think about them. They then are able to handle quality problems and thus keep their customers and get new ones.

Perhaps the most well-known practice of this is that of requesting a customer to comment on the product or service. If you've bought a new car recently, you've most likely received in the mail a questionnaire about how the car is performing for you and asking if the service the dealer has given you has been prompt and satisfactory. If you eat many of your meals away from home, you have probably noticed that some restaurants ask you to comment on the food and service in a space on the bill. These companies want to know if the quality of their product or service pleases you. They realize the importance of quality, and they want to be aware of instances where they failed to provide it or could have done a better job. Some companies ask their own employees for help on improving quality.

Case-in-Point: Because they wanted improvement, Western Electric's Hawthorne's Works[2] conducted a survey of about 200 questions for their maintenance craftsmen. The craftsmen were asked to rate such things as the accuracy of engineering instructions, the availability of tools, the cooperation of fellow-workers, and other job-site activities. By studying the responses, management determined where changes needed to be made. Consequently, innovations occurred at Hawthorne and better communications resulted.

Consultants are frequently hired today to provide direction and assistance to a company in solving operational problems. This is particularly true when management feels they need help to reduce costs. Experts in various types of manufacturing and business can help a company reduce waste and inefficiency as well as improve the quality of their product or service.

Case-in-Point: Two of the major rubber companies in Akron, Ohio in recent years hired The Emerson Consultants, Inc., New York, to study their engineering and maintenance functions. In both cases the companies were able to reduce operating costs and improve work procedures by adopting the recommendations of Emerson. Planning and scheduling, preventive maintenance practice, and better supervisional control were the outgrowths of the help provided to the rubber companies.

11.10 What to Do About Poor Workmanship

By eliminating or reducing the causes of mistakes you can increase the quality of output of your people. This is true in the office as well as on the production line because the results of a clerical or typing error can be just as costly as a tolerance error on a product.

Attitude toward the job is a big factor in workmanship quality. People who are interested in their work and like their company make few errors. One of your supervisory objectives, therefore, should be to promote interest in the job. Another should be to set a good example by being extra careful in your own work. And a third should be to let everyone know that you believe it is within their capabilities to do error-free work.

Boredom is a common cause of poor workmanship, particularly with repetitive jobs. The best you can do to overcome it is to rotate people in different jobs to provide them some variety. You can also make certain that the right person is on the right job—a person doing a job that requires only a small portion of his or her abilities becomes bored quickly. Learn to recognize when a

---

[2]From *Maintenance Engineering*, January, 1976.

person is bored so you can try to expand the work, vary it, or add responsibility to it.

Some people find it difficult to do good work when there is a lot of noise or distraction in their work area. Ringing phones, noisy typewriters, and people talking can be distracting to efforts which are other than routine. You can solve such problems by seeing that noisy machines are individually enclosed or put in separate rooms. You can also relocate people away from the noise. Discouraging unnecessary talk and visiting in work areas are other ways to improve workmanship and raise the efficiency of employees.

Misunderstandings are sometimes the cause of poor workmanship. Study the incidents of misunderstandings which your people have experienced. Were your instructions too complex? Did you use technical terms that were unfamiliar? Did you tell them everything they needed to know to do the job? People may say they understand rather than admit they don't. You can overcome this problem by asking them questions or encouraging them to ask you questions. Whatever, let your people know that it's much better to ask questions than to make mistakes.

11.11 Tips on Solving Workmanship Problems

When you find that a quality problem is the result of poor workmanship, you must look for the cause immediately. You can do this by getting the answers to the following questions concerning the employee involved:

1. Does the employee need more training? If so, the training should be completed as soon as possible.

2. Does the employee understand the close tolerances or limits required? Nobody can consistently meet job specifications unless they understand them.

3. Is the employee careless? The person may need to be counseled on his or her work habits and shown why they must improve.

4. Does the employee lack the ability to do the job? If so, it would be better for everyone if the employee were given a job more in line with his or her ability.

A supervisor cannot tolerate poor workmanship on the job. You must determine the reason for it and do what is necessary to correct it. This step may include going to your boss for help if it appears that a major change is needed.

11.12 How to Combat Poor Quality Excuses

Some of your people may be reluctant to put forth extra effort on the job to maintain or assure quality. They will, of course, have excuses for their behavior. For one thing, they may not understand why quality is so important. For another, they may say that other people aren't going out of their way or working extra hard on quality, so why should they?

You have a job on your hands when you encounter such excuses because you've got to justify quality and get those people to agree.

How-to-Do-It: The way to combat excuses is to eliminate the logic behind them by establishing practices conducive to good quality and seeing that the practices become standard procedures. You can accomplish this in several ways:

1. Make sure that shortcuts are not taken on operating procedures.
2. Don't permit improper or defective tools to be used.
3. Have a definite policy on what is to be done with defective material.
4. Give recognition to quality workmanship.

People will not be able to come up with excuses for poor quality if you take steps to always promote it and literally make it a way of life.

11.13 Stress: A Factor Affecting Quality

Quality of your product or service won't maintain itself. You've got to continuously work at it. You've got to put the pressure on both yourself and your people if you expect to keep quality under control.

There's nothing harmful about some pressure or stress on the job. If people are not occasionally under pressure, they simply don't produce to their ability, much less give you a high level of performance. But the stress must be the right kind.

Stress which induces fear, anger, or frustration is wrong and usually results in more negative than positive effects. People who fear making mistakes, being criticized, or even losing their jobs waste energy and drive in combatting this fear. The quality of their performance usually suffers. People who are angry from a feeling of injustice or frustration similarly do not perform well. They may simply refuse to be productive or their efforts may become destructive.

The right kind of stress is that which challenges, which encourages initiative, and which raises competitive feelings. Such stress is positive in its effect. People who feel called upon to use all their knowledge and skill on the job to compare favorably with others will put quality into their efforts. They will not waste time on thoughts of resentment and actions of retaliation.

11.14 Five Mistakes to Avoid in Quality Control

Some management people consider quality control a necessary evil. They see the persons that practice it as do-gooders, narrow technical specialists, and police-type checkers. The reasons they give for such dim views of quality control people deserve examination since they contain a few truths about the way some supervisors handle quality control. But since the ways are faults and weaknesses, you should consider them as pitfalls. The effective quality control supervisor avoids:

1. Relying too much on statistics, not enough on good judgment. The problem here is that technical data are often not available or cannot be obtained fast enough when a decision must be made. Decisions should be made on the information that is available plus good judgment.

2. Spending too much time trying to find defects, not enough time trying to prevent them. The job of quality control involves more than just preventing poor products from leaving the company. It includes preventing their creation. You may be handicapped in this inclusive effort if you don't know how to go about it. You may need to learn more about the process or service of your company so that you can be of greater value on the job.

3. Paying too much attention to the technical aspect, not enough to cost. You must be more concerned with the practical side of the function. Analytical evaluation is only as good as its ability to get results with the least cost.

4. Doing too much nit-picking, not showing enough concern with major issues. Too many quality control people believe that if they solve most of the quality problems they are doing a good job. They could contribute more if they solved the major problems even though those may be only a small percentage of the total.

5. Dealing too much with things, not enough with people. The quality problem which causes the most trouble usually involves people. Therefore, if you usually concern yourself more with things than with people, you fail to do your best on quality control. Being aware of what's happening on the production line is more important than knowing what the quality control figures and charts say.

An Expert's Comment: "A crucial question in American industry today is whether companies will listen to and support their quality control specialists," says Robert N. Reece,[3] President of the American Society for Quality Control. Reece points out that industry wastes over $100 billion a year correcting sales of

---

[3]From *Plastics World*, Oct., 1978.

defective and unsatisfactory products. "Our best estimate is that 15 percent of net sales of all these companies is spent on this 'fire fighting' activity, whereas competent 'preventive' quality control programs could reduce that figure to 2 percent of net sales," he says.

"If you're in charge of quality control," Reece comments, "you cannot be inflexible, but you've got to be willing to make decisions and stand by them. It's no surprise that sometimes the goals of sales, marketing, and production people are going to clash with those of quality control."

12

Sure-Fire Ways
to Control
Costs

Every employee must participate in controlling costs if a company is to prosper and grow. Supervisors can't do the job alone. But they can get help and cooperation in the effort by selling their people on why costs must be reduced and controlled. Workers need to be convinced that their company must make a profit. It will follow logically that profits will be better when costs are lower.

Supervisors prove their worth when they become interested in cost control and keep costs down. They become experts at the job by learning how to attack specific cost problems and how to prevent little costs from becoming big. Proving one's worth in this respect is not difficult because almost everything that a supervisor controls is a cost to the company in one way or another. The ways by which costs can be controlled are many and varied.

Efficient use of labor, care in the handling and use of material, reduction of waste, and minimizing overhead charges are the main ways which a company adopts to control its costs of operation. The supervisor has a responsibility in all of these areas in that he or she can promote productivity of employees, control the amount of overtime they work, and see that utilities, operating items, and supplies are used with discretion.

12.1 Communication: Key to Selling Cost Reduction

When your company is making an effort to reduce costs, one of the first things you must do is pass this word to your people. It's only with their cooperation that you can accomplish any significant reduction except for layoffs or shutdown of your department. Although your people may see the situation as beyond their control, it's up to you to convince them otherwise. The way to do this is to explain how they are directly involved and what they can do to help.

Consider how you would feel if someone in authority were to talk costs to you, and let that guide you in what you say to your people. Obviously, you are going to suggest operations that should be looked at and changes that should be made. And you're going to talk about why costs must be reduced.

Point out that reducing waste and scrap is one of the most logical ways of cutting costs, and that employees are in good positions to do this. Tell people that doing their work safely avoids accidents which are costly; add that good housekeeping promotes safety. Be sure to get across that extra effort on their part benefits them as well as the company, that they will be cutting costs for the sake of their own jobs rather than being cooperative with you or the company.

People on the job often do not understand why their company makes changes in equipment or procedures because nobody takes the time to explain such matters to them. The key to selling cost reduction is to give people the facts and to point out how raising the profits of the company helps them. You should talk to them in words and terms they understand.

Quote figures on how the cost of the raw materials they use have risen. Tell them about the production schedule, what it was last month or last year, and what it is now. Mention who the company's competitors are and what they're doing in the market. When you talk about profits, show how making a profit is necessary to stay in business and to provide jobs for people.

Your goal in talking to your people about costs is to be sure they get the facts and that you clear up any misconceptions they may have about how much profit the company makes.

Case-in-Point: Frank W. Mohney, president of the Stationary Power Tool Equipment Div. of Black and Decker, said, "Planned cost reduction programs in some companies have not achieved their potential because they were not the primary goal. Therefore, the first step in establishing an effective cost reduction program is to clearly communicate from the top down that cost reduction should be a primary objective of each employee. It sounds obvious, but it's surprising how many firms never do it.

"Next, all of the company's resources—its people, its capital, its equipment—must be geared to making cost reduction a way of life. Then, there must be an overall plan to release these resources fully and effectively and then sustain momentum."

12.2 How to Get Across the Need for Profits

Louis H. Meyer,[1] president of the Material Handling Institute, recently stated at a seminar, "There is a great deal of evidence to indicate that the most misunderstood subject in the United States today is profits." He went on to give facts and figures that are needed to deal with this problem. He said that leaders should pass along such information to their people on the job.

Supervisors should do this to convince people that their livelihood and their future depend upon a system that permits the company to make a fair profit. You can sell the need for profits of all businesses by pointing out some reasons such as:

1. Profits create more than a million new jobs in the United States each year.

2. They provide federal, state, and local governments more than $40 billion in annual tax revenues.

3. There are over 30 million shareholders in the country who depend on profits for part of their income.

4. There are over 33 million workers whose retirement funds are invested in stocks and bonds, and who depend upon the profits these companies make to increase investment values.

This kind of information relates profits to people. The supervisor's task is to get the message across to those who do not understand the relationship. Profits are vital to all of us—people on the job and management, alike.

12.3 Five Painless Ways to Sell People on Cost Reduction

You've got to have the cooperation of your people when you set out to reduce costs. Unfortunately, you may encounter some resistance because cutting costs often means getting along without some things, eliminating some

---

[1]From *Modern Materials Handling,* May, 1977.

expenses, doing more work, and doing jobs differently. People naturally resist change even when it is for their good. Here are five ways to overcome that resistance and sell your people on cost reduction:

1. Ask for their help and cooperation. Let them know you appreciate their suggestions and recommendations. Get them interested in finding ways their work can be performed at lower cost. Compliment them on their efforts to do so.

2. Set specific goals to shoot for. Don't just ask for cutting costs as much as possible—set a figure or amount such as "25 percent less overtime this month," or "10 percent less waste of materials this week."

3. Point out costs of specific items. Many employees don't realize what various items cost the company. Explain what the company pays for utilities, telephone service, and such items as stationery, work gloves, and tools.

4. Talk about company profits. Get their point of view on these matters and straighten out any misconceptions they have. Explain that wages and salaries can't be maintained or increased if the company isn't profitable.

5. Give reasons why the company has made changes in procedures to cut costs in the past and what they might have to do in the future. Compare the company's ways to what employees do personally under similar circumstances. Give examples such as turning off unneeded lights and fixing leaks.

12.4 How to Become an Expert at Cost Control

You might think that you as a supervisor can't do much about cutting costs significantly short of suggesting a major process or equipment change. Although it's true that big cost reductions can result from such changes, it's also true that real cost savings can be made by conscientious supervisors in their daily routines. You can become an expert at cost control if you want to be one and put forth the effort to do so.

How-to-Do-It: Study and learn about costs from the purchase of raw materials to the selling of the finished products, from the training of personnel to the doing the work in the plant or office. Investigate the various costs of the company. Most important of all, familiarize yourself with cost areas where you have direct or indirect control.

By understanding the overall picture, you can see where your efforts may be applied. You can study those areas in particular so that if those costs start to rise you know what to do in order to control them. Get in the habit of applying value analysis in your decisions.

Case-in-Point: At a Philadelphia electrical products company, the value engineers studied switch and battery housings and found them to contain many nonfunctional and marginally functional components. They were simplified with an annual cost and labor avoidance estimated at $11,650.

Plant and office procedures were analyzed similarly. Each step was challenged by the question: "What if this were eliminated? Would it make any difference?" In many cases, steps were eliminated, and in one case, the whole job was eliminated.

Don't wait for your boss or other people to push you into cost control. Develop the skill and knowledge on your own. You'll be a more effective and successful supervisor as a result.

12.5 Seven Tried-and-Tested Ways to Control Costs

Since almost everything you do as a supervisor has an effect on costs, you must be constantly aware of the value of material, labor, equipment, and supplies. Every good supervisor knows ways to cut costs and realize savings on the various operations he or she controls. Here are seven such ways which successful supervisors use to keep their department costs in line:

1. Plan and schedule work. By planning you can eliminate idle time, avoid duplication of effort, and handle job steps in proper sequence. Scheduling enables you to avoid waiting for materials, tools, and instructions. Jobs take less time and are done more efficiently if they have been planned and scheduled.

Case-in-Point: A tire plant maintenance engineer had difficulty in scheduling preventive maintenance for the busy production lines until it was suggested that the production department notify the maintenance department prior to the scheduled shutdown of any production line and indicate approximate duration of the shutdown. After this was done, the planner/scheduler had no difficulty in having the production lines inspected and minor repairs made.

2. Become adept at recognizing wasteful practices. Resist assigning too much labor to a job, such as putting two people on when only one is needed. Be aware when machines and equipment need maintenance or repair. Notice when more material is being used than required.

Caution: Simply reducing the amount of something that is used on the job may not necessarily reduce costs—it could actually be a wasteful practice. For instance, saving material may not be economical if you increase your labor costs. Similarly, saving labor is worthwhile provided it does not excessively run up your equipment or material costs.

3. Remove material, supplies, and equipment that aren't being used in the work area. Such things hinder safety, make housekeeping difficult, and cause inefficiency. Their value is probably also deteriorating by being idle; see if they could be used elsewhere.

4. Study processes and equipment, the flow of material, and the use of labor in order to find ways to eliminate procedures and get optimum performance from people.

5. Work at reducing tardiness and absenteeism. Talk to your people who have those problems, explaining the difficulties and cost to the company of their not being on the job on time and every day.

6. Eliminate high cost operations and overtime. Adjust operations to fit the standard workday. Simplify jobs to get them done faster.

7. Eliminate duplication of effort. Combine operations and jobs. With job enrichment you can get more work done by one person while at the same time making the work more interesting.

12.6 How to Attack a Specific Cost Problem

If you have been asked to work on a cost problem, you had better try to do the job quickly. Your boss will be looking for an answer to justify assigning you instead of someone else to the job. Upper management may also be aware of the problem and your involvement. They are expecting you to deliver.

If the cost problem is a major one, you should plan your attack and how you'll proceed so that you'll get the most from your efforts. Decide, too, how to keep management informed of your progress. Set your mind to stay on top of the project to a successful conclusion. Here is how to go about it.

First, find out what you are expected to accomplish. How serious is the problem? How much must costs be reduced? Your boss should give you a clear goal to shoot for.

Second, accept the fact that you must make some changes. Costs will not automatically drop just because you are assigned to the task. You are expected to eliminate something or introduce a new technique that will result in lower costs. If your people are aware of the situation and your role, they may suggest some changes you can make.

Third, set up a course of action to reach your goal. Make it as detailed as possible. Get your boss's approval, and make your people aware of what you hope to do. Ask for their cooperation.

Fourth, make periodic reports on your progress. Management is concerned, and they want to know where the project stands even if you haven't made a lot of progress. The briefer your reports, the better. You want mainly to keep management up-to-date.

Fifth, evaluate the changes you make. Don't hesitate to alter them if they don't work, but be sure of a failure before you make a new decision.

Last, show progress and success with evidence of improvement. Wrap up the project with a report documenting your accomplishment.

12.7 Eliminating a Procedure: An Easy Way to Reduce Costs

Most companies have standard procedures which have been in effect a long time. They may be inefficient and uneconomical but because "they have always been done that way," nobody questions them. It pays to study procedures periodically to see if they are practical as well as necessary. More often than you may think, you may be able to change or eliminate one to achieve a significant savings.

A common example of a wasteful procedure is the large amount of paperwork generated in many offices. Surveys show that most companies turn out many unneeded reports, memos, letters, and other papers. The low, per-copy cost of putting out paper is a trap. Overlooked are the costs for filing, storing, retrieval, and eventual disposal.

You can cut paperwork costs in several ways. Start by taking an inventory of all the reports and documents routinely and repetitively produced in your department to see if they are essential. If you can't eliminate a report, try cutting down on the number of copies produced. Also, don't issue a lot of detail information if summary data will do the job.

Another way to reduce a procedure cost is to review work assignments after a process or equipment change is made in the plant. Such a change may cancel the need for a continual inspection or eliminate the need for periodic adjustments or cleanup operations.

Case-in-Point: Benson Wayne, plant supervisor in Mahwah, N.J., wrote an editor of *Supervision* magazine, "I've found in my experience that a careful time utilization analysis periodically conducted on an employee-by-employee basis invariably pays off." In one of Wayne's recent studies, he found that an inspector's actual working time amounted to less than one-half of his shift. The rest of his time was spent waiting for production to be ready for inspection. His supervisor assigned him compounding jobs which reduced the need for compounding personnel from three employees to two. The move saved the company considerable money.

12.8 Four Ways Ways to Hold Down Labor Costs

Any cost cutting program must include examination of how labor is handled. If you are not getting the fullest potential from your people, you are wasting one of the costly items of running a business. Here are four ways you can hold down your company's labor costs:

1. Use only as many workers on a job as are actually needed.
2. Give on-the-job training to all workers. They will be more efficient, make fewer errors, and create less waste.

3. Assign skilled people to skilled work and unskilled people to unskilled work.

4. Provide enough people on the job to assure that overtime work isn't necessary.

The proper use of labor is a key responsibility of a supervisor. Labor costs can be minimized if you get the most from each worker's ability, knowledge, and experience.

12.9 Overtime: Overlooked Reasons for Reducing It

Working your people overtime is costly to the company in salaries and wages. It's costly to the company in other ways, too. An enigma is the fact that the more you use overtime, the greater the problems become which you use it to solve. Four reasons other than direct cost for reducing overtime work are:

1. Quality suffers and there are more mistakes and errors made when people work overtime.

2. The efficiency of people working overtime drops each hour they continue to work.

3. Worker's efficiency will be lower than normal the day after they work overtime, especially if the overtime was considerable.

4. Constant, day-to-day overtime will often cause an increase in absenteeism.

Note that every one of these effects of overtime increase a company's operating costs in one way or another. If you're out to cut costs in your department, reducing overtime work is one of the sure places to start.

12.10 Reduce Waste: A Positive Way to Cut Costs

One of the quickest yet effective ways to cut costs is to reduce waste. Many wasteful practices go on in today's factories and offices. Supervisors are often unaware of them or simply ignore then under the pressure of other problems. When ways to reduce waste are being sought, the prime areas to look at are idle people and machines, underutilized skills, and mishandling of materials and supplies.

To reduce waste you must apply controls and set up standards for people and machines to meet. Do this where mistakes are being made, high scrappage is occurring, and maintenance is lagging. Check the reasons for high overtime, inventory problems, and production delays.

Case-in-Point: Leaking hydraulic systems are responsible for the worst lubricant waste in industry, according to Mobil Oil Corporation[2] engineers. The solution to the problem is to train oilers to look for leaks and to keep track of hydraulic oil makeup (machine-by-machine). Another answer is to put the job of checking and tightening of the system on the preventive maintenance or lubrication schedule to be sure it's done regularly.

Excessive wear of tools and equipment shortens their life. You can slow the wear as well as prevent it by making frequent inspections and by promoting preventive maintenance. See that tools are not abused and that the right ones are used on the job. Tools should be cleaned and stored at the end of the workday.

Wasted time probably costs a company more than the waste of anything else. Although unforeseen events will always result in wasted time, you can plan and schedule many jobs so that people, material, and equipment are coordinated to save time.

12.11 How to Cut Material Handling Costs

A recent study revealed that the cost of handling materials amounts to between 25 and 40 percent of the total cost of manufacturing. If you review the material handling operations in your company, you likely will be able to find ways to cut the costs by improving the work flow, adopting better inventory control, and reducing waste. Here are some ways to do it:

1. Examine where materials are stored in relation to where they are used. The farther they are from their point of use, the more they must be handled. You'll find that materials and products may not follow the most direct route in manufacturing unless your plant is a new one. When processes are changed and steps added or removed, relocating materials accordingly can reduce handling costs. Any time a step in handling can be eliminated, the work flow will be improved.

2. Make supplies handy for the people who use them. Also, make sure your skilled labor don't waste their time in looking or traveling for material if such things can be done by unskilled labor or if material can be better placed.

Case-in-Point: A large petrochemical plant in Houston, Texas provides pipefittings, gaskets, nuts and bolts, and the like in bins and cabinets close to the process piping and equipment. Maintenance craftsmen needing these items in their work save considerable time in not having to go to the maintenance shop or the storeroom for this material.

3. See that the best equipment is available for moving materials and that it is used properly. For example, drums can be moved faster and more efficiently

---

[2]From *Maintenance Engineering,* March, 1976.

than by use of hand, manually operated trucks if forklift trucks are equipped with drum handling attachments.

Case-in-Point: Joe Heffernan, Manager, Material Handling Engineering Dept., Ford Motor Co.,[3] says, " 'Learn to do the job the correct way' should be everyone's theme. There are many causes of equipment damage that can be easily eliminated. For example, running forks through the side of a wire mesh container, or failing to close a down gate on a container before lifting, are nothing more than sloppy handling. Damage to racks and pallets can be eliminated by making sure the truck forks are the correct length. Similarly, when lifting long items from the side, there's less chance of dropping the load if the forks are properly spaced."

4. Have planned procedures and assign specific employees to receive materials as well as ship them. Demurrage charges can be avoided on receipts by being prompt and efficient in handling them. Also, people trained and experienced in shipping and receiving procedures take better care of materials.

12.12 Avoid Losses: The Big Answer to Lower Material Costs

The objective of a supervisor who tries to lower material costs is to see that material is used productively and that losses are minimized:

How-to-Do-it: Develop standards for the handling and use of materials plus train people to meet them. Although training and instructing people in the proper handling of materials may take time and cost money, the benefits will far exceed the costs. For instance, here are a few losses that can be avoided when people are careful in handling material:

1. Damage in the warehouse and storeroom, in receiving and in shipping.
2. Damage from poor stacking, inadequate protection, and failure of racks and bins.
3. Spillage and loss in handling.
4. Spoilage from aging or contaminating.
5. Taking more material than needed for a job.
6. Waste from rejection of off-quality finished product.

To do a good job of controlling material cost, you must continually stress three matters with people: care in handling, value, and conservation.

---

[3]From *Modern Materials Handling,* August, 1975.

12.13 How to Keep Little Costs from Becoming Big

If you take the time to study your areas of responsibility where costs have increased, you should be able to spot the time when the increase began. If you have been aware of what was happening at the time, you might have been able to prevent it from going so far. However, with matters like this you don't just give up and accept them—you may still be able to take corrective action or at least stop further cost increases.

Alert and experienced supervisors are aware of how little costs become big. When they observe a change in operations, a slowing down or speeding up, a decrease or increase in a function, an omission or inclusion of a factor, they immediately investigate to see if costs will be affected. Here are some examples of such incidents along with advice on what to do if they happen to you:

1. An increase in operating costs occurs which is not explainable by current trends, rate increases, or new acquisitions. Look for work being repeated because of something wrong with either equipment, materials, or workmanship. Check also on customer complaints and returned goods.

2. An operation or process slows down for no apparent reason. Since there must be a reason for it happening, and it probably will get worse, you must find the problem. Search for it and take corrective action.

3. A small increase in the use of a supply item takes place without an accompanying increase in work output. Since it is a single item, tracing it should be easy. It deserves your attention to determine if a more serious problem is behind it.

Cases-in-Point: Dennison Travis, works superintendent at a Rhode Island metal foundry, makes a pertinent comment on the matter of costs: "Employees who are trained to be less wasteful of so-called trivial items will be more careful of costly items as well." Travis's company monitors the use of virtually everything issued in the office and plant from paper clips and ballpoint pens to precision equipment costing thousands of dollars.

A New York laundry posts on its bulletin board a total expense account of low-cost supplies. The figures show dramatically how nets, pins, aprons, coverings, pads, and other items which some people may consider insignificant add up to $500,000 a year.

A west coast aircraft manufacturer points out the high cost of everything from paper towels to memo pads by giving usage and cost figures in the company publication.

4. The accounting department bills your department a new item in the overhead area. Has your department picked up a research or development

charge? Has a new tax gone in effect? Whatever, a call to the accounting department is in order for an explanation.

5. You have a feeling of something not being right and you've sensed it more than once. Don't pass this off lightly because your experience on the job is telling you that a problem is developing. Talk it over with people who could be involved. Observe how individuals are doing their work. Be alert for abnormal behavior and unusual remarks. The quicker you can learn what is wrong, the quicker you can do something about it.

12.14 Tips on Cutting Overhead Costs

Every business has its overhead costs. These are the costs which are not affected by variations in production volume or service performed. Whether the office is operating or not, whether the plant is producing or not, costs such as insurance, taxes, maintenance, and the salaries of management and staff continue to be incurred by the company.

Before studying them, you might think that overhead costs are beyond your control—you would be only partially right. Certain overhead items are within the responsibility of supervisors. The problem is that some of these costs have been accepted for so long that no one thinks of trying to cut them.

Although many overhead costs are minor, they add up to rather large amounts of money, particularly when they are not controlled. Some costs of this type are: utility leaks, overuse of air conditioning, poor housekeeping (which runs up janitorial costs and accident costs), inadequate fire protection (which causes high insurance rates), extra telephones and extensions, and rented equipment not being used. Larger overhead items which supervisors share some responsibility for and can do something about are pollution control, energy conservation, spill prevention and control, safety controls, and the training and instructing of workers.

Case-in-Point: An energy survey conducted by Goodyear Tire and Rubber Company[4] at six of its plants revealed that much could yet be done to conserve energy. Thomas Leary, manager of corporate engineering, pointed out that some plants are only interested in energy conservation if they can get $500,000 in savings through 10 to 20 big items. They overlook the fact that they can achieve those savings by correcting 500 smaller items.

---

[4]From *Maintenance Engineering,* January, 1976.

13

Tested Ways for Evaluating Performance: Handling Appraisals Effectively

Planning and preparing is required in order to conduct an effective performance appraisal. You will learn more about the person and be better able to help him or her if you know what you are going to talk about. Employees need and want to know their strengths and weaknesses, and what they should do to improve. A number of benefits to the company and the person result from a frank and friendly discussion.

To be able to evaluate performance and do a good job of counseling, the supervisor must know much about the person and how he or she is doing on the job. The person should be encouraged to talk about the job and problems concerning it.

An interviewer needs to be adept at asking questions and listening for the answers. To be effective, you need to know what to say and what not to say to motivate and encourage a person. For the company's benefit as well as the person's you should also be consistent in your evaluations. Evaluating on points is a common method for comparing the performance and the accomplishments of employees.

Successful appraisers are aware of the pitfalls to avoid when interviewing people. They also realize the importance of following up after interviewing.

13.1 Tips on Preparing for an Appraisal Interview

A performance appraisal interview will be easy for you to handle, and you'll do a more complete job if you prepare for it. Here are some tips on how to do this:

1. Review the record and personal history of the person by collecting all the information you have, including that received from other people. Look into the person's background, service with the company, previous jobs held, and what progress the person has made since being hired. Study any notes made of previous appraisals with the person.

2. Consider the job the person is doing. Become familiar with the standards and responsibilities of the job in order to judge how he or she is doing. Determine what a person in that type of work must do to be a success.

3. Decide where you will talk with the person. You must have a place where you have privacy and your conversation cannot be heard; this is important to the person. Recognize that a place other than your office would probably put the person more at ease and would therefore be preferred.

4. Pick a time for the interview. Avoid scheduling it for when you or the person might be very busy or could be interrupted. Plan to not start the interview unless you're fairly sure you can finish it.

13.2 How to Get Started Right

The secret to a good performance appraisal interview is to have the interviewee at ease, willing to discuss the job, and wanting to learn how to improve. To put the person in this frame of mind, you should begin by explaining the purpose of your meeting. Say that you are talking to all your people, and that your main purpose is to help each person. Tell the person that you want to talk about the work and how it is going, and that you also would like to talk about any problems the person may have.

Case-in-Point: Roy Leedy, former Manager of Engineering at Goodyear Tire and Rubber Company's synthetic rubber plant in Akron, Ohio told me how he began an appraisal interview. The words he used after greeting the individual and putting him or her at ease went something like this: "We see each other several times every day but in the rush of doing our work we do not have much of an opportunity to talk. So I plan to take some time now and then to sit down with you and with every other person in the department for a personal talk.

"I would like you to tell me how you feel about your job. Also, I want to give you a chance to talk about any ideas you have about your work and problems that have come up. At the same time we can talk about the work you have been doing. We can probably help each other."

13.3 Guidelines for Handling an Interview

When you counsel with your people you let them know how they are doing and what they can do to improve their performance. Since an appraisal interview is like a progress report, most people consider it important and will take it quite seriously.

The interview is equally important to the supervisor because it presents an opportunity to learn more about the person and to motivate him or her through encouragement and praise. Because both of you have a lot to gain from an interview, it's essential for you to do the best you can with it. Here are some guidelines to help you:

1. Listen carefully when the person talks. This may be difficult for two reasons: first, you may already think you know what the person is going to say, and second, while the person is talking you may be thinking about what you are going to say. But, you must remember that if you don't listen carefully, you may not understand completely what the person is saying. Consequently, you'll be unable to provide the right motivation for better performance.

2. Allocate equal time to praise and criticism. Resist the inclination to spend a lot of time discussing a person's weakness or area of below average achievement. Recognize that too much finding fault can cause resentment.

3. Be friendly and sincere. You are trying to help the person, not tear him or her down. Be encouraging and positive when suggesting how performance can be improved.

4. Limit the goals and objectives you set for the person both in number and degree. Recognize a person's capabilities in anticipating what can be accomplished. Don't expect a complete change of behavior during or immediately after a single interview.

13.4 Ways to Encourage a Person to Talk

Successful interviews require an exchange of ideas between participants. Unfortunately, many supervisors find it easier to talk than to listen. You must realize that you are not learning anything when you are talking—you need to get the other person to talk. Here are some good ways to do that:

1. Listen intently when a person is talking. Nod your head and encourage the person without interrupting except for saying, "I see," and "Mm--hm."

2. Repeat the person's words in your own. "Let's see if I understand you."

3. Persuade the person to explain further or in more detail. "Tell me more." "That's interesting. What else?"

4. Turn the person's questions back with "What do *you* think?"

Be friendly and reassuring in what you say because the person is much more conscious than you are of your difference in rank. By all means, be yourself. Any person who knows you well on the job would be quick to see any falseness in your manner and immediately be on guard.

A good way to measure your success at getting the other person to talk is to watch how much you're doing. If you're talking less than half the time, you're on the right track. Try to keep it that way.

An expert's comment: A personnel manager for a large chemical company once gave me a tip on talking during an interview. I had expressed a fear that I and the person I was interviewing would run out of something to say. He replied, "Don't panic if the conversation stops during the interview. Be glad of the silence and use it to think a bit. Rest assured, the interviewee will think of something to say."

13.5 Asking Questions: The Sure-Fire Way to Get Information

An interview may be difficult for you and not seem to go smoothly if the interviewee is nervous and hesitates to say much. What can you do? First, you must try to put the person at ease. Talk about a subject that you know the person is interested in, such as a hobby. The person should soon be more relaxed because you'll be talking his or her language. You can then go on to talk about the job.

An excellent way to get a person to talk is to ask questions. Most of your questions should be ones which cannot be answered with a yes or no. Here, for example, are some questions which would be appropriate:

About the job: What part of your job do you find challenging? What parts do you consider more important? How do you feel about the job overall? What suggestions do you have for improving our department?

About performance of the work: What part of your job gives you the most satisfaction? What part do you find easiest? How can I help you to do a better job?

About ideas or problems: What is your biggest problem on the job? What are your goals with the company? How do you feel about the other people you work with? What do you think about interviews like this?

Caution: Try not to fire one question after another to avoid making your meeting seem to be a simple interrogation. Mix in a few comments, such as how you would answer the questions. You'll put the person more at your level when you do so, and talking is easier on that basis.

13.6 Three Questions You Shouldn't Ask

The supervisor who is skilled at performance appraisal interviewing avoids asking certain questions because they don't help in getting information and may also be disturbing. The most annoying and troublesome of these are questions which put the other person down in some way or set the person up for embarrassment. Here are three types of questions which a good interviewer doesn't ask:

1. The leading question. This question is phrased in a way that it suggests a correct answer. Examples are: "You agree that ... don't you?" "Aren't you in favor of ... ?" "I'm sure you like ... don't you?"

When you ask a leading question you put words in the interviewee's mouth, literally forcing him or her to agree with you whether the person feels that way or not. You can't learn how a person truly feels with a leading question. Many people will agree so as not to put themselves in jeopardy, especially if their job is important to them.

2. The loaded question. This question is closely related to the leading question in that it also anticipates agreement. The loaded question, however, has an added feature—the person answering it is never sure what impact, if any, his or her answer will have. Examples are: "That isn't a very good reason for acting that way, is it?" "When did you stop wasting time on the job?" "I thought he was wrong. What do you think?"

The loaded question is a poor one for several reasons. The interviewee may not know the answer, may resent you asking the question, or may answer it the way he or she thinks you want it answered. Whatever, the result is the same; you learn nothing new about the person. Like the leading question, it only stifles communication.

3. The stress question. This question puts the interviewee under tension because of its grilling connotation. Examples are: "Are you positive that ... ?" "How do you explain ... ?" "Why didn't you ... ?"

Stress questions often are leading or loaded questions, asked to test how sharp and alert a person is. But they don't always reveal that. Instead, they put the person on edge. They also tend to break any trust you may have attained. And since stress questions may make you appear as an authority figure as well as a judge, they simply hurt any communication link you may have established.

13.7 How to Use the "Sandwich" Technique

Experienced and effective counselors often use the "sandwich" technique when talking to someone about the person's behavior or performance. They are careful to make an unfavorable comment only after giving a compliment, and they follow it with a favorable remark. In this way, they soften the blow of criticism while still getting it across.

For example, if you were to use the technique when talking to one of your people you might say, "John, I like the way you tackle a job without delay. It shows me you've got the right attitude about the job and want to do your share of the work. But, you should try to cut down on the amount of waste you make because that runs up our costs. I'm sure you can do this because you're one of the most skilled people we have in the department."

Astute supervisors look for opportunities to use this technique in handing out their work assignments to their people. When they find that they must give an employee a distasteful job, they fit it in with easy or pleasant tasks. They've learned that a person is more willing to accept a dirty job under such circumstances.

A word of caution: You must be careful in your use of the sandwich technique—don't become so predictable in your approach to people that they become suspicious whenever you compliment them, expecting that a criticism will follow. The way to avoid this is simple enough—be more liberal with praise and appreciation for work done as you go along.

13.8 Answers to What to Say to an Outstanding Person

It's relatively easy to talk with a person who is doing well on the job because your attitude toward the person is good and your compliments are very sincere. As a result, your conversation will be high key and positive in almost all respects.

Although you may be tempted to talk about achievements, you should resist this. Your responsibility to the person should be with his or her future. The greater the person's abilities, the greater the obligation you have to see that these skills and attributes are directed to the advantage of both the person and the company.

Talk to the person in a way that shows you appreciate his or her talents and good performance. Say words such as, "How can I help you rise to a better position with the company? Tell me what your goals are—I want to help you reach them." An outstanding person appreciates such comments and will continue to do a good job for you. You will also be able to work together toward the advancement of the person with a corresponding benefit to the company.

13.9 How to Talk with a Failing Person

Nobody likes the job of telling someone that he or she is not doing well on the job and that something will have to be done about it. Yet, it is an obligation that should not be put off by the person's supervisor. You should face the problem early while there still is some hope of saving the person. Because of that, do not postpone the task to the time when you normally conduct appraisal interviews with your other people.

Don't be surprised to learn that the person is aware of his or her failing on the job. He or she may even welcome the opportunity to discuss it with you. Both of you will likely feel better after talking about it whether or not you find a solution to the problem.

Sometimes you can help a person to find a job more suitable to his or her talents and liking. You seldom do a man a favor when you keep him on work he cannot handle. You should be helpful rather than critical when you talk with a failing person. Say, "How can we solve this problem together?" Never say, "Here's what's wrong with you," or similar faultfinding words. Get the person to talk and to offer an answer to the problem. Don't try to solve it yourself. You can't do it unless you simply transfer the person to another job or take action to terminate his or her job with the company.

Caution: Avoid getting involved in emotional problems when you counsel someone who is failing. Leave such matters to psychiatrists and psychologists—you do not have the proper training unless this is your field. Besides, it is very easy to become trapped by your own feelings which then add to the problem. Only if you can tactfully do it should you recommend that the person get professional help. The best person to suggest this should be the company doctor or a very close friend.

13.10 Handling an Appraisal with an Angry Person

Talking constructively with an angry person is difficult if not impossible. If a person becomes angry or emotional at an interview, you must listen, not talk. Let the person get rid of the emotion. If you become angry, you will fail to learn much about the person. You will also not be able to suggest ways that the person's performance may be improved because you cannot do your best thinking when you are upset.

An angry person is expressing one or more feelings which include resentment, frustration, fear, prejudice, and disappointment. The person may not mention these feelings but they will be apparent to you if you listen carefully. Only by listening and trying to understand can you have any hope of helping.

Don't try to explain, persuade, or convince a person of something while he or she is emotional. Nor should you suggest that both of you talk about something else. When a person is emotional, his or her mind cannot be put on any subject.

If you see that a person continues to show emotion after a few minutes with you, it may be wise to give up the interview attempt for the moment. Tactfully suggest that you meet again sometime soon, assuring the person that you understand the feelings he or she has. Show an interest in the person the next few days and express your desire and willingness to again sit down to talk.

13.11 How to Be Consistent in Rating People

One thing you want to be sure of when you rate your people is that you are fair. Don't let bias or prejudice influence your thinking. Just as important, and a way of being fair, is being consistent.

To be consistent, rate your people on only one factor at a time. For example, if you're rating them on their attendance, rate the person who is never absent as excellent, the person who misses a day every three to four months as good, and the person who is absent more than once a month as unsatisfactory.

Resist the tendency to let one favorable or unfavorable trait of a person affect your feeling toward the person as a whole. For instance, because a person may have a poor attitude should not cause you to forget that the person's workmanship is excellent. Along the same line, a perfect attendance should not impress you so much that you overlook an inability to get along with other people. You do your best rating when you rate all your people on one factor before going to another factor.

You can check your ratings for consistency by observing whether you have a variation among your people on each of the factors. You should have a range on each factor such that the great majority are in the middle of the range with lesser numbers at the top and at the bottom.

13.12 Evaluating on Points

The way to make an evaluation of people specific and relative is to rate them on points. Some companies do this as a means of determining the amount of pay increase they award to their people. Others use a point system for advancing workers to higher classes.

A typical evaluation system may contain more than ten traits or perform- ance items. Depending on the responsibilities of the people being rated, the items would include: accuracy, alertness, attendance, creativity, courtesy, dependability, drive, friendliness, housekeeping, job knowledge, personality, personal appearance, quantity of work, safety, and stability. If the person were in a supervisory position you might include the items: control of costs, control of waste, company-union agreement, handling people, meeting the schedule, and specifications.

To convert these performance items to points, the usual procedure is to use a scale of 1 to 5 points for poor, fair, good, very good, and excellent. Evaluation and judgment of performance of an individual is based on the total number of points the person is given on the selected performance items.

Caution: A common problem some supervisors have in rating their people is their proneness to rate nearly everyone as good or average on every item instead of being more critical in judgment. People are not this similar in actuality. To be realistic you should use the ends of the scale as well as the middle.

13.13 Repeat Interviews: How to Handle Them

After you've gotten into the routine of having periodic appraisal inter- views with each of your people, you may wonder what you should talk about at subsequent meetings, especially in the case when a person is doing all right and nothing of importance has happened to change the person's situation.

You may make a repeat interview brief and very informal under such circumstances. But, take heed: the other person may not see it as the routine matter that you might assign it. For one thing, you probably have not talked about the person's accomplishments or goals for a long time. For another, the person's viewpoint about the job may have changed. You must again persuade the person to talk—don't assume everything is just as it was when you last met.

You're never out of style to thank a person for doing good work. And you can always talk about the future. It pays to tell a person that you appreciate his or her cooperation. You might also add that you hope the two of you can continue to work together in the future.

13.14 Evaluating Performance: A Prerequisite to Promotion

Although the most common use of a performance appraisal is to help a person develop on the job, appraisals are used also for determining rates of pay and promotions. You should know a person quite well when you promote him or her in order to be reasonably sure the person can handle more responsibility. You must also consider how the company and your department will be affected.

Will productivity of the people involved increase? Will you have a smoother operating group?

Case-in-Point: "You should promote an individual only on the basis of frank, honest appraisal," says Clyde M. Hyde, department supervisor with Tucson (Ariz.) Gas and Electric Co.[1] in a recent issue of *The Supervisor's Memory Jogger*. "Your recommendations for promotion to your superior should be based on your knowledge of what is best for your department and the company irrespective of personal friendships. At times it is not easy to pass an unbiased opinion on the work of your men. Years of association with them will always tend to influence the decisions you make. Nevertheless, you must make an effort to be honest with yourself." Hyde's thinking is respected by management in his company. He's had three promotions since he started to work for them.

13.15 Five Pitfalls to Avoid in an Appraisal Interview

Several stumbling blocks are in the path of the supervisor who wants to get the most from an interview with one of his or her people. You can overcome them by thinking about what you are going to say before the meeting and by keeping in mind that your main objective is to help the person. Here are five pitfalls to avoid when you talk to a person about performance on the job:

1. Avoid comparison with other people, especially peers. Nobody likes to hear that someone else has done a better job. Say, "Here are some ways you can do better," rather than, "Here is what you have done wrong."

2. Don't dwell on a person's weakness. Focus on improvement in the future, not on past mistakes. Talk about what a person has done, not about what the person is. Speak more about the work than the person. Be constructive in order to motivate.

3. Be careful about discouraging a person by saying that his or her goals are impractical or impossible. You could very easily be proven wrong. If you feel you must say something about a person's goals, go only so far as to tactfully point out the difficulties which might be in the person's path.

4. Refrain from using words which connote poor performance or failure. Words such as *guilty, faults, mistakes,* and *weaknesses* are better left unsaid. Also, words such as *reasonable, common sense,* and *logical* are antagonizing to some people.

5. Do not make promises. You can't predict the future, and you shouldn't

---

[1]Reprinted from *Supervisor's Memory Jogger,* Oct. 1970. By permission of the publisher. Bureau of Business Practice, 24 Rope Ferry Road, Waterford, Connecticut 06386. Copyright, Bureau of Business Practice, Inc.

try. Never, for example, promise a raise or a job. Circumstances may change or events may occur which would make it impossible for you to deliver.

13.16 Follow-Up: An Important Part of Appraisal Interviewing

For everyone to gain from appraisals, you may need to take care of some matters after the interviews. The people you interview will gain more from it if you carry on after your talk by showing interest in them and their work. You have the responsibility also of following up on matters you discussed with them.

For instance, you may have promised to take action of some sort on changing the work assignments or responsibilities of an individual. The person will be expecting some word on this matter—you must not let him or her down. Or, you may have decided during the interview to look into the person's history or job experience in order to correct the record or add some information—this should not be allowed to drag or be forgotten.

A planned program of development and progress of your people often is an outgrowth of your appraisal interviews. Your people need your help if they are to advance in the company as well as get satisfaction from their work. They look to you for guidance and direction. Such developments and plans for the future should not be left to memory. Make notes immediately after an interview. You may put them on the appraisal form or on a separate paper for the person's record file. They'll be of value to you at the time of the next interview.

14

Proven Methods
for Getting Along
with the Union

The presence and influence of the union in business and industry make supervisors better leaders in that because of the union they become more aware of the needs of people on the job. Although the union may make their job more difficult at times, supervisors should realize that it is a waste of time and effort to fight it—they must accept it.

Knowing the agreement and what it covers is a requisite for getting along with the union. Of particular interest, in this respect, is the grievance procedure. Since employee grievances are costly in both time and money, supervisors must constantly work to reduce their number. Supervisors can take a big step in this direction by being on good terms with the union steward. Getting this person's cooperation in handling people problems means much because the union and management don't always agree on the best ways of working toward the company's goals.

The company has the right to discipline employees for infractions of rules and poor performance, but the union may express a difference of opinion on the discipline imposed. Arbitration by an umpire is the way such differences are settled. Supervisors should be familiar with the procedure and have proof to support their action since they may be participants in umpire hearings.

14.1 Collective Bargaining: What It's All About

Collective bargaining is a procedure. It's the getting together of represent-atives of management and the union to discuss and agree on wages, hours, and working conditions. Almost anything that affects a person on the job is a fit subject for collective bargaining. The union bargains for something it feels its members should have. Management has to bargain in good faith on whether it can grant all, part, or none of what the union proposes.

Both the union and management present their arguments in attempting to reach agreement, the outcome of which depends on several factors: whether the company feels it can pay for its cost, how desirable it is to employees, management, and stockholders, and whether it is reasonable under the circumstances. Issues are also decided on the bargaining strength of each of the parties.

Collective bargaining usually starts when the union and management begin negotiating on the contents of the agreement or contract which they will eventually sign. Both sides hope a good agreement will be reached since everyone must live with it for its term like any other contract. Agreements between the union and management are seldom changed during its life but the contract by no means is a forgotten document. Supervisors and employees will refer to it many times during its term to carry out its meaning.

14.2 Answers to Why Employees Join a Union

Supervisors should know why their people may want to belong to a union. Such knowledge provides insight to getting along with it and an understanding of what people expect of the company they work for.

Most workers decide they want a union to represent them when they see that management doesn't listen to them and when they believe that management is indifferent to their needs. Employees show these feelings in many ways. Turnover and absenteeism increase, productivity is erratic and usually declines, scrap and waste are high, and safety records are poor.

Yet, discovering what the real issues or differences of opinion are may still be difficult at times. Management typically believes that money and benefits lie behind most dissatisfactions, but these things often are not the real problem.

Money becomes the big issue only when employees feel they are ignored. And that is the major reason why employees join unions.

An expert's comment: Psychologist Milton Blum in his book, *Industrial Psychology and Its Social Foundations* admits the importance of collective bargaining in the formation of unions, but he points out, "Some employees also believe that membership in a union gives them an opportunity to develop more self-respect. The importance of this need must not be underestimated ... 'Telling the boss off' is often a compelling desire, and a person sometimes avails himself of an opportunity to do so when he has a group, such as a union, in back of him."

14.3 Attitude: The Controlling Factor in Getting Along

As a supervisor, you must recognize that once your company has made a contract with a union, you will be working with it from then on. You may as well accept the union and do your best to get along with it. You will only cause trouble for yourself and the company if you fight it.

You would not be carrying out the responsibility of your job, however, if you gave up interest in your people and their welfare solely because they belong to the union. Management expects you to be a leader and to guide employees in their work. If management felt that union leaders could do this, you wouldn't be needed as a supervisor.

Employees expect their union to protect their economic interests and to make their job more secure. You cannot fault your people for wanting this. An employee who works for a considerate supervisor, one who recognizes this relationship of the employee to the union, usually will be easy to get along with and will try to do a good job for the company.

14.4 How to Promote Good Union-Management Relations

A company's supervisors can contribute much toward achieving and maintaining good union-management relations. The relationship between the supervisor and the individual employee is an important one because when employees think of management or the company, they think of their supervisor.

A poor supervisor can harm relations more than any other level of management because he or she is the closest management person to the employees. Thus, it is important that supervisors create and promote confidence and trust among their people. Supervisors can do much, for instance, to promote a team spirit by letting each employee know how valuable his or her contribution is to the company and how people working together can improve productivity.

Another way that supervisors can help union-management relations is by being good listeners when employees are dissatisfied with their work, want something, or have other matters to talk about. This is not to say that supervisors should give employees whatever they ask for, but that they should try to understand employee problems and explain why not all of their requests can be granted.

Compatibility between the supervisor and an employee is a plus toward maintaining harmony because small differences of opinion can easily be handled when they arise. If you can resolve problems before they become grievances, you serve to cement the union and management relationship.

14.5 Knowing the Agreement: A "Must" for Supervisors

To get along with the union you must be informed on the union-management agreement and understand it. Without this knowledge you cannot fully carry out your responsibility as a member of management nor can you always be right in how you handle and treat your people. Rest assured that your counterpart, the union steward, is well-versed in that document. To be his equal in the eyes of your people on matters covered in the agreement, you must be just as well-informed.

Most companies see that their supervisors receive training on the agreement. Such training and instruction is usually given by the industrial relations or personnel people who know the contract provisions well. The training should include briefing on past practices and the unwritten understandings which the union and management have reached over the years.

The grievance procedure presented in the agreement is very likely the most important part of the document to the supervisor. As for other matters contained in the agreement, you will never regret taking time to study and discuss them with your peers and your superiors. As a result, you will have an easier time in getting along with the union.

14.6 How to Get the Cooperation of the Union Steward

It pays to be on good terms with the union steward. Although you may personally resent the person because of the problems he or she gives you, realize that the steward is the elected representative of your union people, a position which carries a lot of responsibility.

The key to getting the cooperation of the union steward is to treat the person with respect and show that you feel he or she is important. You can do this in several ways.

One way is to always let the steward know what's going on and keep him or her up-to-date. See that the steward is the first person to be told of changes that affect the union people. Another is to show the person you understand the problems of being the union representative. Always do your best to answer the questions that the person asks and to solve the problems that the person brings up.

Get to know the union steward as well as any other employee. The better you know the person, the easier it will be to get along with him or her. You and the steward will have many mutual problems in your daily work. Just as the steward will frequently come to you to straighten out matters, so should you periodically ask for his or her help on your problems. The fact that you do will help you to get the cooperation you need to be a successful supervisor.

14.7 How to Work with the Grievance Procedure

To get along well with the union you must know how to handle a complaint. Once you acquire this skill, you will be able to resolve differences of opinion on the job more easily as well as carry out the responsibilities of your job with more authority.

The supervisor should not consider a grievance as a personal attack on his or her authority but as a way the union communicates to management a complaint or the existence of a problem. With this viewpoint you will not be resentful or antagonistic when you handle grievances. It makes for a more equitable solution of problems for all concerned.

Winning a grievance is not as important as promptly settling it so that an employee can be productive with a minimum of dissatisfaction and loss of time. A supervisor should recognize the need to settle a grievance as soon as possible. The longer it is put off, the more unhappy and discontented the submitter becomes. If a grievance is promptly and properly investigated by the supervisor, the chances of outside arbitration being required are greatly decreased.

14.8 Tips on Successful Handling of Grievances

If you can discern the nature of a grievance you have taken the first step in successfully handling it. A majority of them fit one pattern or another, and two types are most common in companies where management tries to treat their employees well

The first type is imaginary or arises from a misunderstanding. Of course, it is real to the employee, and a supervisor should accept it as such. You should still give a grievance your full attention no matter how illogical or impractical it may appear. And be especially thorough when investigating a grievance which seems to be far out of line—it may be the surfacing of a serious hidden problem.

The second type is simply the expression of an employee asking that he or she get a fair deal. The person may be wrong and not sure, but wants to be checked out. Give the employee the facts and a fair answer. You may have to say that he or she is wrong, but the person will know that you took a personal interest and tried to help. If, however, you ignore or slough off the complaint, the employee will feel that it was not important enough to you. The disappointment and discontent resulting may bring you more trouble later.

14.9 Effective Ways to Reduce the Grievance Problem

No company likes to receive grievances from their employees. Yet, few companies which have unions are able to completely eliminate them, try as they may. This is not to say that a lack of grievances means that everyone is pleased on the job. Frank discussions of problems are better than silent discontent.

However, when management receives numerous grievances, they should search for the reason or reasons. Disgruntled employees are not productive. The company is the loser when employees are unhappy and feel ignored.

The effective way to avoid grievances is to discuss proposed changes in the work with the union before putting them into effect. Another way is to ask for the union's help and cooperation in solving problems and resolving differences of opinion as soon as they become known.

Perhaps the most realistic approach to reducing the grievance problem is to take a less rigid view toward the agreement, to be more liberal when interpreting it. Both the union and management should recognize that conditions involving people on the job change—the agreement must change accordingly. If the agreement is looked upon as a guide for solving problems and reaching decisions rather than as a group of inflexible laws, both parties may be more willing to concede on issues more often.

14.10 Three Mistakes Supervisors Should Avoid

A study of the grievances of employees that end in arbitration hearings revealed that about 90 percent of them reached that point because of mistakes made by supervisors. This indicates that today's supervisors need more instruction and training in human relations and in how to handle people on the job. The three most serious mistakes that supervisors make are:

1. Making light of or brushing off legitimate complaints. When an employee turns in a grievance, at that time the matter is more important to him or her than anything else. The employee will not be satisfied until the grievance is answered. Too often, a supervisor misjudges the seriousness of a person's complaint.

2. Handling a complaint without getting all the facts. This mistake is an outgrowth of not placing enough importance on the matter to justify a thorough study of it. The problem is aggravated when the supervisor isn't aware of the true feelings of his or her people and hasn't been interested enough to know their likes and dislikes.

3. Imposing severe discipline for a minor offense. The union often feels that discipline meted out by the supervisor is too severe. The problem of consistency must also be contended with. If you suspend one person for a rule violation, you can't give a simple warning to another person for the same offense.

14.11 How to Interpret the Agreement on Discipline

Union-management agreements invariably give management the right to discipline or discharge employees for just cause. There has to be discipline, obedience to authority, and respect for the rights of others in any successful organization. Without them efficiency would be impossible.

The supervisor fits into the picture in that he or she evaluates a person's need for discipline and metes out penalties for infractions. Through progressive steps of more and more severe discipline, the point may be reached where discharge is the final step. Supervisors who are concerned with the welfare of their people will counsel them and try to prevent this from happening, but they aren't always successful.

Under the agreement, employees have the right to protest disciplinary action they feel is unfair, discriminatory, or too severe, and they have the right to have the union represent them in these protests. Many cases of discipline or discharge of employees eventually reach the arbitrator because the union and management are unable to resolve them.

Case-in-Point: Grievance No. 3-1512-285-77, submitted to arbitration by the United Rubber, Cork, Linoleum, and Plastic Workers of America AFL-CIO-CLC, reads: The grievance claims that a 30-day disciplinary suspension imposed by the Company was unjust, and the Union requests that the grievant be made whole for all monies and benefits lost.

Arbitrator Peter DiLeone resolved this grievance after a hearing with both the Union and the Company. The Facts section of his analysis read, in part:

"The Union does not argue that the Company need negotiate penalties for any rules violation, nor does it even contest the point that discipline is warranted in this case.

"The thrust of the Union's case is that the Company can impose discipline only where there is violation of a reasonable rule that has been properly promulgated and that once a violation has been established, the penalty for such violation must be evenly applied. It is the Union's contention that the 30-day suspension imposed by the Company in this case is clearly excessive when viewed in the light of penalties previously assessed by the Company for the identical violation—fighting in the plant.

"To further buttress its argument, the Union submitted 17 variously dated suspension letters issued at this plant. All of the suspensions were for fighting, pushing, or threatening in the plant; out of the 17 suspensions, there was one 14-day suspension, the remaining 16 suspensions being for either a three-day or seven-day period.

"Therefore, the Union urges that the penalty be found to be excessive and it requests that the penalty be reduced so as to be consistent with previously imposed penalties for similar violations."

Also in the Facts section of the document was the Company's viewpoint, reported, in part, thus:

"The Company argues that the attack upon Supervisor Jones was without provocation or mitigating circumstances and that discipline must be maintained if the Company is to fulfill its obligation to provide a safe work environment free of both violence and threats to the well-being of its employees, be they supervisors or members of the Bargaining Unit.

"The Company also asserts that it was in compliance with Article V of the contract in that all the facts and circumstances surrounding this incident were properly considered, and further that the 30-day suspension imposed upon King was a proper exercise of its authority when viewed in the light of those facts and circumstances."

In the Analysis and Opinion section of the document the arbitrator stated the following, in part:

"The fact that this grievant received a 30-day suspension, while of the 17 suspension letters referred to by the Union, only one was for a 14-day suspension with the remaining 16 being for periods of either three days or seven days, fails to demonstrate an inconsistency, in the opinion of the Umpire. Any given suspension is meted out for very specific reasons and under very specific circumstances. The Union has shown the penalty in this case to exceed those applied in the past but does not demonstrate any equation between the facts and circumstances of this case and those of the previous suspensions referred. From what the Umpire can determine, the majority of those previous suspensions were for employees fighting in the plant; or pushing, shoving, or threatening a

Supervisor, with varying degrees of provocation and mitigating circumstances present. Significantly, the 14-day suspension was imposed on an employee for striking a Supervisor.

"Thus, although the Umpire might find a certain consistency present in the handling of disciplinary measures, it is not found to be as urged by the Union. The only consistency or practice that can be solidly established is that the Company has considered each case on its individual merits and acted accordingly. The penalty for any given rule violation need not be *identical* to other such penalties to be *consistent* if the variation is attributed to differing facts and circumstances."

In the Award section of the document the arbitrator states: "The Umpire can only come to one conclusion in this case. The grievance should be, and is hereby, denied."

14.12 Tips on Providing Proof to Back Disciplinary Action

A large share of all arbitration cases today question the disciplinary action imposed on an employee by supervision for violation of plant rules or for poor work performance. In most cases arbitrators consider what the degree of proof must be to support the supervisor's action. Some type of proof is usually a necessity.

The supervisor frequently is the star witness in such situations. The specific facts relating to the case must be established by your testimony and by the written record. You must be prepared to show, for instance, that your worker, Tom Johnson, was absent on specific days and that he was warned on particular occasions that his attendance would have to improve.

Nobody in a supervisory position likes to take disciplinary action with one of his or her people. But you must prepare to do that well in advance of the time that it becomes necessary. An efficient supervisor keeps a record of events and incidents at the first sign that disciplinary action may eventually have to be taken. Since the testimony of other people could be needed at an arbitration hearing several weeks or months later, a wise supervisor records who was present and who witnessed a violation. Unless a record is made, one that identifies people with places and dates, time will obliterate the memories of everyone.

14.13 Proven Ways of Promoting and Transferring

One of the most difficult problems management has concerns the promotion of union people. Management needs the maximum amount of flexibility in selecting persons for promotion and also wants to avoid basing promotions on straight seniority. Unions often do not trust the judgmental factors involved with promotions; they prefer to base decisions on a known and measurable factor like seniority. Despite the opposing viewpoints, management and the union usually try to find a common ground on which to compromise.

The right of management to employ the most skilled and efficient people in key positions is one of the basic rights that must be understood in any contract with the union. Supervisors should always interpret the contract in that light. When a job applicant is rejected, it should be done on the grounds that he or she is not qualified. The ruling may be backed by the employee's personnel record which gives in detail the educational qualifications of the person as well as what his or her work experience has been.

Management should insist on proper qualifications also when an employee puts in a bid to be transferred. Many grievances are written on this matter. Frequently an employee may claim the company is guilty of discrimination when his or her request is denied.

Case-in-Point: Tom Shannon, maintenance supervisor at Ace Products in Springfield, Illinois was faced with a problem of job qualification when a utility worker left his department for another job. Following company policy, Shannon posted the vacancy on the bulletin board. The first person to bid for the job was Mary Campbell, a slightly built four-year employee in her mid-30's who performed light maintenance duties. Shannon told Campbell that the job would be too difficult for her because it included handling crates and cartons that weighed up to 75 pounds. Campbell replied that if she needed help she would ask for it. Shannon said that too much time would be wasted doing that.

Mary Campbell told the supervisor that he was simply looking for excuses not to give her the job because she was a woman. "That's not true," Shannon pointed out. "We have women working in all kinds of jobs in the plant."

"Then there's no reason a woman can't do this job as well," replied Campbell. "I may be small, but that doesn't mean I'm not strong enough to handle it. The union will back me at arbitration if you don't give me a chance."

Shannon went to his personnel manager for advice on how to handle the case. The manager supported him in his stand, saying, "The fact that we employ women in a number of jobs formerly held by men is proof that we don't discriminate. And the requirements of the job itself show that Campbell lacks the qualifications needed to fill it. Going out of our way to avoid discriminating against someone is one thing. Hiring a person who isn't qualified for the job would be going too far. I don't think that Campbell's claim that she was turned down because of her sex would get very far with an umpire." Apparently union officials agreed with the personnel manager's analysis because Campbell and the union did not take her complaint to arbitration.

14.14 How to Handle a Promotion to a Supervisor

Management may some day ask you for your opinion on who of the union workers would make a good supervisor. If you are not prepared to recommend one of your people, you could begin your search for the person by asking the union who they would suggest. Union nominees often turn out to be very capable.

Be aware of your objective: to help the company achieve its goal by putting its most skilled and efficient people in key positions. If the union recommends someone whom you feel does not have the proper qualifications, don't accede without giving the matter considerable thought. You must rely on your own evaluation of the person's performance and your own estimate of the person's potential. Usually this is not easy to do because not all good workers make good supervisors.

To be able to make a good recommendation to management, you should evaluate your people for the qualifications of a good supervisor long before you are asked about it. Potential supervisors should be recognized early and be brought along on the job by guiding and counseling. It is also wise to talk with other supervisors about who has the capabilities for the job. You want to be sure you are not overlooking someone as well as confirming that your choice is a good one.

15

Productivity and What to Do About It

Supervisors who put a sincere effort into improving the productivity of employees are a real asset to their company. A highly productive labor force means that people are efficient on the job enabling the company to keep up with competition and be profitable. Supervisors play a key role in productivity improvement programs because they are close to the workers and have a great influence on their performance.

The productivity of people can be raised in many ways other than the obvious "making good use of time." Motivating and training people on the job are two of the most successful ways. Supervisors contribute best when they spend most of their time in direct leadership working with their people. By planning and scheduling work, they can more fully use the skills of workers as well as assure that materials, tools, and equipment are available when needed.

Supervisors have other resources to call upon to help them do something about productivity. With work sampling studies they can determine its level and where they should direct their improvement efforts. A company that has a suggestion system and encourages employee participation usually reaps worthwhile benefits. Supervisors themselves should become skilled in presenting and selling ideas to their supervisors.

15.1 Direct Supervising: Key to Good Labor Efficiency

The supervisor is the main driving force in any program to improve productivity. You can influence morale, job attitude, and workmanship of your people by what you say and do on the job. The stronger your influence and direction, the better the productivity of your people.

Productivity improvement efforts fail when supervisors do not spend enough time on direct supervision. Inadequate attention is reflected in excessive idle time of people and machines, poor safety records, cluttered work areas, excessive overtime work, and high absenteeism among other things, all of which add up to high labor costs.

If you spend a lot of time on administrative functions you will be a less effective supervisor because close, forceful leadership is required for good labor efficiency. Being on the job with your people enables you to search out problems and bottlenecks, to stay on top of the job. Your efforts will be rewarded with an increase in productivity of your people, and you will carry out your responsibilities better besides.

Case-in-Point: Researchers at the University of Wisconsin discovered that individuals are not as productive working alone as they are when other people are around. A study group found that the mere physical presence of other people generates alertness and stimulation; conversation or eye-contact is not necessary for this effect.

Supervisors who have their own office or desk will carry out their responsibilities better, it seems, by leaving it periodically during the workday, arranging their desks to afford a view of their people, and occasionally working in places used by others.

15.2 How to Raise Productivity by Talking to People

Effective use of manpower and good productivity of the workplace requires that people communicate with each other. Employees must work together to achieve company goals. Supervisors should stress the importance of communication when directing work activities.

Many employees want to know what other employees of the company do. They are interested also in the problems of other departments as well as how their company is doing as a whole. Giving them such information prompts greater interest in their work and leads to more cooperation among departments. The result is quicker and more effective handling of problems and greater productivity.

If you want your people to be more efficient, you should periodically talk to them about materials and equipment. Workers in the office and in the plant have ideas on how to do jobs quicker, where they run into delays, and how materials can be handled better. By discussing these things and taking corrective action where needed, you can raise the productivity of your group and help your company. Even the simple act of talking to employees about their work, how they feel about their jobs, and what they need will result in an increase in productivity on their part.

Case-in-Point: Back in 1927, Western Electric was concerned about the productivity of their employees. Management had tried everything it could think of to increase performance, but nothing worked. In desperation, one of the managers decided to talk to some of the workers to see if they had any suggestions. Although he didn't get many worthwhile ideas, a strange thing happened. Production rates began to increase and rejection rates began to go down. Overall performance was higher than it had ever been before.

Not knowing what brought about the change, the manager interviewed the workers once more. Again, few ideas came out of the talks, but production again improved. When the manager talked to some other departments, the same thing happened. Production increased and rejects went down whenever people were talked to about their work, their needs, and their attitudes.

Since 1927, Western Electric has conducted a formal program of talking to their employees, getting their opinions and suggestions, and listening to their complaints, followed by acting on them. Western Electric, as a result, is one of the most efficient industrial companies in business today.

15.3 Promoting Productivity Through Better Use of Time

The inefficiency of people on the job is principally the result of poor use of time. Recognizing this, supervisors should be continually looking for ways to get their people to put more of their time on the job and less on personal matters.

Employees today waste a lot of time with late starts and early quits, excessive rest and coffee breaks, long lunch periods, nonbusiness conversations, and just plain loafing. Regardless, effective supervisors combat the waste of time by their people in various ways.

How-to-Do-It: The best way to get people started on the job is to stay with or near them after giving them an assignment until they begin work. Of course, you have no assurance they will continue to work after you leave, but you can return a short time later.

About the only way you can control the time people take for rest and coffee breaks is to put in an appearance if the privilege is being abused. Although most supervisors dislike doing this, it provides the opportunity to inquire how the work is going, if assistance is needed, or to ask other specific questions related to the job.

One way to break up bull sessions is to join the group, asking if you can help. You imply that the persons have a problem they are discussing—you would like to help. Another answer to break up idle conversations is to approach the group and ask for the help of one of the members, help that requires the person to leave with you to go to a workplace or office. Removing one person from a group often gets the point across to the others that they should be getting back to their jobs.

Nonbusiness conversations have a place in work areas to promote good relations among employees and to relieve stress and tension on the job. You will find that people are more productive if they have a friendly, relaxed atmosphere to work in, one where they can freely discuss their families and their hobbies with their fellow-workers. You should participate in such conversations, too. When employees see that the company is interested in their welfare and personal lives, they are more willing to cooperate on the job and do a good day's work. However, you must guard against excessive visiting which reduces productive time.

Case-in-Point: "The problem of people wasting time by visiting with one another can be handled by making it difficult or inconvenient for them to get together," says Eugene Sankey, former section manager of factory accounting for Goodyear Tire and Rubber Company. "I remember that we had this problem years ago before we remodeled the offices. A suggestion was turned in by a conscientious fellow who had, with others, a desk along an aisle between two departments. People going from one department to another continually stopped to talk with these employees. His answer to the problem was to have a 6-foot partition wall put on both sides of the aisle; so that the partitions were not too unattractive, the upper portions were constructed of glass. It took a lot of shouting if people tried to converse."

15.4 Training: Supervisors Can Make It Pay Off

Training is probably the best way of helping people to perform well. Many companies could reduce their costs, increase safety, and improve productivity if they gave more of their employees training. Workers really do want to do a job well. A lack of knowledge and skill often prevents them from being as productive as they could be.

On-the-job instructing is the most common way that companies train their employees today, although classroom instruction and attending seminars also is popular. Training by supervisors is more practical than by professional teachers, administrative personnel, or consultants. Supervisors are in the best position to measure the effectiveness of the training and place emphasis where it is needed. Since most workers want to please their supervisors, trainees are more receptive and their retention is better when they are taught by their supervisors. Other advantages to using supervisors to train people are that the supervisors also learn from the program and are committed to it more than other instructors would be.

You should be sure to cover the basics when training on the job. Training which consists only of telling people what, how, and why to do something is usually not adequate. Many people need to do the job or task in order to learn it. Certainly, this is the only way for people to really become proficient and raise their productivity.

Day-to-day problems should not be permitted to interfere with training lest the participants see the training as unimportant. Training pays off the most when people are conscientious in how they go about it and put their full efforts into it. The optimum benefit is realized when the training is on how to do the job itself or closely related to the work to be performed.

15.5 Positive Ways to Prevent Obsolescence of People

While aging of your people is natural and expected, obsolescence should not be. The company should be concerned and try to keep employees knowledgeable of developments which affect their work. Maintaining and improving the productivity of people on the job requires that they be kept abreast of technology in their type of work.

Most workers are interested in new ideas, new products, new tools, and better ways to do a job, especially if these things will make their job easier. You can prevent your people from becoming obsolete in the way they handle their work in several ways.

How-to-Do-It: Provide the appropriate training for them when a work procedure is changed or when new equipment is put in use. Usually the vendor or manufacturer of new equipment which the company acquires will provide instruction on how to operate and service it or will supply a manual which does this. See that such instruction and information are made available to your people.

Encourage your people to take courses at the high schools and universities in the area. If your company will pay tuition costs, you have a good selling argument. Emphasize the value of improving one's skills on the job and how such education can lead to a better position with the company.

Rent or buy films to show your people on subjects of interest such as safety and health. Bring speakers and lecturers to the company to make presentations. And don't overlook payroll inserts, bulletin boards, and the company newspaper as other ways to keep your people up-to-date and informed on new products, new tools, and better ways to do a job.

15.6 Motivation: The Sure-Fire Way to Raise Productivity

Most management experts agree that motivation is the key to good productivity. The supervisor's task is to create the right atmosphere conducive to motivation, using all the resources and skills he or she possesses. This is difficult. It takes time, intuition, and a sensitivity to people to accomplish and maintain enthusiasm. You should never give up, however, even though you may often be discouraged and feel frustrated.

A way to motivate people is to see that they get satisfaction from their work. Try to provide the factors that fill their needs. Make the work challenging and interesting. Give people a reason for doing a job and compliment them upon its completion.

Believing in your people and having confidence that they can do the work will increase their level of performance because they will attempt to live up to your expectations and be worthy of your trust. Training is a motivational tool if your people want to learn more about the technical side of their jobs. This is particularly true with craftsmen.

Public recognition often maintains motivation. Formally congratulating skilled people after they successfully complete a demanding job is very effective. So is recognizing work done under unfavorable conditions such as bad weather, poor location, and hazardous situations.

A temporary promotion is an effective way to motivate a worker in many companies. Acting as a temporary supervisor, for example, will motivate a person to raise his or her productivity when the person returns to the job.

15.7 Tested and Proven Benefits from Planning and Scheduling

To have high productivity, emphasis must be placed on the supervisional functions that promote efficiency and job accomplishment. Planning and scheduling of work is the way to go about it.

Planning determines what work needs to be done, when it should be done, and what will be required to do it. Scheduling assigns people to jobs at a specified time. The procedure involves coordinating people, material, tools, and equipment to assure that all are available at the time to start the work. Here are six proven benefits which a company gains from planning and scheduling its work:

1. Attention and action based on priorities. You can make sure first things come first. When supervisors consider customer orders, work situations, availability of labor and material, and the other factors which affect service and production, they can make decisions to get the optimum from their resources within the time available.

2. Better procedures for getting work done. Planning and scheduling prompts study of the job which results in finding the best method. If a supervisor gives a worker a job without instructions, the worker may do it in an inefficient manner as well as waste material. The worker may also run into a problem on the job and wait for the supervisor to come along to ask for help. When a job is well-planned, such waste of time and material is avoided.

3. Better coordination of labor and materials. Planning enables you to decide what materials and tools are required. You can then see that they are on hand before starting a job. A worker doesn't have to wait for material or be unable to complete a job because of the lack of it.

4. More efficient utilization of labor. When planning a job or project, you consider its scope and size. This prepares you to assign the optimum number of people and time to get it done. Estimating the time to do a job helps with scheduling people, thus improving their efficiency. It also enables you to avoid or minimize overtime.

5. Reduction of errors, mistakes, and omissions. Planning and scheduling permits you to provide written instructions for jobs, thus reducing errors which occur with oral orders. Drawings and specifications prevent omissions as well as result in better workmanship.

6. Better credibility of supervisors. Good personnel relations between departments of an organization promotes more cooperation and teamwork, thus raising the productivity of all employees. Planning and scheduling enables supervisors to be more accurate with job completion promises. This enhances credibility and reputation along with confidence in ability to get the job done.

15.8 Three Pitfalls to Avoid in Keeping Productivity Up

Successful supervisors avoid the roadblocks in their procedure of attaining and maintaining high productivity of their people. Three pitfalls they are particularly alert to are:

1. Allowing employees to set their own methods for doing work and the time to do it. This practice can be especially unproductive with maintenance

work if craftsmen are sent to a job site by their supervisor to see what the job for the day will consist of and what tools and materials will be needed. These decisions should be made by the supervisor before sending the men to the job.

2. Failing to consider time span and man-hours required to get a job done. The supervisor should know how long it will take to do a job and insist that employees meet the standards or come close to them.

3. Neglecting to place a value on cost in determining how work should be performed. Examples of abuse are assigning too many people to the job, using inefficient work methods, using more expensive material than required, and resorting to overtime.

15.9 Work Sampling: A Useful Tool for Measuring Productivity

Work sampling is a technique whereby supervisors or personnel department people observe workers to determine how productive they are. The principles of work sampling are based on the laws of probability. These laws conclude that a large number of observations made at random intervals and classified into distinct activities will provide a fairly reliable story of what percent of the time each activity is occurring. A key point is that activity observations must be taken randomly to assure unbiased results.

Work sampling procedures are designed to:

1. Measure the amount of control that supervisors have over their people.
2. Determine the percent of time people are working.
3. Reveal activities which are preventing people from putting more time into their work.
4. Provide a base against which future performance may be measured.

Caution: Work sampling should not be used to measure a worker's performance nor should it be used as a disciplinary tool. You lose the trust and confidence of your people if you use it for these purposes.

15.10 How to Make a Work Sampling Study

A definite procedure must be followed when work sampling if the information you get from it is to be valid and reliable. Here is how you should proceed:

1. Predetermine what activities you are going to look for so that you can classify your observations. The usual activities are: working, idle on job, idle away from job, traveling, getting instructions, and cleaning operations.

2. Make your observations in all areas of the office or factory where people may work, covering it entirely during one tour period.

3. Make tours on a random time basis throughout the work day. Determine the times by the use of random number tables.

4. Limit the tour period to 15-20 minutes. If you cannot complete it in this time, have another observer help you.

5. Include the canteen and lunchroom in the areas to be observed. Do not include locker and washrooms unless you have a problem locating people.

6. Know the total number of people to be observed on each tour and compare the number of observations you make with the number of people available. People not observed should be less than 10 percent.

7. Make a minimum of 12 observations of each person over the period of the study. The more observations you make, the more reliable the information.

8. Record your first impression when you observe a person. No additional observation time is needed.

9. Calculate the percent of time you found each person in each predetermined activity.

10. Summarize your study and put it in writing so that you will have it for comparison purposes on future work sampling studies.

15.11 Four Steps to Management by Objectives

A generally accepted mark of an efficient supervisor is a proficiency in setting and achieving his or her department's objectives. Management by objectives is a currently recognized and practiced procedure for carrying out the functions of management. It involves setting job responsibilities and performance standards for each job in a department. Although each person has specific objectives, all persons work toward a common goal, directed by the manager or supervisor.

People do a better job if they are aware of the level of performance expected of them. Also, managerial functions are more efficiently carried out if responsibilities are understood by both manager and subordinates. The four procedural steps to management by objectives are:

1. Analyze the person's job responsibilities. Supervisors frequently are surprised to learn what subordinates believe their responsibilities are. The issue is best resolved by having both the supervisor and the person list them independently. When the lists are compared, agreement should be reached on those functions for which the person will be held accountable.

2. Specify the person's level of performance. People on the job need guidelines to enable them to determine how well they are doing. By setting

standards for performance, the supervisor gives them a yardstick to measure the quality and quantity of their work. The use of standards makes possible an individual's determination of where more effort is required.

3. Set goals for the person to attain. The goals should be agreed upon by both the supervisor and the person. The supervisor may limit a person's goals to assure a good showing within a specified period of time. Discouragement because of failure can be minimized or avoided if goals are not set too high.

4. Assess the person's degree of accomplishment. Follow-up is essential to evaluating accomplishments. The supervisor should have an appraisal interview with the subordinate regularly to cover the objectives and goals previously agreed upon. At this time, the supervisor and the person usually set goals for the future.

15.12 Five Selling Points for Suggestion Systems

Every company should have a suggestion system if for no other reason than to raise the productivity of its employees. The Bell Telephone Laboratories[1] in Raritan, New Jersey made a study a few years ago of their system and reported that a good one will return from $3-$8 for every dollar invested in it. At that time the average suggestion plan cost about $28 per employee yearly. John Main of Bell said the indirect benefits included:

1. Release of employee frustration and boredom.
2. The opportunity for employees to demonstrate their value to the company and their peers.
3. A sharpening of healthy competitive instincts.
4. The focusing of employee's attention on what is of primary importance in their jobs.
5. Involvement of employees in the firm's procedures and objectives.

15.13 How to Promote More and Better Suggestions

To raise productivity, you've got to think of efficiency and be cost conscious of all the operations and services your people perform. Why not ask your people to think about better ways to do their work?

You can start by explaining the company's interest in suggestions from employees. Suggestions from people on the job help to reduce costs and improve productivity. Point out some of the problem areas where improvements

[1]Excerpted from *Administrative Management*, © Nov., 1973 by Geyer-McAllister Publications, Inc., New York.

are needed. Mention the need to reduce waste, to overcome a bottleneck, and to simplify some of the work.

Build up enthusiasm for submitting suggestions by talking about the awards people are eligible for and how they have a lot to gain with nothing to lose by participating. Say that you're available to answer questions and to help anyone in writing up suggestions.

Case-in-Point: Victor A. Dams, general supervisor with the Calgary Transit System,[2] Calgary, Canada says, "Make your people feel they're working for a human organization, not some kind of impersonal machine. This can be encouraged by acting on employees' suggestions." He adds, "Don't ignore the ideas of subordinates. They can't identify with the organization and its goals if you won't let them. Unless they do, they won't produce any more than they have to, and you'll have to spend more time closely supervising them."

Caution: When you promote suggestions, be sure you make it clear that turning in suggestions is an entirely voluntary matter—suggestions are not a requirement of the job nor are you telling people that they should be submitted. Some people will find suggestion systems more palatable when they are presented this way. Also, you avoid any arguments that may arise concerning pay for time spent developing an idea on nonworking time.

15.14 Selling an Idea: The Positive Way to Do It

A sometimes heard complaint of supervisors is that their bosses are unwilling to listen to them or that they cut them short when they propose something. Although there are autocratic people in middle management jobs today, most managers are interested in their subordinate's ideas. Supervisors should not use the excuse of a nonreceptive superior to put off trying to sell an idea. Getting your boss to listen to you and accept your idea may not always be easy, but you can improve your chances of success if you go about it in the right manner.

How-to-Do-It: Whether you're trying to sell your boss or someone else an idea, the first thing to do is look for the feature or part of it which would interest the person. It's difficult to sell anybody anything if they're not interested or cannot see anything in it for them.

Think out your idea thoroughly. This means compiling as much information as possible about it and deciding what part you will present. Try to have facts rather than opinions for support.

---

[2]Reprinted from *Supervisor's Memory Jogger,* Oct., 1970. By permission of the publisher. Bureau of Business Practice, 24 Rope Ferry Road, Waterford, Connecticut 06386. Copyright, Bureau of Business Practice, Inc.

Pick an appropriate time to do your selling. Don't burst in when the person is busy nor at the end of the day. You may decide to ask the person for a time to meet when it would be most convenient for him or her.

Be enthusiastic. You can't expect someone to accept your idea if you're only lukewarm or half-sure about it yourself. Present the benefits and the advantages. Include savings. Show that you've spent some time working on the idea, that it's not just a whim on your part.

Look for agreement and acceptance. If you have a good idea and present it well, you should get approval. Offer to take whatever steps are necessary to put the idea in practice.

15.15 Tips on Controlling Your Paperwork

One of the major stumbling blocks to being productive are the tasks you must perform that are nonproductive, such as paperwork. When you put in a lot of time on paperwork, you have less time to devote to your supervisory responsibilities. Of course, you'll never be able to eliminate all paperwork. But here are some tips on how to get around much of it:

1. Do the paperwork when it arises rather than postponing it. The papers and records won't accumulate and become a big job later.

2. Handle the paperwork on the job whenever possible instead of carrying it to your desk or office. The quicker you can handle it, the less of a burden it will seem. And you won't have to handle the paper twice.

3. Keep a minimum of records but know where you can get information if you need it. You'll avoid clutter and distraction, not to mention having to decide where to file something.

4. Don't recopy records or forms. Avoid making duplicates of anything. The less copies, the less paper to keep track of. Most copies are seldom referred to again.

16

Successful Ways for Getting the Most from Skilled and "Special" People

People are different, one from another, in their education, skills, experience, and how they feel about their work. This is especially true with people who have the potential to accomplish much. Professional people look at their work and their jobs differently than nonprofessional people, and they expect to be treated in respect to their position. Creative people also view their work and perform it in ways which are fitting to the way they think and their lifestyle.

Young workers and old workers also think about their jobs and perform their work differently compared to each other. Older workers in many cases have demonstrated a superiority over their younger peers by outperforming them. Supervisors are more successful in getting the most from their older people.

To work successfully with the minorities, the handicapped, and other "special" people, you must care about these people and be patient with them. They usually need more training than other workers in order to perform on an equal level. Once they have been trained, however, they will often be more consistent in their work. They should be given the same consideration on the job as you give others. The best way to do this is to have them work side by side with other employees.

16.1 How to Recognize People with Potential

Recognizing people who have potential and who will certainly advance in the company is usually a simple matter. Such people perform their work in a positive and enthusiastic manner. The ones who are ready and capable of taking on greater responsibilities show it by the following behavioral characteristics:

1. They display good judgment and common sense. They have the ability to see the simplest approach to a problem rather than the more complicated.
2. They communicate well. They get unspoken messages quickly and they are at home with the jargon of the various people with whom they are involved.
3. They are optimistic. They believe the future will be better than the present, and that confidence in themselves leads to success.
4. They readily accept change. They are concerned only with what is to be changed and how it is to be accomplished.
5. They are goal oriented. They understand that achieving objectives is what pays off.

Technical knowledge and stamina are desirable but not vital for most supervisory jobs. However, you should hesitate to promote someone who doesn't have most if not all of the above characteristics.

16.2 Ways to Determine Where People Will Do Their Best

If you put a person on a job for which the person is not suited, you do not make the most of the person's skills nor do you enable the person to get satisfaction from the work. Even worse, if you misfit a person to a job you may disrupt the department organization and cause poor morale as well as low productivity. Fortunately, effective supervisors know how to match people with jobs and work situations which will turn out best for both the individuals and the company.

You can give employees psychological tests to help you discover what type of work best suits their preferences and interests. But, you must recognize that tests merely indicate the niches employees should occupy. Furthermore, employees like to feel they have some choice in the matter. Supervisors should draw on human inclinations for insight to proper placement of their people.

People do not like to fail on the job. Thus, they will prefer jobs which they feel they can handle and at which they will be a success. They do not want to be embarrassed, which they would be by failure. And they like to feel they are contributing in turning out the company's product or providing its service. If you are sensitive to people's feelings about their work, and fair to them without bias or prejudice, you will have no trouble in finding the best spots for them in the company.

An expert's comment: People who dress unusually and men who wear beards or long hair may be trying to tell you they want to be recognized as individuals but feel that they aren't. More serious symptoms accompanying the feelings are lack of commitment, no drive or enthusiasm, and general apathy along with inefficiency. Dr. Norman B. Sigband,[1] professor of marketing and business communication, University of Southern California, Los Angeles, says the solution is relatively simple: effective internal communication by management in defining goals, directions, and values with the worker. This way the person becomes somebody.

16.3 Three Keys to Capitalize on People's Strengths

Supervisors who have strong people to work with should take on the responsibility of inducing them to grow on the job, accept challenging work, and strive to utilize their abilities to the maximum. Exceptional talents should not be wasted anymore than a company would waste its expensive raw material or its complex equipment. The keys to effective capitalizing on human strengths lie in the way you treat and work with people. Here are three approaches you should take:

1. Look for and expect the best from people. Supervising with high expectations gives strong people the incentive and drive which they need to see purpose and get direction for doing good work.

2. Build on and promote people's strong points. Ignore and play down their weaknesses. Publicize accomplishments and report progress. Relate achievements to company objectives.

3. Classify strengths and abilities of individuals. Then design and make work assignments accordingly, measuring the individuals by the progress they make. Increase responsibilities as you see that capabilities to handle them are attained.

---

[1]From *Industry Week*, Aug. 28, 1972.

16.4 How to Maximize the Output of Highly Potential People

One of the attributes of successful leaders is a sensitivity to the potential of their people. The skill enables them to help individuals discover and attain their full potentials and to guide individuals to levels of accomplishment which they might not otherwise reach. You can maximize the output and productivity of your highly potential people by dedicating yourself to such efforts.

How-to-Do-It: Study a person's background, interests, and motivations. Line these up with the job positions and opportunities in the company where the person can apply himself or herself and advance to the level where the person's potentials will be reached. Then, show your interest in the person's future by discussing with him or her this long range program as you see it. Provide stimulation and encouragement to persuade the person to pursue this course.

If you can inject some flexibility in your plan and provide adequate time for the person's development, you are more likely to get understanding and acceptance. You should also point out the logic of your proposal. This will help motivate the person to overcome roadblocks which occasionally may appear along the way.

Case-in-Point: An industrial plant manager told me how he brought along one of his people to a high position in the company. "I recognized that Bob Rollins had managerial capabilities the first day I talked to him. But I also saw that I would have to do a real selling job to convince him of it. Thereafter, I took steps to see that he had opportunities to learn all the operations, and I encouraged him to accept temporary supervisor jobs whenever possible. Rollins consistently did a good job as I was convinced he would. He continued to move up in the organization and recently accepted the position of Production Manager."

16.5 Successful Placing and Use of Professional People

Professional people are different from other employees in that they feel they are professionals and resent any treatment that suggests they are thought of as ordinary workers. Therefore, the key to getting along with them is to treat them as special people.

Professional employees want to be recognized as members of a profession. They are often more career-oriented than company-oriented and dislike regimentation. If professional people work for you, remember that their job titles are important to them and they are jealous of their own ideas and accomplishments.

Scientists and people doing research work develop information. They are creative and usually have quite a bit of education. They get the advanced degrees at the universities and their viewpoint is more theoretical than most people's. Engineers use and apply the information which the scientists develop. Although they may also be creative, they usually don't have the advanced degrees. They are more practical and less theoretical than scientists.

Professional people expect better working conditions than rank-and-file people. They also want fewer personal restrictions. You may not be able to go along with all such desires, but try to do so if you can. They will appreciate it. If you can assign creative work and work that is challenging or complex, you give professional people the chance to show their worth. They like work that is investigative in nature and not routine or repetitive. Be sure to give them recognition for what they are and what they accomplish if you want to get the most from them.

Case-in-Point: Technical ideas conceived by Research and Development employees at the Goodyear Tire and Rubber Company,[2] Akron, Ohio, are evaluated by a recently instituted Genesis Program. Joe Gingo, director of Projects and Materials Coordination, and chairman of the R & D Genesis Program explains, "The program is designed to create a route through which technical people can originate ideas for new products and processes not necessarily in their line of work. The keynote to the program is recognition—to let the idea generator's colleagues know that he or she went above and beyond the call of duty." Employees who submit ideas are eligible for recognition and rewards not only under the Genesis Program, but they may also receive recognition and cash under the company's suggestion award program, providing the ideas meet the criteria of the suggestion award program committee.

16.6 Sure-Fire Ways to Keep Exceptional People Enthused

Exceptional people, in addition to being skilled, creative, quick, and having other attributes not found in average people, are often impatient. They may lose interest in their work much faster than other employees. You must be aware of such tendencies and be alert to combat them.

Varying a person's job assignment and rotating the work keeps a job from becoming dull. It also promotes creativity in that the person is exposed to different situations and runs into more problems where the individual's ingenuity and skill may come into play.

Always listen to the suggestions of exceptional people, and avoid being critical in judging their ideas. At times it may pay to let persons further investigate a suggested idea even though it may not seem practical or plausible at the time. You will keep them interested in the work and you will not overlook any bets in searching out solutions to difficult problems.

---

[2]From *The Innovator,* Vol. 1, No. 3, March, 1979.

Above all, avoid misusing the talents of exceptional people. Although you must give them some routine work along with other assignments, try to limit servile jobs as much as possible. Two major reasons for talented people leaving jobs are: their company fails to give them challenging work, and too little is expected of them in the way of performance.

16.7 Tips on Managing Creative People

People who are very creative present problems for supervisors sometimes because they handle their work differently than people who are not creative. Recognizing their traits and characteristics is essential to understanding and getting along with them. Here are some tips on how they think and what you can expect from them:

1. Creative people want and expect personal freedom. They are independent in their thoughts and judgments; they should be given latitude to pursue and develop new ideas. Although they desire challenge and responsibility, they prefer these matters to be in areas of their special interest.

2. They tend to work on their own ideas, not those of others. Their concentration in this respect may extend to intolerance with disagreement. They may become impatient when they are not understood. They prefer to avoid group activities and thus do not do a good job of cooperating with others.

3. The creative urge which they possess is stimulated by challenge and inhibited by routine. They thrive on intricate problems that only their intelligence and talents can handle. Creative people are very competent and take pride in their accomplishments.

4. Although creative people expect and appreciate recognition for work well done, they are prone to judge what you think of them by the nature of the next assignment you give them. You must try to make it appropriate for their capabilities, the more difficult the better.

5. Creative people lose track of time. They may work for long stretches without rest or relief, and then require a longer than average break time to recover. You will find that their productivity over the long run is better than that of people who don't possess their creativity.

6. Creative people with scientific training often are perfectionists. Their preoccupation with checking and double-checking often makes it difficult for them to meet deadlines.

16.8 How to Handle the Person Who Prefers to Work Alone

It is important for you to know if an employee is most suitably a "group" worker or a "lone" worker. Such knowledge helps you in motivating the person, making the best work assignments for him or her, and in assessing the capability of your department.

Don't think of lone workers as being people who prefer to be physically separated from other people. Although some people are of this nature, most loners simply prefer not to interact with others or be team members. They want to work *in* groups rather than *with* groups. They prefer to be inconspicuous on the job.

Supervisors should accede to such people's desires as much as company regulations and work situations will allow in order to have such people like their work and be productive. Promotional moves as well as transfers to different environments should be carefully thought out and discussed before being implemented. A loner may leave the company rather than make a change, even though the change may appear to be to his or her best interest.

16.9 Young Employees: Understanding and Motivating Them

Today's supervisors are finding it more and more difficult to motivate their people. The problem is particularly acute with young employees. But, it is a mistake to believe that young people do not want to work—they want to work provided they have the proper incentive—the incentive isn't always financial. Several social and economic changes which have taken place in recent years explain why young people now want more out of a job than just the pay.

Young people today are better educated than their parents. Their aspiration levels are also higher. They become bored more rapidly with routine work; thus, they shun such work for that which is different and challenging. Most young people have not experienced a lack of jobs available to them except for the minorities; they don't know the hardship of being without work. So they are more demanding of the type of job they will accept.

The increasing power of unions has made members more militant. Job security is not a motivator to union members. They do not hesitate to express their grievances because they have no fear of retribution. Supervisors must listen to and do something about the complaints of young employees if they expect them to be productive.

As the affluence of today's society increases, the needs of workers have become more difficult to satisfy. With the basic needs of food, shelter, and clothing satisfied, the higher level needs become the main motivators. But these needs are more difficult to satisfy under today's style of management unless supervisors allow employees to participate in making decisions.

16.10 Proven Advantages to Employing Older Workers

The number of retired and older people who seek jobs has been increasing as the elderly population of the country steadily increases. More and more businesses are using older workers with great success. Here are seven proven advantages to employing them and why supervisors like to have them in their departments:

1. They are usually more reliable and steady workers, particularly in jobs where no advancement is possible.
2. They have a high standard of ethics and feel a strong responsibility to do a good job.
3. They are almost always on time and are absent less than other workers.
4. They are exceptionally cooperative. They are not impatient for promotion.
5. They set an excellent example for others and exert a stabilizing influence on younger workers.
6. They are more receptive to odd jobs and will readily substitute for other people. They are invaluable for fill-in work and sometimes may agree to work partial days.
7. They are not usually concerned about pay rates nor varying wages since in most cases they have other income.

16.11 Hostility: Pitfall to Young Supervisor/Old Worker Relations

Young supervisors sometimes encounter hostility from workers who are older than themselves. Since you can contend with hostility better if you know the reasons for it, here is some insight and advice on handling this problem.

The most common reason why an older person may be hostile to a younger supervisor is fear. The person may be afraid that he or she may be looked down upon, discriminated against, even lose the job. The degree of fear depends on the amount of uncertainty which exists within a particular work situation.

Jealousy is another reason why older persons may be hostile to their younger supervisors. Older workers may wish they were supervisors or held positions which carried higher status and received more pay. The older workers may resent their younger supervisors even though the younger persons had nothing to do with their plight.

Hostility is usually shown by antagonism or withdrawal. Then again, lack of motivation and job satisfaction as well as lack of self-confidence may be behind hostile actions. The best way to contend with hostility is to take the person aside and talk to him or her about it. Explain that you sense that the person is uneasy in your presence and that you would like to be on better terms with him or her. Try to learn the reason for the hostility so that you can refute it. Assure a hostile person that you are fair and treat all people equally. Then, be sure that you do so.

16.12 How to Criticize a Top Performer

Most supervisors have a person in their department on whom they depend more than any others. You probably do, too. The person may have many years of experience, be the most efficient one on the staff, and know all the ins and outs of how your department functions. But, since nobody is perfect, the person will occasionally make mistakes. Although you can ignore a minor miscue, perhaps joke about it, you should not pass off lightly a big or serious mistake. You must let the person know that you're aware of it and offer advice on how to correct the mistake as well as avoid a repetition.

Since top performers take pride in their work, the person will probably readily accept your advice. Good workers, those who also have the right attitude, generally regret their lapses and express their regrets. Some top performers, however, may resent your concern and not willingly accept your criticism.

If you must get tough with a top performer, do it. You really have no choice in the matter unless you are willing to give up control and the responsibilities of your job. If the person doesn't accept your criticism or reacts negatively to your comments, maintain your position. The poor performance will probably not reoccur after the person gets back on the job, thinks a bit, and understands why you had to act as you did.

16.13 Positive Ways of Working with Minorities

Supervisors should not consider minorities as problem employees but as people who may require attention to assure that bias and prejudice are not factors in how they are treated. Most of these people are eager and able to prove how good a job they can do. All they need is a fair chance. Some of them may require a little extra training because of lack of experience.

Because of limited education as well as lower-than-average cultural advances, many minorities are ignorant of what is expected of them on the job. They may not be aware of the accepted procedures nor of how to conduct themselves in certain situations. They hope you will consider these matters and make allowances for them. Minorities can be just as good workers as other employees. You should not expect them to be exceptional in order to gain your acceptance. Nor should you condemn their group on the basis of poor performance of one or more of their members. Majority workers also fail occasionally.

Don't segregate minorities on your work teams. Put them on jobs where they can be most effective and where they'll do the best job. Minorities don't want preferential treatment. They may be embarrassed if you give them very easy work. Doing that might also bring on a discipline problem as well as result in your being accused of showing favoritism. Expect and insist upon the same standards of performance from minorities that you do from other employees.

Case-in-Point: When talking about hiring a Negro for a job, Whitney M. Young, Jr.,[3] executive secretary of the National Urban League, said, "A Negro will usually value the job more than his white counterpart because his opportunities are fewer. Where the white fellow may be taking an ordinary job as a stop-gap until he can find something better, this may be the best job the Negro ever dreamed he could land." This attitude of the Negro toward the job means more loyalty to the company and more dedication to succeed. Records of companies who have placed Negroes in other than hand-labor jobs are endless with testimonials to this fact.

16.14 Guidelines to Avoiding Charges of Discrimination

It is accepted that business and industry should not discriminate against people because of their color, race, religion, sex, or anything else that does not pertain to the job. Reverse discrimination that favors a minority person over a more able majority person is equally wrong. Supervisors need to take every precaution to avoid charges of discrimination in the treatment of their people.

But, under no circumstances should a supervisor put up with incompetence or rule breaking to avoid discrimination charges. The best way to help people who perform unsatisfactorily is to counsel them and give them a chance to meet acceptable standards. No one benefits if standards are lowered to make it easy to get along with poor performers. Here are some procedures to follow which will help you avoid charges of discrimination as you carry out the responsibilities of your job:

1. Set performance standards for people. Explain the rules and what you expect from people on the job.
2. Warn people when they do below average work. If they cannot improve, try to find jobs for them which they can handle.
3. Offer a second chance after a poor performance. But do not be more lenient with minority persons than with majority persons.

---

[3]From *What Every Supervisor Should Know* by Lester R. Bittel. Copyright © 1974, McGraw-Hill. Used with permission of McGraw-Hill Book Company

4. Tie salary increases to performance. Treat everyone alike in this respect.

5. Keep records of performance on each person. Also document discussions you have with people about their performance.

6. Discuss serious nonperformance which could result in termination with the Personnel Department. Make sure your records are complete.

Most people are unhappy in jobs they cannot handle. They will feel better on different jobs, and the people who work with them will also benefit from a change. Although you may risk a charge of discrimination now and then, you must rotate assignments and move people into work where they will do their best. You are responsible for keeping up the efficiency of the people who work for you.

16.15 Effective Techniques for Working with the Handicapped

Supervising handicapped people is really not much different from supervising normal people, providing they are properly trained. Many companies feel that the handicapped people in their employ are better in several ways than normal employees. Supervisors get greater respect, much better attendance, and a low rate of turnover from them. Furthermore, once you train them to do a job a certain way, they won't make variations—they'll do the job the same every time. The techniques for working successfully with handicapped people are simple:

1. Show that you care about them. Don't begrudge the extra time required to train them. Adjust jobs to their abilities and arrange the people accordingly.

2. Don't ever lose your temper. Patience is very important. Learn what provides the strongest incentive to good performance and try to provide that.

3. Treat handicapped people with the same consideration you give normal employees. Emphasize cooperation and team effort. Have them work side by side on the same jobs with normal labor.

Case-in-Point: Eighty percent of the employees at Markade, Inc., Knoxville, Tenn.[4] are mentally or physically handicapped. Most of them are mentally retarded; many were trained at Knoxville's Sunshine Sheltered Workshop. "I have more problems from the normal people on my shift than from the handicapped," says second shift supervisor Bob Simmons. "You can do a profile of work quality of five normal employees. If the handicapped employees are trained right, their work will be better nine times out of ten."

---

[4]From *Supervision Magazine,* Nov., 1978.

16.16 How to Help the Mentally Slow Person

It is up to the supervisor to make the most of a mentally slow person on the job. You cannot afford to neglect this person for both his or her benefit and the company's. People who are mentally slow often suffer from their own frustrations. They are frequently hurt because fellow-workers abuse them. You can help a handicapped person overcome these problems and make the most of his or her abilities.

Try to build up the person's ego by encouraging and praising good work. Practice patience—don't rush the person with new or strange work. Get the person's confidence so that when something isn't understood, the person will tell you.

Always give orders in slow and simple words, repeating if you sense you are not getting through. Explain in great detail. Then ask if the person understands what you want done and how it should be done. Above all, never imply or suggest that the person is slow to understand or is inferior in any way to other workers. Recognize that you may have to spend more time with the person than with your other people. The person will appreciate your help. Your company will also benefit from your efforts.

17

Working Out Answers to Your Problem People

Supervisors' work would be much easier if they didn't have to contend with problem people on the job. However, supervisors would find their work less interesting and lacking in challenge if they didn't have to make use of their skills in solving human relations problems.

Understanding human nature, being perceptive, and knowing what makes people tick are invaluable in coming up with answers to your problem people. Of equal value, if not more, is being able to reason with people and persuade them to change their behavior because this is the skill you need to work out personality conflicts, referee arguments, handle complaints, and cut down bickering. The problem people who talk too much, the know-it-alls, and the prima donnas may appear minor in comparison to other people problems, but they also must be solved if you are to have a productive, enthusiastic, and efficient work force.

Serious problems facing many supervisors today are those having to do with people's weaknesses. Typical of such problems are absenteeism, alcoholism, and drug abuse. However, companies are successfully dealing with such problem people in many cases by training their supervisors in how to handle them.

17.1 How to Work Out Personality Conflicts

When you have a personality conflict between two of your people you have a serious problem to contend with. If permitted to continue it may cause hard feelings, affect productivity, and hurt team effort. You must take steps to improve the compatibility of the individuals and do it quickly.

Although a transfer of either person to another job would probably handle the matter, this move is not always possible or desirable. One or both of the individuals may be highly skilled and not easily replaced. Then, too, no other job may be open in the company. The best way to solve a personality conflict problem is to work out the disagreement with the persons involved.

Bring the two individuals together to discuss the situation. Point out the disorder they are causing by their failure to get along with each other, and how the failure is affecting other people and the company. Say that you want to help them settle their differences.

Tell each person what he or she means to the company and that you do not want to lose either one. Show them how their disagreement has affected their work, and as a result you cannot permit the present conflict to continue. Give them the opportunity to have their say but do not take sides with either person. If the two do not seem to be able to work out a peaceful answer, suggest compromises. Push for commitments from both on how they intend to act in the future, and end your meeting on as friendly a basis as possible.

If you learned that one of the individuals was mainly at fault, approach this person later. Talk to the person privately to save his or her face. Discuss the fault and ask again for a promise to change.

If better relations don't materialize from your talks with both persons, discuss the situation with your superior. You may have to insist that one or both persons must change or leave the company. More people lose their jobs today because of their inability to get along with other people than because of their inability to do the work.

17.2 How to Referee an Argument About the Job

No place of business where work is performed always runs smoothly. Inevitably, two or more of your people will have a disagreement either about who is to do a job or how it is to be done. Since you as supervisor are responsible to see that the work gets done, the dispute becomes your concern. Here are the steps to take when you must act as a referee:

1. Don't call a halt to the discussion or dismiss the problem. This doesn't reach the issue or solve it.

2. Keep your cool as you listen to both sides of the story. Don't become emotional or let the problem get out of proportion to its importance.

3. Check the stories and make sure you have all the facts. Keep company rules in mind and confirm company objectives.

4. Try to be fair to everyone concerned. Put aside bias and prejudice, personal likes and dislikes.

5. Make a decision. You are responsible for getting to the bottom of arguments which affect your department and its efficiency. Carry out that responsibility to the best of your ability.

There will be times when you must act as referee on matters other than the job but still related to your department functions. In most cases, you will find that the steps to follow given above will work equally well in those cases.

17.3 How to Tell People Their Work Is Unsatisfactory

Nobody likes to tell someone that their work is unsatisfactory, yet supervisors periodically must do this. The reason why you must criticize people about their unsatisfactory performance on the job is to get better work from them. To get that, you must tell them specifically what is wrong and what you expect of them. Your manner, how you control yourself, and how you treat people determines how your words are received as well as how quickly and completely people make a change for the better.

Case-in-Point: Fred Schmidt, supervisor in a machine shop in Akron, Ohio, told me, "I don't put up with sloppy work in the shop. I feel I'm much better off telling machinists what I really think than what I think they want to hear, and I believe people respect me for it. In fact, a fellow once told me I was very tactful after I let him know what I thought about the waste he created."

If an employee is not doing what is required or expected, the person should be talked to privately about the matter. However, before you talk to a person about failing on the job, plan what you intend to say and what you're going to ask of the person. Realize that the person may not expect this criticism and that the occasion may be a traumatic one.

Be sure you have the facts about the performance of the individual. Have specific cases and situations to talk about so that you don't generalize, such as saying, "Your reports are always late," or "You make too many errors." Go over the performance and history of the person's deeds, making notes which you can refer to during your conversation. Never accept hearsay or rumors about the person's performance. Dig out and document facts.

To lighten the blow to a person's ego from your criticism you can accept part of the blame for unsatisfactory work. You might say, for example, that you perhaps didn't completely explain what was expected of the person or that you didn't make yourself clear. Another way to share responsibility is by making statements that contain the word *we,* such as *we* take pride in our work in the department, or *we* seldom if ever get behind in our schedule.

When you talk with people about poor work performance you must, of course, listen to their side of the story. If you don't, you won't be able to help them. Most people will defend their actions and want to explain. When they do, you will usually learn how to help them.

Never ridicule a person or be sarcastic about his or her efforts. When you do this you are finding fault with the person rather than the work. Better to tell the person what's bad about the work. Explain exactly what's needed and follow up later to make sure you are getting what you asked for.

17.4 Tips on Dealing with Rule-Breakers

When one of your people breaks a company rule you must take action. Overlooking the offense and saying nothing about it is equivalent to condoning it. You must do something because the incident can affect the person's future behavior, your department's morale, and even your company's relations with the union, if you have one. Here are some tips on dealing with rule-breakers.

1. Know the company rules, and see that your people also know them. You can't maintain discipline without knowing what is permissible and what is not.

2. Get all the facts when you believe someone has broken a rule. Try to establish exactly what was done or what happened.

3. Give the person who is guilty an opportunity to explain his or her actions. Don't expect the person to volunteer an explanation—take the initiative and ask for it.

4. Decide on the most appropriate disciplinary action. Keep in mind what you hope to achieve—a change in the person's behavior, not punishment or revenge.

5. Administer the discipline, telling the person why you are doing so. Never give a person a penalty without explaining it.

17.5 Sure-Fire Ways to Overcome Slowness on the Job

Slowness of one or more of their people is a common problem for supervisors of work crews. Too many people are slow to get to work, slow to get started, slow to understand orders, and slow to get the job done. If you want to keep up the productivity of your department, you've go to solve such slowness problems.

One of the several ways you can go about this is to simply talk to the slow person about it. Of course, you must be careful of what you say. Question the person in a soft-spoken manner or you may have an angry employee on your hands instead of a cooperative one. Point out that you feel the person can be more prompt and efficient, and that you would appreciate the effort to do so.

Often a person is slow because he or she has no interest in the job and is simply bored. With this person you must talk about the work in detail. More variety or responsibility may be an answer—can you enrich the job? Or perhaps the person should have a different job. If a change would likely improve matters, go ahead with the move with the understanding that if the person doesn't improve his or her performance, the former job will be the permanent one.

Sometimes a person is slow on the job because of fear that speed will result in errors. You can solve this problem by giving the person work where the chances of errors being made are few. Both the person and you will be glad of the change.

If you learn that one of your people has always been slow regardless of the job assigned, you may as well give up trying to change him or her. Your best bet is to find work for the person where speed is not a factor. Look for a job where precision, care, or perseverance are required of the worker.

17.6 How to Handle Slowdowns

A slowdown of the work force can be very costly to a company. Not only does the work not get out and jobs are not finished, but also the need for overtime work is created. People working extra hours are paid additional money and are usually more inefficient besides.

You must notice when people are making a job last too long, when their rest and coffee breaks take too much time, and when they're doing more talking than working. If you suspect that one or more of your people are deliberately slowing down, act immediately. Handle slowdowns in one or more of the following ways:

1. Break up bull sessions promptly by joining the group, asking if they have a problem and if there is anything you can do to help. Another way to

break up a session is to give one of the people a job, saying that you need it done right away.

2. Point out to inactive workers that a job is urgent, that the department is behind schedule, or that the order must be gotten out today. Express your concern over progress of a job.

3. Mention to a person the time standard for a job. Say you know the person is capable of meeting it.

4. Increase your coverage of a trouble area. Make your presence felt. Do what you can to assure availability of materials, tools, and supplies so that there can be no excuses given relating to those items.

5. Warn guilty persons that disciplinary action will be taken if the inefficiency continues. Take that action if your warning isn't heeded.

17.7 Tips on Effective Handling of Complainers

You're bound to find someone who has a gripe in most work groups. All workers are not happy with their jobs or get satisfaction from their work. Unfortunately, the person who frequently complains can be a problem for you because he or she is detrimental to the morale of the entire group. You cannot afford to let such a situation continue. Here's some tips on how to effectively handle complainers.

Learn all you can about a complainer in order to understand his or her attitude. What work did the person do before joining the group? Is the person lazy? A poor performer? Does the person suffer from a psychological or physical handicap? Look into the person's needs since they evidently are not being satisfied. Does the person feel superior to the job or the people he or she is working with? Perhaps there is a feeling that the work is demeaning or degrading. What specifically does the person complain about?

Talk to the person. Say that you noticed that he or she is unhappy. Ask if there is something you can do to help. Explain that you want people to get satisfaction from their work and that you don't want the morale of other people to suffer if one person isn't satisfied.

If there is something you can do to please the complainer, get busy at it. But, if ending the complaining is a matter of changing an opinion or viewpoint, mention this. In either case, try to get a promise for no more complaining on the job.

17.8 Eight Ways to Attack Absenteeism

Absenteeism costs business and industry in many ways. The manhours not put into the work result in low productivity and lost profits, the replacement labor is inefficient, and the overtime costs are excessive. Solving the problem of absenteeism of their people requires a strong effort on the part of supervisors. Here are eight ways that you can join other successful supervisors in attacking it:

1. Know your people and show an interest in their personal lives. Encourage discussions of problems that affect attendance.

2. Insist on prior requests to be absent for personal reasons rather than explanations after the fact. Ask for real explanations rather than dubious excuses.

3. Have personal discussions with the people who cause most of your absentee problems. See if someone in the Personnel or Medical Departments can help.

4. Insist on prompt notification *always* when someone must be absent unexpectedly. Don't treat such incidents lightly.

5. Avoid the serious effects of unexpected absences by having standard procedures to follow when they occur. Designate replacements and who is to do someone else's work.

6. Keep good records of absenteeism. Examine them for Monday and day-after-holiday occurrences to alert you to problem people.

7. Have a group meeting to discuss it if absenteeism becomes serious. Point out the costs to the department and the company to emphasize its seriousness.

8. Set up a progressive discipline system for offenders. Carry out its terms religiously all the way to dismissals, if necessary.

Case-in-Point: "The solution to chronic absenteeism or tardiness can be a simple matter of keeping accurate records or a properly given suggestion," according to Andrew Filicky,[1] supervisor in the anodizing and painting department of General Extrusions, Inc., Youngstown, Ohio. Producing his attendance record, Filicky told an habitual offender, "This shows a consistent pattern. Are you deliberately avoiding the cleanup detail? If I let you get away with it, pretty soon I won't have anyone left on cleanup."

"The record did it," says Filicky. "He hasn't been off since."

17.9 Company Checkup: An Effective Absence Deterrent

Recent surveys in business and industry have revealed that when employees take sick days by single day absences, actual sickness is the cause only

---

[1]Reprinted from *Supervisor's Memory Jogger,* July, 1973. By permission of the publisher. Bureau of Business Practice, 24 Rope Ferry Road, Waterford, Connecticut 06386. Copyright, Bureau of Business Practice, Inc.

50 to 60 percent of the time. Employees go shopping, visit relatives, or take care of personal business the remainder of the time.

Among the various ways that employers use to fight such absenteeism, company checkup is rated by personnel experts as the most effective of them all. Simply telephoning the absentee to ask how he or she is feeling and whether he or she plans to come to work the next day can have a powerful effect. And it's embarrassing and incriminating if the person isn't home to receive the phone call.

Where chronic absentees are involved, some companies send the company nurse to the home. Merely knowing that this can happen is enough to make most people think twice before taking that desired day off.

17.10 How to Handle the Know-It-All Person

In most work forces you'll find at least one person who will participate in every argument and has an answer to every problem. The person may be likable as well as competent but still is disruptive because of his or her distrubing interference, egotistical attitude, and superior manner. Your effectiveness in handling your people depends in part on what you do about the know-it-all. Here are some tips on how to handle this type of person.

You must be firm with know-it-alls. They generally try to get away with as much as possible. Let them know where they stand, making sure you are clear. Plug up any loopholes they might find to twist your instructions and orders.

Avoid disagreements and arguments. Know-it-alls are usually clever, enjoy showing off, and even delight in confusing an issue. Such behavior can make your supervising job difficult. Show know-it-alls that you know what you're talking about and they'll usually respect you.

Give them more responsibility. It will tend to make them settle down, especially if you let them know you're sure they can handle it and you are counting on them. Expect more of them in quality and quantity of work but don't make an issue of it if they don't come through—simply let them know that you noticed their failure.

Let know-it-alls try new ideas and procedures, and let them make mistakes. Give them credit if something new is successful, but also explain when something fails. A failure may cause them to realize that they're not always right—they'll be less ready to question your decisions in the future.

17.11 Effective Ways to Cut Down Bickering

Many team efforts have failed to pay off because of one or more argumentive, sarcastic, and backbiting employees who just can't seem to get along with other people. Too often, supervisors may tolerate such behavior with the result that the efficiency of the group is not what it could be. Some supervisors, fortunately, have found ways to handle the problem.

You can, for example, not permit extensive conversations on superheated subjects such as religion and politics, even to the extent that they are banned entirely. For better compatibility, you can pair up people who have similar interests and viewpoints.

Another approach to cutting down bickering among your people is to take aside an offender and talk to him or her about the problem. Surprisingly, the person may not have realized the aggravation that he or she was causing. It's up to you to lay the groundwork for the future by being firm in making the point that such behavior won't be permitted.

Bickering among people or between individuals sometimes occurs because the persons aren't speaking the same language. This happens because of differences in age, sex, racial, and cultural levels. You can watch for such communication roadblocks and do your best to translate and straighten out word meanings. Learn to listen carefully to your people and help them understand one another.

17.12 How to Control the Person Who Talks Too Much

Similar to the know-it-all, the overly talkative person is often a problem in group discussions or meetings. Because the person dominates the discussion, other people experience difficulty joining in. Although you may at times tolerate such a situation if the person is contributing greatly to the topic being discussed, if he or she is simply showing off or exaggerating to appear important, you should take action.

One way is to ignore the person, hoping that he or she will get the message that you prefer to hear from the other members of the group. Another is to challenge the person, forcing him or her to justify a statement or idea, particularly if it is farfetched.

You may decide that the best course to follow is to talk to the individual after the meeting. Tell the person that you recognize that he or she is far ahead of the others in thinking and reasoning. Ask the person to withhold comments in future meetings until all of the others have had a chance to contribute.

Caution: Recognize that an overly talkative person can keep a discussion active and moving. If other people in a meeting are reticent and reluctant to speak up, the talkative person may be the catalyst to draw them out. Thus, you may not wish to suppress this individual completely. Consider the hostess who, when making out her guest list, says, "I'll be sure to invite her because she's a good 'mixer.'"

17.13 Pitfalls to Putting Up with the Prima Donna

A supervisor sometimes runs into a temperamental worker, one who goes about jobs in an unusual manner or who on occasion displays extreme behavior. The supervisor might be inclined to overlook or not react adversely to it, yet sight should not be lost to the pitfalls of accepting it. Here are three such pitfalls you should be aware of:

1. A supervisor's favored treatment of a prima donna suggests the wrong performance criteria for doing a good job. Instead of promoting the fact that outstanding work is most important, what is indicated is that the person who puts on the best performance is most accepted.

2. By overlooking the temperamental individual, the supervisor wastes a possible good performer or prevents the person's replacement by a person more steady and productive.

3. Special treatment of the prima donna by the supervisor arouses resentment in other people. This can result in a letdown on the job as well as a loss of respect for the supervisor.

Temperament on the job may not be a problem if it is backed up by exceptional performance. But, as the person's supervisor, you must be sure that you are not letting the prima donna get by on only nerve.

17.14 How to Contend with Extreme Emotion

Contending successfully with extreme emotion on the job requires that you be very tactful and discreet. Emotion is particularly difficult to handle when it interferes with the normal routine of getting the job done. Experts in the field of human relations generally agree on the best way to handle it. Here's what you should do:

1. Don't take emotional outbursts as personal attacks. The person displaying the extreme emotion is usually venting his or her feeling to anyone who will listen. If you take the words or action personally, you will not be able to do a good job of handling it because your own emotions will be strained.

2. Don't try to stop the emotional flow—let the person work it out and get rid of it. The person will feel better much sooner than if you interfere.

3. If you are expected to respond, agree with the person's expressed reason for the emotion. Say that you would probably feel and act similarly if you were in the same situation.

4. Don't attempt to reason or discuss the work with the person; say that you will return later when the person feels better.

5. Return to the person when he or she has unwound. The person will probably be very considerate because of your previous tact. However, don't bring up the incident. If the person wishes to discuss it, he or she will bring it up.

17.15 What to Do About Alcoholism

Many companies today have a program for dealing with alcoholism of their employees, and some organizations have instructed their supervisors on procedures to follow in working with their people on this problem. The immediate supervisor is the key to the success of any program of this type. You must act promptly when an employee's job performance drops off. If the cause is alcoholism, the situation can only get worse.

Companies which have employee assistance programs want their supervisors to encourage people who are failing on the job without clear cause to discuss the matter with appropriate personnel. The program consists of diagnosis, counseling, and treatment by professionals. Usually the alcoholic must first be talked to personally by his or her supervisor. A good start is to say, "I've noticed that something is affecting the way you handle your job. I think I know what the problem is, but I can't help you until you *tell* me about it." If the person is honest with you, all to the good. All too often, however, the person will claim ability to handle alcohol and to stop drinking anytime if it is necessary. Whether or not the person admits to the problem of drinking, you must tell the person that the company will not continue to accept the particular failures in job performance of which the person is guilty. You must point out that failure to do better will eventually cost the person employment with the company.

An alcoholic values his or her job and will do almost anything to protect it. The problem drinker must believe that you are serious when you say that he or she must give up drinking or suffer such consequences. If the person doesn't believe you, you will probably not get results.

Talking with and trying to help the alcoholic isn't easy. While you may feel sorry and want to be protective, covering up for the person doesn't help—you will only delay solving the problem. Encourage the person to get professional help. You cannot depend on promises made by an alcoholic. Although the person may mean well and fully intend to do better, having this disease often makes the person incapable of changing. An alcoholic may also lie as well as offer all sorts of excuses. You should see these for what they are and realize they are of no benefit.

Being patient and not losing your temper may be difficult but you won't get anywhere with lecturing, criticizing, or scolding. Helping the alcoholic requires the best you have in dedication and human relations skill, realizing that the person probably is incapable of handling the problem without your own or someone else's help.

17.16 How to Handle Drug Abusers

A supervisor faced with having a worker suspected of using drugs should be concerned and want to help the person. Whenever the job performance of someone begins to decline because of drug use you should act immediately. Similar to handling alcoholism, a big help in rehabilitation of a person on drugs is getting the person to admit to the problem. The person whose job performance has begun to be affected by drugs should be told that he or she has to decide between holding the job and continuing on drugs.

You must be practical and levelheaded about drugs to not alienate a person who is inclined to use them. Encourage the person to discuss the problem and try to present the arguments against drugs, but be careful in how you do it. Scare techniques usually are ineffective because the person most likely has firsthand knowledge which can contradict them.

As a supervisor you can demonstrate that people can enjoy life and have fun without resorting to the use of drugs. The person who is enthusiastic and gets satisfaction from his or her work shows the world that happiness and enjoyment can be realized without taking drugs.

The problem of drug abuse cannot be solved easily, but success is possible if several elements of a withdrawal program are adopted. Most important, the drug user must be determined to overcome his or her dependence on them. Professional help, both medical and psychiatric, is usually needed. The drug user must be persuaded to get it.

18

Tried-and-Proven
Ways to Handle
Safety and Health

Responsibility for the safety and health of workers is one of the most, if not the most, important of all the responsibilities of supervisors. Many people on the job resist safety, requiring that supervisors constantly promote it and insist that safety rules be followed. Supervisors who can get their people to share the responsibility for safety are going to have better safety records in their departments.

There are many ways by which accidents can be prevented. But, in general, you must search out unsafe conditions and unsafe acts of your people—then take steps to eliminate them. By observing people on the job and making accident investigations, you can learn how accidents happen and what you must do to prevent them.

Federal laws require that companies protect and maintain the health of their employees. The task is not an easy one, especially when people are exposed to toxic materials and some are reluctant to wear protective clothing or use protective equipment. Companies are doing the job by process changes, material substitutions, isolation, ventilation, providing personal protection, and maintaining sanitation.

18.1 Effective Methods of Promoting Safety

The safety of employees in business and industry places a tremendous responsibility on supervisors. It also presents a challenge for supervisors to show initiative in the prevention of accidents.

Safety can never be taken for granted. No organization attains a good safety record through luck or chance. Behind every good safety record that a company achieves you will find much planning and a great deal of hard work.

You promote and communicate safety by creating an awareness of it in the minds of your people. You accomplish this by setting up a safety program and carrying it out conscientiously and thoroughly.

You and other supervisors play key roles in your organization's safety program. Aside from the obvious demand of knowing the company's safety rules and setting a good example for your people, you must actively participate by instructing your people in safe work methods. You should also encourage workers to discuss accident prevention through anticipating unusual risks in the work areas and following up by providing safety equipment. When you see a hazard you must immediately do something about it. You must also investigate, analyze, and report every accident.

No job is so important or so urgent that time cannot be taken to do it in a safe manner. This means that you must always see that your people are performing their work safely and that they are not taking shortcuts that could lead to an accident or injury. Continuous training in safety is a requisite of an effective safety program.

Case-in-Point: At the Russellville, Ark. plant of Morton Frozen Foods Div., I.T.T. Continental Baking Co.,[1] hoses on the plant floor were getting run over, stepped on, and, worst of all, tripped over. Glen Ray, a receiving supervisor, solved this problem with a hose reel. He put the reel and hose in a box, mounted it on wheels, and designed it with an inlet and coupling on the outside for quick hookup. Now floors are clear, hoses aren't damaged, and people aren't having tripping accidents.

18.2 Four Positive Ways to Get Your People Involved

Efficient production or service today has come to mean safe performance. You achieve it by reducing and eliminating accidents. Although there are many

---

[1]Reprinted from the November, 1977 issue of *Occupational Hazards Magazine.* Copyrighted 1977 by Penton/IPC Incorporated.

ways to do this, four ways stand out above all others from a supervisor's viewpoint. All of them relate to working with people: planning with them, training them, communicating with them, and motivating them.

Planning involves considering the work factors. You must have the correct tools for a job your people are to do because the right tools not only make the job safer, but they also make people more efficient. You should plan which people will be asked to do the work, preferring experienced people for safety reasons. However, if more than one person is required, you might assign one inexperienced person to learn the job. When planning, always discuss the work with the people who will be doing it. You will be able to point out hazards that exist as well as talk about safe work procedures.

Training your people to work safely is especially important because many accidents today involve an inexperienced employee. Begin by showing a person the main steps of the job slowly and thoroughly, going only as fast as the person learns or understands. Then, test the person by letting him or her show you how to do the job. If a mistake is made, tactfully correct the person and help him or her to do the job properly and safely.

Talking to your people daily about safety and observing them on the job enables you to learn how they do their work, if they take chances, and if they tend to be careless. By paying attention to them and what they are doing you will be able to spot a weakness or omission which could lead to an accident. When you explain safe practices, be sure that you also follow them to the letter. See that your people abide by no smoking rules and wear the safety clothing required in certain work areas.

Motivating your people to work safely is a never-ending task. An effective way of doing it is to point out to a person what an accident would mean to his or her family, doing this especially when you sense a laxness toward safety or a violation of safe procedures. Another approach is to ask a person "What would you do if ... ? inserting a specific incident which has a possibility, however slight, of occurring to a person on the job. If you can get people to think about an accident which could happen, they may go just a little bit farther in trying to do their work safely. That little bit may be all that is needed to prevent an accident.

18.3 Guidelines to Overcoming Resistance to Safety

When people on the job resist safety they do it subtly and shrewdly, not outwardly or defiantly. Thus, you may misjudge the magnitude of the problem of selling them on the importance of safety.

Some people resist safety because they associate it with work—work which doesn't give them satisfaction. They can see the effects of not following safe practices but they cannot see any reward for doing so.

Most workers like to make their own decisions on how to do a job. They feel they know best what is safe for them. Following safety rules sometimes restricts their activities and insults their intelligence, they feel. People naturally resist conformity. They do not always agree on how serious a safety problem is in their area.

Employees may turn a deaf ear to safety if their supervisors don't show interest in it or enforce the rules. Why should they be compelled to wear safety clothing if their supervisors aren't? Effective supervisors meet the challenge of their people resisting safety by continually stressing the advantages and benefits of it. You've got to do this daily if you want your people to be safety conscious.

18.4 Getting People to Share Safety Responsibility

You have the responsibility to provide safe working conditions for your people and you must insist on safe work practices on the job. To carry out these responsibilities you need to make equipment and work area inspections, train people on procedures, and make accident investigations. Yet, since safety should be everyone's business, why shouldn't you ask your people to share these safety burdens? After all, no one is in a better position to spot safety hazards and to make sure the work is done in a safe manner than each and every person on the job. Besides, you can't be in all work areas at the same time. The answer is to get people to share safety responsibility.

How-to-Do-It: Explain to your people that the company intends to meet all federal, state, and local regulations on safety. This means that safety devices will be provided and must be used, protective clothing will be provided and must be worn, and safe practices will be established and must be followed at all times. Tell them that you cannot enforce all rules by yourself, so you are going to share this responsibility with them. Say that you will see that each person is well-informed on safety so that anyone can immediately report to you conditions and practices which are not safe. Show that you are serious about safety—you're bound to get results and have a better safety record in your department.

18.5 Tips on Using a Suggestion System to Improve Safety

Don't overlook your company's suggestion system as a way to promote safety. Here are some tips on how you can use it to give a boost to your safety program:

- Give your safety program lots of publicity. Put up posters in the office or plant calling attention to the campaign and stating the awards which will be given for safety suggestions which are adopted. Use the company newspaper and the bulletin boards. You can even send letters to employee's homes.

- Get the union or employee's committees involved. Suggestion systems are good for promoting cooperation between labor and management on mutual problems.

- See that supervisors, foremen, and managers support the program. Positive attitudes on their part will help put it across. These people can aid employees in clarifying ideas and getting them in writing.

- Announce winners and awards as soon as possible. This adds to the authenticity of the program as well as creates interest in the people who were undecided on participating.

18.6 Five Common Accidents—How to Prevent Them

The ways to prevent accidents are often simple and direct, yet supervisors may overlook them or not enforce the safety rules concerning them. Here are five common accidents which people experience on the job along with what you can do to minimize their happening:

Improper Lifting—Many people suffer painful back injuries because they do not know how to lift properly. You must explain to your people how to do it. The six steps for safe lifting are: 1) Stand close to the object. Have firm footing. 2) Squat down keeping your back straight and bending your knees. 3) Grasp the object firmly making sure your grip won't slip. 4) Breathe deeply to inflate your lungs. 5) Lift with your legs, slowly straightening them. 6) Hold the object close to your body.

Failure to Lock Out—The failure to guard against power being turned on during repair or maintenance operations on equipment has caused many deaths and injuries. You can prevent such accidents by adopting a lockout procedure. Each person who works on a machine is issued a lock and key. Locks are put on the start switch using a multiple hasp if more than one person is involved on the job. Keys are retained by the lock owners and locks are not removed by the owners until they have completed their work on the machine. With this procedure no one can turn the machine on until all locks have been removed and everyone is clear of the machine.

Falling into Excavations and Pits—Often not respected as a serious danger to people is a hole in the ground or an uncovered pit. Yet such things are potential cripplers or killers simply from falls into them. The walls of an earth excavation can also collapse to crush or smother a person. Protection against collapse of the walls is accomplished by shoring them but a person should also take the precaution to never work alone in pits. Although barricades and roping off can warn people of the danger of an excavation or pit, if you also cover the opening with a supportable material, you provide additional protection against an accident. And it's a wise move to see that the area is well-lighted at night.

Experiencing Electrical Shock—Electrically operated tools are potential killers, especially if they are used around water. Every tool should either be double-insulated or fitted with a three-wire cord and plug. Many people minimize the danger of 110-volt circuits and are not careful when using extension cords. Temporary wiring is also a shock hazard—you should see that it is eliminated as soon as possible.

Using Tools in Poor Condition—All cutting tools such as knives, chisels, bits, saws, and planes need to be kept sharp. Sharp tools are safer and do the job more efficiently. Dull tools often are the causes of serious cuts in addition to turning out poor quality work. Other tool-related accidents are caused by chisels with mushroomed heads, hammers and axes with cracked handles, and screwdrivers with chipped or bent tips. You must get rid of tools that are damaged or in poor condition to protect your people from needless injuries.

18.7 Answers to the Accidents Which Keep Repeating

The accident repeater, the person who continually has accidents, is usually well-known to supervisors. Most supervisors are concerned, as they should be, about this person and they search diligently for the human factors to explain how and why the person is so accident prone. But, not receiving as much attention usually from supervisors are the accidents which keep repeating but involve a different person each time. Supervisors should be just as concerned, if not more so, about those, particularly because there are definite steps which can be taken for preventing them. You can get at this problem by analyzing all reported accidents for their *causes,* picking out the causes which are repeaters, and taking action on them.

A second matter for you to handle is to tell your people you want to hear about near accidents and other accidents, small and large, which don't result in injuries. When you learn of two or more with the same or similar cause, take definite action to eliminate it.

Correcting unsafe conditions and unsafe practices are sure ways to improve the safety record of your department. By following up on accidents which keep repeating, you will be able to learn of those conditions and practices.

18.8 How to Promote the Wearing of Safety Clothing

Supervisors can accomplish much toward increasing the safety of their people if they can convince them of the importance of safety clothing and persuade them to wear it. When workers understand how safety clothing protects them, and when they've been trained how to use it, they will more willingly wear it. Here are some of the ways you can promote it:

1. Set an example. Wear safety glasses and other appropriate clothing such as a hard hat or safety shoes. And point out to your people that you would not be without these things to feel safe.

. 2. Get the backing of the union or the informal leaders. If those people set the pattern for proper clothing on the job, others will follow.

3. Let people participate in decisions relating to the type, style, and model of protective clothing they're going to wear. Discuss with them the hazardous conditions and the kinds of clothing that will provide them the best protection.

4. Be firm and persistent that the safety clothing be worn, going so far that you take disciplinary action if it is not. Point out that some companies make the wearing of safety clothing a requirement for being employed. Remember, you are responsible for the safety of your people.

18.9 Sure-Fire Ways to Prevent Office Accidents

Accidents don't happen only in the plant, at the construction site, or on the road. They occur in other places where people work such as in offices, stores, and recreational areas. A recent report from the Federal Occupational Safety and Health Act Agency stated that office workers alone suffer 40,000 disabling injuries and over 200 deaths every year. If you are a supervisor in an office, here are some of the hazards you may have to contend with there along with advice on how to make the place safe for your people.

1. Watch out for loose rungs, carpeting, or other floor coverings which could lead to falls. Highly waxed floors are a hazard, too, and even a paper clip or thumb-tack on the floor can cause a slip.

2. Provide adequate lighting and a contrasting color scheme to make furniture, files, and machines stand out. Such things also delay fatigue, a common cause of accidents.

3. See that desk drawers, file drawers, and desk slides are not left open. These can cause serious injuries when a person inadvertently bumps into or stumbles over them.

4. Prohibit running in the aisles or up and down steps. Tell people that hurrying results in accidents.

5. Advise people to not leave sharp-edged tools loose in table or desk drawers. Also, broken glass should never be put in wastebaskets.

6. Don't permit papers, books, and other material to be stacked on top of filing cabinets or lockers. This practice is not only an example of poor housekeeping but also the cause of injuries when such things are knocked or fall off.

18.10 Three Keys to Preventing Falls

Falls have always been the cause of many preventable disabling injuries and deaths. You should be continually alert to anything that you might do to eliminate conditions which lead to them. Three key moves you can make are:

1. Study the equipment, material, and work areas. Look particularly for oil and grease spills, waste, damaged floors, poor stacking of material, and obstructions in aisles and walkways. Promptly clean up spills and put absorbents on grease or oil. Provide racks and bins for material. Keep aisles open and clean.

2. Study people's work clothing and protective equipment. Look for poor fits, frayed or torn material, and floppy trouser cuffs. Check for good repair of rips and tears. Observe if clothing is appropriate for the job. See if protective equipment is being used properly. When you find a variance or exception, speak to the person involved, pointing out how the item should be used properly.

3. Study the accident records. If an injury resulted from a fall, determine how and why it happened. Look for unsafe work habits. Survey areas where falls took place to see if there is a change you could make such as providing additional lighting or relocating equipment.

18.11 How to Make an Accident Investigation

Supervisors rather than safety engineers or directors are expected to make accident investigations in most companies. The reasons for this are that supervisors know the operations better and have the responsibility and authority to take whatever corrective action is necessary. If you make a prompt and thorough investigation of an accident, you gain the trust and confidence of your people because they see that you are looking out for their interest and are concerned with their safety. However, your investigation must be more than simply reporting the explanation of the person who saw or had the accident. The report should include recommendations for corrective action.

Investigating an accident requires that you be patient and tactful in getting information about it. Talking to the person who was involved is the first thing to do. Try to put the person at ease. Point out that the purpose of the investigation is not to put the blame on anyone but only to prevent a similar accident from happening again, and that you need help to do this.

Go to the accident area, if possible, and also do your talking in private. The person involved will be more at ease if the two of you are alone; also what you report will not be influenced by comments and opinions of others in the person's presence. Let the person describe what happened without interruption. If you don't understand something, ask about it later.

Avoid judging what happened or is said. You don't want to put the person on the defensive. Limit your questions to asking for facts rather than opinions to learn what happened, what was done, and how it was done. "Why" questions may make the person defensive. Ask your questions in a friendly, helpful manner, and ask the type which cannot be answered with only a "yes" or "no."

It's a good idea to repeat the account of the accident to the person after you've heard it and written it down. This will enable the person to correct any errors in your account as well as perhaps add something you omitted. Finish the investigation by discussing what should be done to prevent a similar accident. You thus confirm the purpose of your investigation and prove that you want to help.

18.12 How to Safeguard Your Workers' Health

Federal laws require that the atmosphere of offices, plants, and other work areas be monitored for harmful physical agents and toxic substances, and that these materials be removed if found in quantities hazardous to people's health. Adequate protection for workers must be provided if the substance can't be removed.

An accurate assessment of the hazard is the first step. Supervisors may become involved with this because the procedure requires thorough knowledge of the process, equipment, materials, and by-products which could possibly create a health hazard to employees. To do a comprehensive job you must take air samples with the proper instruments to test for oxygen content and concentration levels of particulate or gaseous contaminants. These samples must be taken in the working area, in the surrounding area, and at the machine or equipment putting out the toxic gas or dust. Some companies bring in a trained industrial hygienist for professional advice on the evaluation of health hazards which the company suspects or knows exist.

The National Safety Council has listed the main elements to consider when evaluating a health hazard. They are:

1. The amount of the material in contact with a body cell that is required to produce injury.
2. The probability of the material being absorbed by the body to result in an injury.
3. The rate of generation of airborne contaminant.
4. The total time of contact.
5. The control measures in use.

When you take corrective action, be sure to consider possible emergency conditions which might arise. Assure that the control equipment is handy and that the procedures for using it are understood by the workers.

Case-in-Point: "The best time for my customers to learn all about air masks is before they have to use them," says Bob Cox, field representative for Mines Safety Appliances Company.[2] Cox conducts training programs for the industrial workers in his California territory. You should train your workers in using emergency equipment such as air masks if there is any likelihood that workers some day may be exposed to hazardous materials and need to wear masks to survive or save the life of a fellow-worker.

18.13 Guidelines for Maintaining the Health of Employees

Business and industry today must give continuous attention to the health of employees and not limit their concern to a one-time examination of them when they are hired. Occupational health must be monitored and managed just as any other responsibility of management. An individual's medical condition cannot be used as a criterion for employment under Equal Employment Regulations. Thus, the preliminary medical exam may be used only to decide in what position a prospective employee may be placed. A person can be turned down for employment for medical reasons only if the person's medical capability is insufficient to do the job or if the person's performance in such a capacity would place himself, herself, or other workers in physical jeopardy.

In many industrial plants, periodic medical exams are performed on employees based on time and exposure to the hazards in the environment to which the employees are exposed. If their state of health has significantly changed, the reasons for the change must be determined. But, regardless of the

---

[2]From *Occupational Hazards Magazine,* May, 1977 issue. Copyrighted 1977 by Penton/IPC Incorporated.

cause, once a negative effect has been noted, thought must be given to reassignment of the employees to a better environment and steps taken to improve their condition.

Case-in-Point: "Change the machine, don't try to change the human body, if you want to protect a worker's health," says Joseph F. Stelluto,[3] corporate manager of industrial hygiene for FMC Corp., Philadelphia. "It is much easier and more economical to modify a machine to do the necessary task than to alter the basic anatomical and physiological functions of a human to fit a poorly designed machine. Efforts are best spent in designing processes and machines which enhance the productivity of the operation, prevent unnecessary safety hazards, and reduce physical stress."

Mr. Stelluto gave an example of what he was talking about when he said, "One electronic firm was able to reduce employees' continued wrist tendonitis by redesigning the pliers used in chassis assembly. When the employees' discomfort and complaints were eliminated, increased productivity and en-hanced employee morale soon followed."

18.14 Ten Positive Ways to Control Health Hazards

The National Safety Council has suggested ten methods by which business and industry can control health hazards. They are:

1. Substitute a less harmful material for one which is dangerous to health.
2. Change or alter a process to minimize worker contact.
3. Isolate or enclose a process or work operation to reduce the number of persons exposed.
4. Use a wet method to reduce generation of dust in operations such as mining and quarrying.
5. Provide an exhaust at the point of generation and dispersion of contaminants.
6. Ventilate with clean air to provide a safe atmosphere.
7. Provide personal protective devices.
8. Maintain good housekeeping. This includes cleanliness of the work-place, waste disposal, adequate washing, toilet, and eating facilities, healthful drinking water, and control of insects and rodents.

---

[3]From *Application of Basic Industrial Health Principles to Plant Engineering and Maintenance,* Nat. Plt. Eng. and Main. Conf., May, 1979.

9. Provide special control methods for specific hazards such as reduction of exposure time, film badges and similar monitoring devices, continuous sampling with preset alarms, and medical programs to detect intake of toxic materials.

10. Train and educate people to supplement engineering controls.

Case-in-Point: During an inspection of the B.F. Goodrich[4] plant in Grantsville, W. Va., an OSHA inspector observed that employees working with toluene solvents weren't wearing hand protection. OSHA cited the firm for an alleged serious violation of section 1910.132(a), which requires "protective shields and barriers" to be used "wherever it is necessary by reason of hazards of processes or environment..." A $280 penalty was proposed.

Goodrich contested the citation, and the case was heard by Review Commission Judge George Taylor. In its testimony, OSHA pointed out that employees who continually dipped their hands in and out of the toluene solvents risked contracting or aggravating dermatitis. Therefore, OSHA concluded, some type of personal protective equipment, be it a barrier cream or rubber gloves, was needed.

Goodrich countered that it recommended both creams and gloves for protection of employees working with toluene solvents; the protection became mandatory if an employee contracted dermatitis. Since employees were urged to take advantage of the hand protection offered them, Goodrich reasoned, plant officials could not be held responsible for the failure of employees to avail themselves of such protection.

Judge Taylor ruled in OSHA's favor, finding that a hand hazard did exist, which Goodrich should have made a concerted effort to alleviate. Merely suggesting that employees wear gloves and leaving the final decision up to them didn't fill the bill, Taylor ruled; a mandatory program backed up with effective enforcement was what was needed.

---

[4]Reprinted from the May 1979 issue of *Occupational Hazards Magazine*. Copyright 1979 by Penton/IPC Incorporated.

19

How to Promote
Creativity and
Sell Change

You or your people don't have to be intellectual or highly educated to be creative. Nor do you have to be born that way. Although creative people have certain traits which distinguish them from others, those characteristics can be developed with practice and determination. Since being creative results in getting ideas, making improvements on the job, and better work performance, supervisors should try to promote and develop creativity in themselves and their people. There are many ways this can be done.

Ideas come easiest to people when they think and study problems under conditions and at times which are most conducive to generating them. But ideas are of little value unless they are accepted and implemented. Knowing how to present your idea and doing it under the most favorable conditions can significantly increase the likelihood of it being accepted.

Change is inevitable yet many people resist it. The supervisor who is adept at selling change will have an easier time on the job and get along better with people. Numerous techniques have been developed to sell change. Communication plays a big part in preparing people for change and in allaying their fears. When people are kept informed and told why a change is necessary, they will accept it much more readily.

19.1 How to Recognize Creativity in People

The experts on the subject of creativity say that there are some key characteristics or traits present to a greater than average degree in persons who are creative. If you can detect or observe these behavior modes, you will be able to recognize creative people when you meet them. The key characteristics which the experts refer to are: imagination, sensitivity, curiosity, persistence, motivation, and flexibility.

The ability to envision and picture in the mind the implementation of an idea and to think in terms of the unorthodox is the trait of imagination. Creative people usually have a stronger sense of imagination than those who are not creative. Being sensitive to a problem or situation is demonstrated by being aware that it has more than one possible solution. A sensitive person goes beyond routine thinking in analyzing and studying a situation.

Curiosity is behind a person's challenge of the obvious way of doing something. A curious person wants to know why things are as they are and why they can't be different. A persistent person doesn't give up easily, continues to search for an answer to a problem or for one better than that on hand.

Creative people are usually self-starters. They don't need someone to motivate them. And they realize that getting started is more difficult than continuing to work. People who are flexible adjust easily to changing conditions and situations. This trait is also reflected in an ability to think of many approaches to a problem and a willingness to consider all alternative solutions.

19.2 Creativity Leads to Better Work Performance

If you are creative you will probably be continually improving your department's operation. But you don't have to be creative to make improvements. Any supervisor can do it if he or she can persuade others to be creative and is able to recognize a good idea when it is presented. There are, however, some contingencies to be considered.

First, you must be honest enough to concede that your department is not perfect and that improvements are possible. You must feel that most if not all jobs can be done better than they are now being done.

Second, you must be confident that your people can come up with better ways of getting the work out and with solutions to problems that arise along the way. You must believe in people and their potentials.

Third, you must be bold and aggressive enough to try new ideas. You must be willing to experience an occasional failure and not let it deter you from trying another idea which looks like it might have promise.

The art of being creative is something that supervisors should try to develop in their people. Creative people like their work and get satisfaction from it. As a result, they do better work and their company benefits.

19.3 Ten Sure-Fire Ways to Promote Creativity

Your people don't have to be highly intellectual in order to be creative on the job. It does help, however, if they are aware of the inevitability of change and they know that change is going to occur whether or not they contribute to it. Here are ten ways you can help your people to be imaginative and innovative:

1. Assure them that they will not be laughed at or ridiculed when they make suggestions or offer ideas that don't pan out.
2. Respect their right to disagree and let them know this. "Yes" behavior impedes innovation and the search for a better way. It also leads to mediocrity.
3. Make the rewards for being right greater than the penalties for being wrong.
4. Be sure people are aware of goals and objectives. Give them things to shoot for.
5. Invite communication. Ideas must be transmitted to the right people if they are to be brought to light and evaluated.
6. Teach innovation and ingenuity. Push imagination. Get people to have open minds to problems and ways to solve them.
7. Encourage people to be curious and inquisitive. Make them want to see how other people handle problems similar to their own.
8. Remove blocks in the way of creative effort. Give people leeway. Downplay rules of the game.
9. Furnish tools and assistance. See that conditions are conducive to coming up with ideas.
10. Display a positive and enthusiastic attitude toward creative efforts. Work to change unusable ideas into usable ones.

Case-in-Point: "The one thing most needed for creative ability is improvement of mental habits," says Robert F. Wells,[1] a creative supervisor at General Electric Co., Schenectady, N. Y. For most people, this means reviving dormant creative skills. Children express themselves freely and are greatly enthused by a discovery largely because they haven't been "burned" by ridicule and social embarrassment.

19.4 Answers to How to Be More Creative

Some people think creativity is something mysterious and to be creative you must be born that way. They are quite wrong about that. Any person can be creative if the person sets his or her mind to it. Creativity in its simplest form is only problem solving; everybody solves problems every day. If you feel that you aren't as creative as you'd like to be, adopt the following thinking and procedures:

1. Grab onto and organize your thoughts. Although only a few of your many thoughts may ever help you solve a problem, if you make an effort to retain those which you *think* may help, you increase the chances of finding answers to problems. When you have thoughts that may be of value, write them down on a pad or notebook.

2. Question what you see and hear. Ask yourself why jobs are done in certain ways, in certain places, and at certain times. By challenging the ways things are, you may get ideas on how to change them for the better.

3. Break up a system or procedure into its elements. Alter the order of steps, rearrange parts, and look at matters from a different angle. Most of the ideas that come to you may not be practical, but eventually a good one will come along.

4. Relate a problem or situation to one with which you are familiar or have come up against before. Ask yourself what something reminds you of, what you can borrow to use elsewhere.

5. Do some "way out" thinking. Don't be afraid to consider some weird ideas. Many things that are done today are because of habit, custom, and tradition, and for no other reason. An answer to a problem doesn't have to be conventional. What really matters is whether it works.

19.5 Roadblocks to Creative Thinking

Although some people, particularly those doing research and development work, may try to be creative, most of the answers to problems they come up

---

[1]From *Industry Week*, Aug. 16, 1971.

with are conventional rather than innovative. Psychologists who have studied creative thinking explain this with the statement that the barriers to creative thinking are inherent with the individuals and with their approach to their job. Many personal characteristics can and do inhibit creative thinking. A lack of curiosity, mental illness, and inadequate motivation are a few. Viewing change as a threat is another. The fear of criticism is a major roadblock with many people, particularly with those who feel they can't afford to make a mistake or appear impractical.

Work habits and degree of familiarity with a subject can also have a negative influence on creative thinking. The person who has little knowledge about a problem area feels unable to be creative in that area. Still, too much knowledge may also be an inhibitor if it leads the experienced individual to know the answer even before the problem is fully defined.

Lack of pertinent data and information limits creativity drastically. Yet, lots of it is no better if it is not investigated and organized. You can do a poor job of creative thinking if you overlook the obvious, but you can also fail if you stick with the obvious. Narrow definition of a problem may prevent finding a creative solution. Then again, too broad a definition can block any solution.

A willingness to accept the first solution that appears to be a logical answer puts a damper on further creative thinking. And it is foolhardy to conclude that the first solution is the most creative one. The work environment can be a block if management philosophy is to make the rewards for innovation small and the penalties for not playing it safe great.

Case-in-Point: L. W. Langley,[2] director of material handling systems management, Rexnord Material Handling Div., recently stated, "The value of creativity to the material handling industry is closely tied to the role the material handling itself plays in business. It is generally acknowledged that material handling is taking an increasing share of the responsibility for profits. It seems safe to say that creativity is thus becoming more important to the material handling industry. It is almost certain that the major material handling companies of tomorrow will not be the suppliers of hardware, but will be the skillful system builders who are able to attract and effectively employ creative people."

19.6 Ten Ways to Generate Ideas

Do you feel that you're not getting your share of good ideas? Do you often say to yourself, "Why didn't I think of that?" You can make a better showing and be more creative if you set your mind to it. Here are ten ways to do it:

---

[2]From *Automation,* December, 1973.

1. Be alert for a change in your or your people's jobs. Look for an unexpected result, reaction, or problem. Noticing these things can prompt you to come up with a corrective idea.

2. Try to continually expose yourself to new places and strange people. In your spare time read about subjects which are not in your field.

3. Work at solving problems when you are fresh, have a lot of energy, and can think things through. Early in the morning is best for most people.

4. Try to be alone part of the day to think. Go over some of your problems without feeling that you must find answers immediately. Let your subconscious mind go to work for you until you again have time to think.

5. Forget about being logical and practical when you're looking for answers to problems. Most of the ideas you'll get with this approach won't amount to much, but there's bound to be one now and then that will pay off.

6. Don't let ridicule or criticism hold you back when expressing your ideas. Keep trying even when other people say you are on the wrong track.

7. Be ready to take time out from what you're doing to think about a problem. Daydreaming is not a waste of time, nor is relaxing and talking with a friend. You can sometimes induce ideas with a walk, a shower, or listening to restful music.

8. Always have a pad and pencil with you so that you can make notes of your thoughts and ideas when they come to you. Many valuable ideas are lost because people don't make a note of them.

9. Make a habit of using checklists when you plan. When it comes to carrying out those items, you'll do a more thorough job. A checklist is worthwhile also because you have to think to make one.

10. Set deadlines for yourself. The need to meet them can spur you to more accomplishment. The fear of failure to meet them can intensify your thinking.

19.7 Six Traps to Being Innovative: How to Avoid Them

If you sincerely wish that you could come up with more good ideas, think about how you're going about it. You may be handicapping yourself by making it more difficult than it need be. Here are some traps which may be preventing you from being more innovative:

1. Noise and distraction. Are you doing most of your mental work under poor conditions such as near noisy machines or where people's conversations can distract you? Get off by yourself in a quiet area.

2. Thinking in generalities. Zero in on the specific problem which needs to be solved. Break up a big problem—try to solve it in parts or steps.

3. Being satisfied with things as they are. You have to believe that anything and everything can be improved. There is always a better way to do something.

4. Having your senses dulled. Beward of too much food or drink if you have some serious thinking to do. Your mind will not be sharp if you eat or drink to excess.

5. Thinking deeply at the wrong time. You can't do your best when you're fatigued or weary. You need to be fresh to be inspired.

6. Unwilling to express yourself. An idea that you keep to yourself or file away for future use isn't worth much—it hasn't a chance of being adopted now. Don't worry about an idea being rejected. Talking about it may even lead to a still better one.

19.8 Positive Practices to Gain Idea Acceptance

People with ideas can significantly increase their selling success if they carefully prepare for presenting ideas and use strategy to put them across. And the more positively and enthusiastically they go about it, the more influential such practices become. If you adopt the following techniques and master them, you will be able to significantly increase the number of your ideas which are accepted.

1. Know the likes, dislikes, and needs of the people who judge and evaluate your ideas. You can then slant a presentation with those matters in mind. If you also know why and how these people resist change, you can search out ways to reduce their resistance to it.

2. Go beyond the economic considerations when talking about benefits and advantages of an idea. Talk up, for example, the social, cultural, or educational aspects. Some persons are reluctant to accept a change unless they can be made to see new or different benefits.

3. Be sure your idea is fully understood. Clear, well-presented proposals reflect a high competency of the suggestor which helps to overcome any doubt of this nature. Avoid jargon and technical terms, if possible; you may appear to be trying to impress rather than inform.

4. Present an honest, complete story. Resist being biased by giving both the positive and negative features of the idea, but be sure to include recommendations on how the negative ones can be overcome. This type of presentation eliminates many questions before they are asked. At the same time, it fosters more confidence in you and what you can do.

5. Share the credit for ideas, even though others may have contributed little. You gain doubly: first, by letting it be known that you listen to others, and second, by acquiring the support of the people you credited.

6. Tie your idea to another which has already been accepted. Point out similarities and comment on the logic of the comparison. This helps to allay the "newness" of your idea, a matter which some people unconsciously object to.

7. Seek cooperation by letting people feel they played a part in the promotion or development of the idea. When people think they have contributed, they will more willingly accept and lend you their support. You may have to modify some part or detail a bit, but that's a small price to pay to gain their acceptance.

19.9 How to Protect Your Idea

Ideas to improve operations, make work easier, reduce waste, and cut costs should be discussed and publicized when they are put into practice. People who come up with such ideas want to receive credit for them, supervisors included. This is natural and to be expected. But, how can you publicize an idea and be assured of getting credit for it if it is not immediately accepted and adopted? You can protect your idea as well as promote its acceptance very easily.

How-to-Do-It: If you get an idea in a meeting or a discussion with other people on the job, write a follow-up memo to the person or persons who are in a position to act on it. You can also use the memo as a way of adding to or refining the idea beyond your original proposal.

Getting your idea in print enables you to point it out to other people who might be interested. This is a low pressure way to show your involvement and interest without blowing your horn excessively.

Another way to protect as well as promote your idea is to carry it orally to a higher level of authority. Avoid letting someone else speak for you, if possible, especially if other people are also promoting the idea. A good idea is worth fighting for yourself so you don't get lost in the shuffle.

19.10 Guidelines to Handling Change Smoothly

It's natural to fear change. Change is seldom welcomed unless people demand it to relieve themselves of a burden or a discomfort. Mostly, this is because people don't know what to expect. Even minor or insignificant changes disturb habits and routines causing worry and stress. It takes time for new habits and routines to be formed, and some people need more time than others to get accustomed to something new.

Change is more acceptable, therefore, if it is managed without a lot of fanfare and publicity. Although it isn't always possible to make a change this way, the less adjustment that is required of people, the less apparent it is that you are making a change. Here are some guidelines on how you can make a change smoothly:

1. Announce a change promptly. The word is going to get out anyway. It's much easier to present truths in the beginning than it is to correct untruths and rumors later.

2. Maintain the status of individuals whenever possible. You get into trouble if you build one person's status at the expense of another's.

3. Avoid decrees. People are offended when you dictate. Suggestions are received much better than demands.

4. Show confidence that the change will be a success. If other people sense that you have doubts about it, they will also have doubts, and the road ahead may then be rocky.

5. Recognize and respect resistance. Don't try to have your way at any cost. Discuss an objection and reconsider. You could be wrong in what you're doing.

6. Be patient. Allow time for a change to gel. People cannot be expected to completely and enthusiastically accept a change immediately after they learn of it.

19.11 Tips on Selling Change

If you acknowledge that there's more than one way to sell change, and you have developed a perceptiveness to people's feelings, you are on your way to perfecting a selling technique. Here are some tips on following through to become an expert in the art.

Play change in a soft key. When you are going to make a proposal, don't give out the whole deal at one time—present only enough so that people can see what you're thinking about, but not enough to put up a strong argument against it.

Proceed slowly by talking to only one person at a time and by giving that person time to think before you bring up the subject again. People need time to adjust to a new idea before they will wholeheartedly accept it.

Watch a person's manner and his or her body language to see if you are getting agreement with what you're saying. Feel your way if you perceive resistance. Tactfully probe for what the person does not agree with or thinks is wrong.

Truly listen to a person's objections and study them. Recognize that you may have to modify your idea, that it may not be perfect. Try to learn how you might improve it so that it is more acceptable.

19.12 Sell by Saying the Right Words

When you feel that a change should be made but you don't have the authority to make it without another person's approval, you are faced with selling that person on the worth of the change. You may have to convince your boss, for example, that your idea will improve a work situation or a process operation. Saying the right words will increase your chances of selling your idea.

How-to-Do-It: Start by emphasizing the benefits. Show how costs will be lowered, production increased, or efficiency raised. Use figures, if you can calculate them, because they enable you to be specific.

Be careful not to exaggerate or make exorbitant claims. Also, admit to extra costs, drawbacks, and difficulties which might be encountered in the implementation of the change. Yet, ask for the full amount of help or money you believe will be needed to accomplish the change.

Condition yourself to answer questions. This means that you must know the details and steps to get started, the people that will be involved, and the problems that might arise.

Finish your proposal for a change by asking for authority to make it. This action is similar to the one a salesperson must take who, after a sales presentation, should ask for an order. Although you may not get a green light to go ahead right at the moment, at least you will have made your point and left the decision up to your superiors.

19.13 Making It Easier: Explain Why

You can sell change much more easily if you explain why it is needed. Too often the "what" of a change is explained adequately while the "why" is handled poorly if at all.

When you tell people why a change is to be made, you help them to understand it. Thus, explaining why strengthens your selling message.

By explaining why a change is necessary, you also overcome part of the natural fear that people have of it. With this knowledge they can be more assured, for example, that their jobs are not going to be lost or that they are not going to have to work harder. The more information you can give people about a change, and the more positive way you can do it, the easier it will be for you to sell it.

19.14 Five Ways to Take the Pain Out of Change

Since employees naturally resist change, supervisors should do what they can to get their people to expect it, understand it, and prepare for it. The more supervisors can do along these lines the less resistance they will encounter when they make a change. Here are five ways you can take the pain out of change:

1. Be sure the change is beneficial and worthwhile. Change for the sake of change is only a waste of time, and you may build up resistance to a later worthwhile change besides. If you don't have a lot to gain from a change, it's better to forget the whole thing.

2. Ask for advice. Employees will feel involved and become committed when they have a voice in a decision, especially if they can spot an oversight or a weakness in a plan and are able to point it out.

3. Make the change as simple as possible. Break it up into steps if you can so that it doesn't have to be taken all at once. Change is less disruptive if you can space it out.

4. Give the change time. Resistance won't disappear immediately. All people need time to adjust.

5. Admit it when a change doesn't work. Back off and return to the conditions before the change. If you persist, you show that you are either stubborn or a poor judge of people and situations, both of which will hinder you on the job.

Case-in-Point: Management at The Cincinnati (Ohio) Gas and Electric Co.[3] tells employees that they can adjust to changes by remembering that fear of the unknown is normal: "Don't be pessimistic—don't convince yourself in advance that change won't work. Take time to consider the past and review some of the personal challenges you have met and overcome."

19.15 Steps to Getting Greater Acceptance of Plans

You can get better acceptance of your plans and ideas if you keep the people who will be affected informed about them. This is best done in steps:

- First, inform people that a change is being considered. Tell them that it will result in benefits and advantages to them.
- Second, after you've settled the details, give the reasons for the change and an explanation of it.
- Third, describe the plan's elements as to who, what, where, when, and how much.

---

[3]Reprinted from *Supervisor's Bulletin for Line and Staff,* Issue No. 357. By permission of the publisher. Bureau of Business Practice, 24 Rope Ferry Road, Waterford, Connecticut 06386. Copyright, Bureau of Business Practice, Inc.

- Fourth, periodically report on progress of the change. Mention any deviation from the original plan.

- Fifth, confirm that the change has been made and is now the standard procedure. Ask for comments on difficulties or problems encountered with the new way.

19.16 How to Enrich and Enlarge Jobs

Attitude surveys have shown that today's job seekers, particularly young people, want more than just a job. They want to get satisfaction and a sense of achievement from their work. Security and money is not as important to such people as a challenge, a chance for self-expression, and an opportunity to make a contribution to society. Educators and psychologists say that jobs must be enriched and enlarged if these desires of new employees are to be achieved. They suggest four ways by which it may be done.

- One way is to create the proper environment or climate. Supervisors and workers must do a good job of communicating with each other, identifying common goals, and trusting one another. There should be no pressure on the workers to obey rules and work harder.

- A second way is to design jobs to permit people to make maximum use of their skills while at the same time motivating them to do so. This involves giving workers more responsibility to run their jobs as they see fit and to make decisions on how the work is to be done

- Another way is to design equipment and systems which promote motivation, create interest, and provide satisfaction with accomplishment. This is done by making the work exciting and challenging, and by providing pleasant, confortable work conditions.

- The fourth way of enriching jobs is for management to provide the means for learning and growth, and to participate with workers in setting goals and solving problems. In this way performance is rewarded on the basis of goal achievement.

INDEX